PARIS AND THE PROVINCES

PARIS
AND THE
PROVINCES

The Politics of Local
Government Reform in France

Peter Alexis Gourevitch

UNIVERSITY OF CALIFORNIA PRESS
Berkeley • Los Angeles

University of California Press
Berkeley and Los Angeles, California

© 1980
The Regents of the University of California

Printed in the United States of America

1   2   3   4   5   6   7   8   9

Library of Congress Cataloging in Publication Data

Gourevitch, Peter Alexis.
    Paris and the provinces. The politics of local
    government reform in France.
    Bibliography: p.
    Includes index.
    1. Local government—France.   2. Regionalism—France.
    I. Title.
France.   I. Title.
JS4895.G65   320.8'0944   79-64666
ISBN 0-520-03971-8

TO MY FAMILY

CONTENTS

PART THREE: COMPARISONS AND CONCLUSIONS

ACKNOWLEDGMENTS

Knowing the life history of a book is not essential to judging its contents, but it is indispensable for giving an account of the author's debts and gratitudes. My fascination with France (rooted in a very recent European family past) was stirred into consciousness at Oberlin College by several faculty members, particularly George Lanyi, J.D. Lewis, Carey McWilliams, and Aaron Wildavsky. At Harvard, this interest deepened and widened. A generation of students has experienced Stanley Hoffmann's extraordinary talent at communicating his passionate concern with France. His lectures, seminars, conversations, critical reading of my drafts, and encouragement over the past fifteen years have been indispensable to this work. A very stimulating group of colleagues associated with the Center for European Studies prevented "premature closure" of my ideas, and through their endless love of argument helped make the whole experience more rewarding: Suzanne Berger, Patrice Higonnet, Peter Katzenstein, Steven Krasner, Robert Jervis, James Kurth, Peter Lange, Victor Perez-Diaz, Theda Skopcol, and Martin Shefter. Several teachers helped shape my thinking about politics in general and local government in particular: Samuel Beer, Edward Banfield, Henry Kissinger, Arthur Maass, Barrington Moore, Jr., Judith Shklar, Michael Walzer, J.Q. Wilson, and Laurence Wylie.

Through the years, several colleagues in the fields of French and European studies have assisted me in numerous ways. As a fellow student, teacher, coworker, colleague, and friend, Suzanne Berger taught me an immense amount about each role. Through a truly remarkable ability to criticize constructively, she has helped me understand what I wished to say and how to say it. Sidney Tarrow read drafts with acuity, shrewdness, verve, and speed; his constant questions, observations, suggestions, and encouragement helped keep me going forward. Nicholas Wahl shared generously his vast knowledge of French politics and political personnel. Yves Mény drew upon his unparalleled familiarity with the regionalism controversy to provide extremely useful comments on the manuscript. Henry Ehrmann, Mark Kesselman, and Ezra Suleiman shared their own considerable knowledge of French politics. Most of the writing was done in Montreal; several friends and colleagues sustained me in that activity, in particular, David Bloom, James de Wilde, Harvey Rishikof, and Janice Stein.

During my stays in France, Catherine and Pierre Grémion, Claire and Jean-Jacques Salomon, Christiane and Georges Vachuad, and Martha and Willy Zuber helped nourish body, mind, and soul with countless kindnesses and much treasured companionship. I feel a special gratitude to the Grémions for their generosity in showing me their work. Michel Crozier helped greatly as both subject and colleague, cheerfully submitting to several lengthy interviews, discussing my ideas, and arranging interviews. Annie Kriegel, Annique Percheron, Jean-Claude Thoenig, Marie-France Toinet, Jean-Pierre Worms and many other persons attached to the Fondation Nationale des Sciences Politiques, the Groupe de Sociologie des Organisations, and the Université de Grenoble all contributed greatly to my understanding of French politics.

Much of the material contained here is based on interviews. Most were done during three separate periods: In 1967–1968, I spent several months in the Isère collaborating with Suzanne Berger, Patrice Higonnet, and Karl Kaiser on a project whose purpose was to see how various elites interpreted the shifts which had taken place in French political life since the war. The interviews were open-ended and loosely structured. I concentrated on local officials and party leaders, and explored attitudes toward the state and the distribution of authority between Paris and the countryside. Our joint essay was published as ''The Problem of Reform in France: The Political Ideas of Local Elites,'' *Political Science Quarterly* 84 (September 1969). I continued with the theme of decentralization through a doctoral dissertation, ''The Resilience of Ideologies in France.'' As its title suggests, the major explanatory thrust of the dissertation was that reforms had failed because of attitudes toward the proper distribution of authority between Paris and the countryside on the part of local elites and national politicians. The argument drew upon the Isère interviews and a case study of the Referendum of 1969.

Between the completion of this first study and the next stage of my research, a considerable shift occurred in the type of reasoning I wished to pursue. Less interested in ideologies of center-periphery relations, I became increasingly interested in debate over policy toward local government as a political problem, one touching partisan and personal rivalries. The present book has been cast in these terms, but the influence of the earlier concern remains visible.

The second round of on-site investigation came during a sabbatical year, 1971–1972, spent in Paris. This coincided with the preparation and passage of the *loi Frey* on the government side, and the elaboration of the Common Program among the opposition. My interviewing focused on these two developments, with some exploration of the 1968–1969 period as well. I spoke with civil servants, party leaders, former members of the government, interest group leaders, journalists, and researchers, and I followed the consideration of the government's legislation by the National Assembly and the Senate.

Finally, I returned in 1976 and 1977 to bring my understanding of events up to date via additional rounds of interviews. In each trip I found people remarkably helpful, accessible, and open, quite unlike the reputation French officialdom usually has. It is impossible to thank everyone I saw, but without that aid, this study could not have taken place. Certain institutions provided assistance with specific problems. The IFOP (Institut Français de l'Opinion Publique) allowed me to consult some public opinion surveys carried out in the Isère in 1966. The SOFREAS (Sema–Organisation Française d'Enquêtes par Sondage) showed me much of the material it had gathered in 1968 on French attitudes toward the state. The Ministry of Administrative Reform allowed me to go through many boxes of reports, based on the questionnaires distributed to elites all over the country during the summer and fall of 1968, concerning the geographic distribution of power in France.

Special help was given on specific chapters. Judy Chubb did much of the basic research on the Italian case. Alessandro Pizzorno, Peter Lange, and Sidney Tarrow labored patiently to improve my understanding of the country they know so well. Sidney Tarrow continued his aid during the preparation of the volume he edited with Peter Katzenstein and Luigi Graziano, *Territorial Politics in Industrial Nations,* in which my comparison of Italy and France was first published.

The ideas concerning peripheral nationalisms were first presented at a conference at Cornell chaired by Milton Esman in May 1975. Subsequent presentations at the Center for European Studies and the Center for International Affairs at Harvard, at an Airlie House Conference in Virginia, and at a meeting of the Quebec-Ontario teachers of international relations in Toronto all provided helpful criticism. In addition to persons already mentioned, I wish to thank for their comments on this chapter: David Bloom, Milton Esman, Michael Hechter, Albert Hirschman, Juan Linz, Charles Lipson, Charles Maier, Tom Naylor, Victor Perez-Diaz, Harvey Rishikof, Michael Stein, and James de Wilde. An earlier version was published as "The Reemergence of 'Peripheral Nationalisms': Some Comparative Speculations on the Spatial Distribution of Political Leadership and Economic Growth," *Comparative Studies in Society and History* 21 (July 1979).

Material assistance came from many sources, all of which I

wish to thank: the American Philosophical Society, the Ford Foundation, the Interuniversity Center for European Studies in Montreal, the Graduate Faculty of McGill University, and, at Harvard University, the Government Department, the Joseph Clark Fund, the Center for International Affairs, and the Center for European Studies.

Many people aided in the organizational tasks involved in preparing a book. I am especially grateful to my mother, Sylvia Gourevitch, for helping me with translations, the index, and proofreading, and to Abby Collins, Leonie Gordon, Debbie Cowper-Higgins, Laura Winer, Kim Reany, Susan Bartlett, and Cathy Duggan. Grant Barnes, Lynn Hovland, and Sheila Levine of the University of California Press aided greatly in transforming a draft into a finished product.

Some of the material contained in this book has previously appeared in various forms: "Political Skill: The Case of Pierre Mendès-France," *Public Policy* 14 (1966); "The Reform of Local Government in France: A Political Analysis," *Comparative Politics* 10 (October 1977); "Reforming the Napoleonic State: The Creation of Regional Governments in France and Italy," in *Territorial Politics in Industrial Nations*, edited by Sidney Tarrow, Peter Katzenstein, and Luigi Graziano (New York: Praeger, 1978); and the two articles cited above, "The Problem of Reform in France" and "The Re-emergence of 'Peripheral Nationalisms'."

The thanks to one's family have a special place. I have been fortunate in being surrounded all my life by people whose idea of a good time is a roaring argument about politics and ideas. My parents, my wife's parents, and my wife have all listened, read, criticized and encouraged. My father did not live to see the fruits of his son's efforts. My mother has seen them and has helped me in innumerable ways, large and small. My son is old enough to dislike the time his father gives to writing, but not quite old enough to realize what joy his existence brings to my life. My wife's contribution to all of this is something only she can understand and only I can fully appreciate.

INTRODUCTION

Local government is simultaneously a determinant and an epiphenomenon. It lies at the heart of a political system, but it is also an expression of it. The values, attitudes, and experiences that citizens learn at the local level shape their behavior in national politics. All politics, it has been said, are parish-house politics. No national government can survive which does not satisfy local needs and aspirations. Questions of great national and international moment have turned on the financing of a local bridge, or canal, or housing project. Analysis of the whole which begins with the parts, constructing the national level from the local one, is thus a time-honored tradition of political theory.

A sharply contrasting tradition derives the local system from the national one. The character of these microcosms depends, in this view, on the properties of the national society as a whole. They have as much individuality or uniformity, importance or irrelevance, substance or shadow as the national system will allow according to its needs, problems, and experiences. The forces which shape the functioning of the local level transcend it; therefore, the whole cannot be reconstructed from the parts. The explanation of the nature of the local structures to be found in a given country must be derived from an explication of the outstanding features of the national system. Centralized regimes, for example, have often been those heavily involved in

1

war (France, Prussia) or wracked by sharp internal political cleavages (the USSR, France, Spain under Franco).

In writing this book I have used both approaches. The original impetus to my study of local government in France came from the former tradition. The argument that a healthy democracy requires involved citizens has always seemed persuasive to me. Citizen involvement requires the opportunity and the incentive to act, which in turn can exist only if political structures offer many points of relatively easy access—which means strong local government. As little as a decade ago, this view might easily have been categorized as American, drawing on a particular fusion of James Madison with Alexis de Tocqueville. Nowadays, it seems clear enough that such views have spread quite widely in Europe as well. Complaints about bureaucracy, impersonality, and inefficiency, demands for cultural autonomy, and for new types of participation have all sustained a very widespread attack upon existing political structures everywhere, in particular, upon centralization and hierarchical control.

It is one of the striking characteristics of political life in the last quarter of the present century that the state is under attack from all points on the political spectrum. As Suzanne Berger recently observed, the renewed awareness of the importance of politics goes hand in hand with renewed disillusionment as to the adequacy of existing institutional arrangements and of the uses of state power per se.

> (I)n the past in Western Europe, movements that formed in response to a newly perceived salience of the state usually tried to *capture* the state and turn it to their end. In the seventies, the dominant political response to the new transparence of the state has been to try to *dismantle* it, not to take it over. While this response is not without precedent in European history—the conservative Right often proposed this in the nineteenth century—never before has this conception of politics shaped new political ideas on both the Left and the Right.[1]

1. Suzanne Berger, "Politics and Antipolitics in Western Europe in the Seventies," *Daedalus* 108(Winter 1979): 27–50.

Existing vehicles for linking populations to policy are found wanting. Neither the opportunity to vote for members of Parliament every four or five years nor the nationalization of industry appear to convince large numbers of people that they participate meaningfully in the direction of collective life. Everywhere we see not only new issues pouring into the political sphere (pollution, nuclear power, women's rights, abortion, and others), but also demands for new political forms. Of these, *autogestion*, the participation of the employee in management of an enterprise, has perhaps attracted most attention. More involvement in local government constitutes another.

For many groups of differing political persuasions, the strengthening of local government structures is now a crucial prerequisite to the realization of essential values, be these libertarian (concerned with the extension of freedom and moral development of the individual), authoritarian (concerned with the maintenance of control), or technocratic (concerned with efficiency and a type of rationality). Chapter 1 explores the ways in which persons seeking one or another of these values have in France come to support some measure of dispersion of power away from Paris toward the provinces.

In coming to this subject, then, my interests were shaped by notions which see local government as "determining"—local government structures shape which goals can and which goals cannot be realized; changing the goals requires changing the local structures. Controversy in France precisely over proposals for such changes seemed to have an obviously compelling importance as a subject matter. In seeking to explicate the results of that conflict, however, the alternative attitude toward local institutions—the nature of local institutions derives from what happens at the center—proved of great utility. The relationship between Paris and the countryside not only shapes policy, but is itself an object of policy. As such, it is affected, like all policy issues, not only by the inputs of individuals and groups, but by forces which can only be understood systemically. The political system as a whole can be said to have properties from which the behavior of the individuals and groups can be derived. It is this reasoning which has led to a study of French local government which is rooted in looking at what goes on in Paris.

The relationship between Paris and the provinces is not an independent cleavage issue in French politics. Opinions on different measures for change do not themselves determine partisan attachments or other political behaviors. Rather, policy toward local government is a byproduct of other forces, and concerns foreign policy, economics, political rivalries. The principal goal of this book is to demonstrate the way policy toward the "areal" distribution of powers in France (as opposed to the capital distribution of power which refers to the allocation of powers among institutions within a national capital, as between the executive and the legislature) has been shaped by such forces and concerns.[2]

The problem of explanation is faced early on. Chapter 2 explores the alternative paradigms that can be used to interpret the relatively limited extent of local government reform in France, and explicates the emphasis given here to party politics. Chapter 3 sets out the principal options debated in the postwar years and summarizes the chronology of major developments. The ways in which party politics shaped policy toward local government are closely examined in Chapters 4–8. These chapters offer an interpretation of French party dynamics, to which local government policy is then linked.

France is not the only European country in which center-local linkages have been a matter of debate in the postwar years. Indeed, virtually every country in Europe and elsewhere has examined the territorial distribution of powers and everywhere changes of one kind or another have been proposed. In comparative terms, France has perhaps been the country where the *least* change has occurred (excluding the recent dictatorships of Spain, Portugal, Greece). Chapter 9 applies the line of reasoning used for France to the most plausibly similar case—Italy, whose administrative structures and party system are close

2. Arthur Maass, ed., *Area and Power* (Glencoe: Free Press, 1959).

enough to that of France to make comparison interesting, and where the outcome of the debate has been somewhat different: Italy went much further than France in creating regional government.

Among the forces pushing for reform of center-local linkages in postwar Europe has been the resurgence of "peripheral nationalism"—Scots, Basques, Flemish, Bretons, and others. In some places, the strength of such pressure has been strong enough to bring about change: Belgium, Britain, and Spain are the clearest examples. In other cases, the pressure has been relatively weak, as in France (also Italy and Germany). An explanation of policy toward the areal distribution of powers must therefore interpret the differential strength of peripheral nationalisms in postwar Europe; this is the aim of Chapter 10.

Speculation about the future is risky but interesting. The concluding chapter offers an appreciation of what has happened to date and some guidelines for thinking about what might happen next.

PART ONE

THE ISSUES

1

THE NEW CRITICISM
The Re-emergence of Anti-Jacobin Analyses of the Areal Distribution of Powers in France

On the eve of World War II, most of the political "families" in France were firmly attached to the Jacobin tradition of a centralized and unitary areal distribution of powers. Both Socialists and Communists alike rejected the syndicalist alternative on the left in favor of a more statist model. Despite the profound differences between them, both parties understood that the tasks of socialism, conceived largely as the supplanting of market forces by the state, would require a strong state apparatus. The non–Marxist left and anticlerical center continued to equate local autonomy with reactionary ends. For them, the grip of conservative forces over local life could be broken only by the application of power from the capital, via the *instituteur*, the prefect, and other agents of the republican state. Conservatives looked to a strong state as a guarantor of order against radical forces, and as a defender of business interests against the hurricane of world market forces. Nationalists thought only a powerful central government could control disruptive forces within France and defend her against enemies from without.

Dissent from the centralizing tradition certainly existed. Catholics, submerged *ethnies,* syndicalists, libertarians, and elements of the far right all preferred a less thorough concentration of power in the hands of the central government, more pluralism, and greater possibility for local control. French political thought was certainly not without spokesmen for decentralization. But Tocqueville and Montesquieu have always been appreciated more outside France than in, and the non-Jacobin dissenters were politically weak. The intense internal strife of the thirties did to the proposals for reform of center-local linkages what political conflict has always done at previous moments in French history: it made experimentation with the state machine seem too risky. It took military defeat to give some of the anti-Jacobins a chance to implement some of their ideas, and even they too quickly found political imperatives to recentralize the system.[1]

After 1940, attitudes began to shift. It is an oft-noted irony that many of the ideas discredited by the Vichy collaboration in fact crept their way into French thought and practice anyway, in somewhat purified form. The debacle shook up everyone; the Resistance and the Liberation added more food for thought; the Cold War, de-Stalinization, progressive Catholicism, Keynesian prosperity, and decolonization made their own contribution to a reevaluation of French institutions.

It is possible to see in the postwar era the emergence of new attitudes toward the areal distribution of authority in France. Within each political camp, new critiques of the Jacobin model are joining forces with latent older traditions to produce a sustained attack on existing institutions. Among Marxists, centrists, conservatives, and nationalists, the traditional equations between party purposes and the massive unitary state are no longer accepted quite so axiomatically. The criticism reflects both new goals such as autogestion and new understandings of how to reach older goals (strengthening the state, for example, by freeing the capital of petty details). In each political formation, the formulation of ends has led to reanalysis of institutional requirements of those ends. Repeatedly, political actors

1. On French ideas about the areal distribution of powers, see Stanley Hoffmann, "The Areal Division of Powers in the Writings of French Political Thinkers," in *Area and Power*, ed. Arthur Maass (Glencoe: Free Press, 1959) pp. 113–149; Henry Ehrmann, "Direct Democracy in France," *American Political Science Review* 57 (December 1963); Roger Soltau, *French Political Thought in the 19th Century* (New York: Russell and Russell, 1959). On the development of local institutions since 1789, see Maurice Bourjol, *Les Institutions régionales de 1789 à nos jours* (Paris: Berger-Levrault, 1969).

have come to think that reform of the links between Paris and the countryside is central to their program: not that institutional reform itself constitutes that program, but that such change turns out at least to be essential for the realization of other substantive goals.

These newer modes of thinking have struggled mightily with the old. The Jacobin tradition has deep roots in everyone. It is naturally not easy to cast off habits of thought, categories of analysis, cognitive maps, sentiments, and understandings which embody generations of experience. The new discourse about the areal distribution of powers produces sharp conflict, not only between groups, parties, and individuals, but within each of them. Indeed, it is more accurate to speak of profound "internal contradictions" in each type of actor than of divisions among them. On the one hand, the French public, politicians, and theorists are profoundly attached to an interpretation of the public good which is unitary and, as such, lends support for the traditional Jacobin, centralized model of center-local relations. On the other hand, these same elements of society have developed an analysis of the substantive problems which confront France for which serious reform of the areal distribution of powers, including some kind of decentralization, is essential. At any given moment, the same people adhere to both sets of ideas.

THE PUBLIC GOOD

French political parties do not, of course, seek the same goals. Nonetheless, despite the variety of ends sought (equality, socialism, efficient capitalism, liberty) one may argue that there is something the various publics have in common in the way they understand these goals: they see them as unitary wholes, as coherent goods. Society, in French discourse, is a reality, not an abstraction, and a unity, not an aggregate. There exists an entity, society, about whose "welfare" or "well-being" it is possible to be concerned. The job of the state is to identify that public welfare, and realize it. To do so requires that the state have autonomy from other forces. No constituent member of the whole can be allowed to block the actions of that agent charged with identifying and realizing the general interest—the state.

Particular forces are, in this view, of inferior legitimacy. They embody partial views, whose sum is never equal to the interests of the whole—a line of reasoning whose most famous exponent is, of course, Jean-Jacques Rousseau. While Rousseau is regarded as a theorist of the Revolution of 1789, much of his thinking has passed into the common domain in France. It has become detached from its original political location and become part of a set of ideas available to all parts of the political spectrum. Thus, in the National Assembly debate of December 1968, which considered the projected referendum of April 1969, both Alexandre Sanguinetti, ardent Gaullist, and Waldeck L'Huillier, leader of the *Parti Communiste Française* (PCF), could evoke arguments inspired by Rousseau, which virtually everybody else in the Chamber would accept:

> Legitimate as the private interests may be—and they are legitimate—necessary as their defense may be, you can never make the sum of private interests equal the general interest. The special virtue, the nobility of public power is that it represents the general interest. No one else can do it, not even the socio-professional groupings: it is neither their role nor their mission. Their mission is to defend private interests—as noble as the general interest—but which still are only private interests. [Applause from several benches of the *Union des Démocrates pour la République*][2]
>
> (Sanguinetti)

> To vote taxes and direct public funds can only be done—as all republican traditions have established—by an assembly elected by universal suffrage.[3]
>
> (L'Huillier)

2. Alexandre Sanguinetti, *Journal Officiel de l'Assemblée Nationale, Débats*, Fourth Legislature of the Constitution of 4 October 1958, first ordinary session of 1968-1969, sessions 104–107, 11–14 December 1968, p. 5463.

3. Waldeck L'Huillier, *Journal Officiel*, loc. cit., p. 5350.

Not only are "particular" (or private) forces of inferior legit-imacy. They can also be dangerous to national unity. Given the opportunity to assert their interests, groups may press their claims so far as to endanger the very coherence and integrity of French society. French political discourse often conveys a fear that France is on the brink of civil war. The straitjacket of the centralized state has forced these centrifugal forces into a co-herent political entity. It is that type of power which managed to harness the energies of particular groups toward the internal development without which France would have been unable to defend and assert her interests in the world. Again, the speeches of Sanguinetti and L'Huillier in the same debate may be taken as typical:

> The whole history of federal nations is marked by the struggle of the federal power against the power of the states. The United States had to weather the atrocious crisis of the Civil War and their struggle is far from over. . . .

> It is pertinent to point out that we owe our existence to cen-tralization, because our existence did not come about naturally. France is not a natural occurrence; she is the consequence of a political will that never let up in the course of the monarchy, the empires, and the republics.

> If the central government had at any one moment dropped its guard, we would have seen the centrifugal forces at work. And anyway, we have seen them.

> It is because we are a centralized nation that we are able to sustain seventeen regimes in one hundred seventy-seven years, three military disasters, and a terrible bloodletting. . . .

> We are today going to repeat what was already done by Louis XVI, destroying the accomplishments of Louis XI, destroying the work of Louis XIV, . . . bringing on the French Revolution.[4]

> (Sanguinetti)

> Any return to a federal system would be artificial and retro-grade. Given the existing centralized structure, it would only lead to impotence.

4. Sanguinetti, loc. cit., p. 5461.

The departments, which date from the French Revolution, were formed to weld together the unity of the nation and to destroy provincial particularisms, finishing with the outmoded expression of semifeudal relations of production of 1789. They still are a solid reality, an element of equilibrium of the economic and social life of the nation.[5]

(L'Huillier)

This view of the public interest, it may be argued, is incompatible with decentralization. Decentralization fragments political power. It creates multiple centers of decision-making, each autonomous, each able to inflect the overall pattern of policy in one direction or another. Groups of all kinds have numerous opportunities to exercise influence. The state, like ordinary groups, must bargain and fight for its point of view. A unitary conception of the public good cannot accept these implications of decentralized decision-making.[6] We would expect that in countries where such views prevail, as in France, it is difficult to legitimate any proposals which call for such change. We would appear, therefore, to have a ready explanation for the failure of wide-ranging proposals since World War II.

THE NEW CRITIQUES

Yet, these traditional French views have been subject to widespread questioning in past years. The very same groups, indeed the very same people, who speak of the unitary nature of the public good, the inviolability of the state, and the menace to national unity, have also spoken out against the existing areal division of powers in France. On all sides, politicians and the public criticize the specific form of rule from Paris as destructive of the ends they seek. To some degree, this controversy reflects

5. L'Huillier, loc. cit., p. 5461.
6. On the contrasts between fragmented and centralized decision-making processes, see the various writings of Charles E. Lindblom, in particular, *The Intelligence of Democracy* (New York: Free Press, 1965); *Politics and Markets* (New York: Basic Books, 1978); and "The Science of Muddling Through," *Public Administration Review* 19 (Spring 1959): 79–88. Also Edward Banfield, *Political Influence* (Chicago: University of Chicago Press, 1961).

the emergence of new goals, such as autogestion. To some degree, it also reflects new understandings of the realization of old goals: Michel Debré, for example, has advocated reform in order to strengthen the state by freeing Paris of lesser business. In either case, the criticisms are strong and pervasive. Everyone in France complains about centralization, even those who have been articulate in presenting the ideas which justify it. The criticisms have developed to the point where they are now capable of legitimating quite a different set of arrangements. Jacobinism, considered so typical of French thinking, no longer holds exclusive sway. An alternative body of reasoning, drawing upon a variety of sources, has emerged. To make sense out of present quarrels, it is useful to examine these criticisms in some detail. They tell us something important about the changes in both reality and perception which support the current controversy and which have led to the "contradictions" in French thinking about the proper distribution of authority between Paris and the countryside.

The critiques may be sorted into three categories, each focusing on a different "end" sought through the areal distribution of powers, or a different "function" it is expected to perform. We may identify those primarily interested in *liberty*, of some kind or another; *political control*, of various kinds; and *rationality*, variously defined. These categories are not mutually exclusive. The same persons or groups may be interested in all simultaneously. Nonetheless, the distinctions do exist analytically, and in practice there tends to be a center of gravity to the concerns of political actors, leading them toward one set of goals or another. Each category comprises a variety of arguments.

1. Liberty or Human Development

English-speaking readers tend to associate the critique of centralization with concern for a particular kind of liberty, constitutionalism. Tocqueville, is, of course, the most famous theoretician of the linkages which make centralization the principal cause of despotism in democratic societies. Quite a range of other arguments exist as well. A theorist commonly taken as diametrically opposed to Tocqueville, namely Marx, found the character of the French state important enough to deplore. To him, it warped French development in ways detrimental to the realization of socialism. This critique of the state from the standpoint of socialism has emerged in recent years with considerable vigor. Other versions of such arguments include a progressive Catholic one, a kind of benevolent corporatism which believes in intermediate bodies, and ethnic nationalist ones, which seek accommodation for cultural diversity. What these arguments have in common is the conviction that the Jacobin model is inimical to the realization of certain human potentials, capacities, and rights, and must therefore be altered.

A. Constitutionalism, Political Stability, Human Development, Human Choice—the Tocquevillian Family of Arguments

For some theorists, of which Tocqueville is doubtless the most conspicuous example, the territorial distribution of powers is more than a "subsystem" or aspect of the whole. It is a structure which shapes the functioning of the entire polity. This happens because the pattern of center-local linkages shapes a whole complex of attributes which are held to lie at the base of the political system: psychological attitudes toward authority, human relations, intellectual categories, capacity for initiative, religion, manners, and so on. The trouble with centralization for Tocqueville is that it inculcates the wrong behaviors. Whereas democracy is more or less inevitable, the type of democracy remains a choice. There can be constitutionalism or an arbitrary executive, the moral development of the individual or conformity and majority tyranny. A "good democracy" requires that its citizens have a sense of civic responsibility, an ability to cooperate with others, a concern for the public good, a pragmatic orientation to politics, and so on. While the Americans meet these requirements, the French, alas, do not. Why?

A famous passage in *Democracy in America* sets out quite clearly the causal sequence Tocqueville postulates: "In shaping society Customs are more important than the Laws, and the

Laws are more important than Geography.''[7] In *The Old Regime*,[8] the argument is more interactive: over time, customs are themselves profoundly affected by other forces, in particular by institutions. Prior to the seventeenth century, Tocqueville argues, the French people were interested in public affairs, did cooperate with each other to undertake collective action, did worry about pragmatic questions. Then the Bourbon kings stripped away all power from local institutions. Local initiative no longer had any effect since local governments had no power. Individuals had no incentive to be interested, cooperative, practical. Gradually, the French became isolated, private-regarding, divided from each other, dependent on higher authority while complaining about it, ideological because their interest in society had no practical outlet to lash down the sails of ideational speculation. They took no interest in local affairs, leaving everything to the crown. The whole political system was thereby corrupted. So deep were these attributes that the revolutionaries after 1789, instead of wrecking the system of centralized rule, perfected it and provided its modern form: departments, prefects, and the Jacobin label. Tocqueville was gloomy. Once ''the civic culture'' is destroyed, it cannot easily be recreated. A vicious cycle is set up: people are dependent on such a state; only a different kind of structure would break them of that dependence, but so long as they are dependent they will either not want to alter the structure, or, if they do, will make a mess of it. Like drug addicts, they know that their dependency is bad, but cannot live without it.

In the present period, these ideas have found powerful exponents most notably in the writings of Michel Crozier, Stanley Hoffmann, and Alain Peyrefitte, among others.[9] Crozier's work

7. Alexis de Tocqueville, *Democracy in America*, vol. 1 (New York: Vintage, 1945), ch. 17.
8. Alexis de Tocqueville, *The Old Regime and the Revolution* (New York: Anchor, 1955), especially chs. 8 and 9.
9. Michel Crozier, *The Bureaucratic Phenomenon* (Chicago: University of Chicago Press, 1964); *The Stalled Society* (New York: Viking Press, 1973);

(particularly *The Bureaucratic Phenomenon*) is the most for-malized presentation. The French dislike face-to-face relation-ships and value equality within their own categories. Rather than work with each other, they prefer, therefore, to refer deci-sions to a higher level, which in turn they view with con-siderable suspicion. They need authority and fear it at the same time. As a result, higher officials make decisions with rather lit-tle input from below, and *la base* periodically refuses to go along with these decisions, and subverts them one way or another.

Like Tocqueville, Crozier links to these psychological charac-teristics many attributes of French society: the alternation between regimes of strong executives and weak ones, the fragmentation of the party system and its ideological character, administrative irrationalities, and the style of industrial rela-tions. And like Tocqueville, Crozier sees a vicious cycle for which there is no clear way out: how can the cycle of institutions producing a psychology, which sustains the institutions, which produce the psychology—how can this cycle be broken? While Crozier gives no clear answer, it is clear enough that for him the health of the body politic depends on breaking out of this deadening pattern.

In contemporary France this line of reasoning has found an audience primarily in the political center, somewhat broadly conceived as ranging from the moderate wing of the Gaullists, through the center parties to the moderate wing of the Social-ists. "Crozierism" influenced the important speech by Jacques Chaban-Delmas to the National Assembly in 1970 in which he called for an attack upon the *société bloquée* (after which he was fired by Georges Pompidou). Alain Peyrefitte has recently brought similar themes to the attention of a large French public through his bestseller *Le Mal français*, where the "mal" is

---

Stanley Hoffmann, Charles Kindleberger, Lawrence Wylie, Jesse Pitts, Jean-Baptiste Duroselle, François Goguel, *In Search of France* (Cambridge, Mass.: Harvard University Press, 1963); and Stanley Hoffmann, *Decline or Renewal?: France since the 1930s* (New York: Viking Press, 1974); Alain Peyrefitte, *Le Mal français* (Paris: Plon, 1977).

precisely an excessive dependence on authority. Echoes of this sort of analysis crop up in the criticisms of centralization put forward by Jean-Jacques Servan-Schreiber and by various members of the Socialist party.

This centrist locus is not accidental. The Tocquevillian line appeals, in a sense, most strongly to those who reject the major alternative grounds for criticism: a socialism rooted in class analysis: a conservative, property-oriented liberalism; or an internationally focused statism. The social-psychological argument lacks the clear connection to substantive policies characteristic of these other arguments. It complains of the character of the decision-making process in France, of the forms and style of politics, rather than its content. This policy ambiguity is important to the argument's strength. Socialists, centrists, *gaullistes de gauche*, and conservatives can all claim it for their own, as the key to unblocking the way to the realization of *their* particular policy objectives.

The clearest policy prescription of the Tocquevillians has been in the realm of center-periphery relations itself. They call for extensive change in the present system. While divided over whether emphasis should be placed on departments or regions, they press for something beyond administrative deconcentration, something which will allow greater opportunities for local initiative, and participation in the allocation of resources.

Among the types of criticisms of present structures, the Tocquevillians are doubtless those who seek the most from change. They derive from present structures a wider range of features of the present political system, indeed of French life in general, than does any other school. They suggest that nothing important will change, or can change, until this feature of French life is changed. If this changes, everything will.

B. Decentralization and Socialism

Typically, the Marxian tradition is associated with justification of a powerful, wide-ranging state and a concern less for liberty than for control. French Marxism has, indeed, supported the Jacobin model. Proudhonian elements of the socialist tradition, critical of statist power and sympathetic to localized, autonomous units, were supplanted by scientific socialism, preoccupied with public ownership and planning understood in ways which required vast extension of the state apparatus; in place of the market, there would be administration. The process of getting to socialism also implied a centralized model. Conflict with the bourgeoisie would be severe and of long duration, and the problems of transition would be difficult; only a disciplined, hierarchical structure, both in party and state, could cope.

Since the war, the equation of socialism with Jacobinism has been *mise in cause*.[10] While public ownership is still regarded as essential, many on the left question whether it is sufficient. Substituting the state for private stockholders does not by itself democratize industry. The work may remain unpleasant, boring, and stultifying; authority may remain just as remote and hierarchical. Even if enough property is socialized to free the state of that form of influence, the public managers may themselves constitute an autonomous force, subverting the realization of socialist values. Socialism, for these critics, involves the actual experience of participation in the direction of common social affairs. In the workplace, this means some kind of autogestion, whereby the worker has a share in the management of the factory, the industry, and the economy through a system of elections and committees organized from the shop floor up. The same principle must be extended to the state. The state must be *socialized* no less than industry. Indeed the socialization of one without the other leads inevitably to the desocialization, in practice, of the first. Returning the state to the people implies a variety of things, in particular, genuine and extensive decentralization. Providing local governments

10. On the growing disenchantment with the state by all sorts of people see Suzanne Berger, "Politics and Antipolitics in Western Europe in the Seventies," *Daedalus* 108 (Winter 1979): 27–50. Some of the left's ideas about decentralization may be found in Yves Durrieu, *Régionaliser la France* (Paris: Mercure de France, 1969); Michel Philipponneau, *La Gauche et les régions* (Paris: Calmann-Lévy, 1967); Robert Lafont, *Décoloniser la France* (Paris: Gallimard, 1971); and the programs of the PCF and the PSF published in 1972, and the Common Program of 1972.

with ample powers would situate decision-making in the community, close to the citizens, allowing them a reasonable share in the direction of their lives. Some argue that power cannot be socialized so long as the *Grands Corps* remain intact, but the major party formations have not been willing to go this far.

Those who have been making such arguments draw on Marx himself for support, particularly on the sharply critical comments about the French state found in *The Eighteenth Brumaire*. Marx links the victory of Louis-Napoléon to the individualism and isolation of French society and economy—the peasants connected only like potatoes in a sack, in the famous phrase, were vulnerable to the appeal of a man on horseback. Not only the peasantry, but all classes are isolated in this way; such isolation is not only a cause of the strong state, but also a consequence of it. Like Tocqueville, Marx points out how the state levels down, creates dependencies, fragments, suffocates. All social classes are deflected away from their "natural" course of development: the bourgeoisie turns away from private enterprise toward state employment and subsidy; the working class is fragmented and mystified by imperial forms; the peasantry cannot act. The result was Caesarism. In short, Marx worried that centralization in France corrupted bourgeois development and would either prevent socialism or corrupt it.

This interpretation of *The Eighteenth Brumaire* conflicts with an older one whereby the problem is not the state, but the character of French capitalism. Lacking, for one reason or another, the dynamism of its British counterpart, French capitalism turns to the state for compensation. The state provides money, positions, and protection for a bourgeoisie not capable of developing the economy on its own. In this reading of Marx, the interaction between state and economy is broken: the flagging economy is taken as primary and prior, giving rise to the omnipresent state, rather than, as in the other interpretation, the state itself being a contributing cause to the nature of the economy.

The tension between these ways of interpreting Marx runs

throughout present debates on the left over reform of state structures. Decentralization has been a confusing issue to the Marxist parties. On the one hand, centralization cannot be the *key* to socalism, since class relationships and the persistence of capitalism occupy that position. On the other hand, in analyzing what socialism would be like, in formulating critiques of Stalinism, the Soviet model, and the Parti Communiste Française, and in discussing democratization of industry, socialists are driven to find structures and institutions very important indeed.[11] They become in fact the very essence of how real socialism differs from state socialism. It is through structures of representation in the state and the factory that the working class comes to govern, and prevents management from becoming a new ruling class.

In this way, these Marxists intersect with the Tocquevillians. There are "socialist Crozierites," and "Tocquevillian socialists." Where the two schools differ is in their thinking about the relationship between the economy and the state, and between autogestion and decentralization. The Tocquevillians tend not to discuss industrial democracy, or are vague about it. The problem is not capitalism versus socialism but good authority relations or bad ones. For the Marxists, better authority relations cannot work unless property is socialized. While the socialization of the state is important to the left, the strongest emotional tug remains that of autogestion based in the factory, hence the economy.

C. Catholic Corporatism

While the Tocquevillian and neo-Marxist critiques of the Jacobin model have been the most conspicuous in postwar France, the controversy has tapped other sources as well, some of them perhaps as politically significant if less visible. Among these may be noted the Catholic tradition. Catholic thinking about society, in France and elsewhere, seeks to root the in-

11. See critiques of the PCF's views of the state by Louis Althusser, *Le Monde*, 25–28 April 1978.

dividual in a context, in a complex tissue of social relationships, which give him identity, meaning, belonging, security, and sustenance. Liberalism, Marxism, and capitalism are all criticized for constricting the individual, pushing him into only one identity, and leaving him alone, isolated, exposed to the full and harsh workings of social forces.

The Catholics do not, therefore, share the central tenet of the French justification of its Jacobin state: the suspicion of intermediate groups. For them, such groups are precisely what is needed. They believe that a network of relationships located in a strong civil society promotes proper individual development and helps prevent the emergence of a crushing state machine.[12] Many kinds of intermediate bodies are useful: voluntary associations, families, professional groups, union and business syndicates, and local governmental structures. These may be regional, departmental, or communal. The general doctrine does not point in any compelling way to one or the other. In the postwar period, it has been the moderate, progressive Catholics who have shown the most interest in local government from this point of view. As we shall see, the success of reform movements depended greatly on the political fortunes of that portion of the French party system.

Here too there are points of overlap with the other arguments. Catholics share with the Tocquevillians an emphasis on the importance of intermediate associations, both as a means for human development and as a guarantor of a sane and stable, constitutional political order. Catholics share with the Marxists a certain suspicion of untrammeled liberalism, of allowing the free market to shape society. Their arguments are less psychological than the Tocquevillian arguments, and they are, in contrast with the Marxists, less concerned with rooting out capitalism than with the proper ordering of society, which will by itself contribute to harmony and the reduction of class tensions.

12. For Catholic thinking about the state, see Soltau, *French Political Thought*, chs. 4, 7, 11.

D. The "Liberal" Critique

A fourth current of French thought attacks the Jacobin model as part of general criticism of the domination of the state over society. The more conservative members of this school want the state to be limited—the night watchman state of the last century. They say that too much interference stifles individual initiative, and sooner or later all liberty. Power should lie in society, not with politicians. While all government is something of an evil, local government is less so than distant Paris. This line of reasoning, so common in the United States, is much less widespread in France because liberals there have always, by and large, accepted the necessity for an active state.[13] It does exist, though, partly in the center (the Radicals descend from Alain as well as the Jacobins), partly on the right.

E. "Progressive Pragmatism"

Another source of "libertarian" criticism of centralization comes from those who stress the inherent virtues of participation and the instrumental utility of local control as a means of correcting the problems which arise from present practice. Such people attack the state for being ignorant, haughty, irritating, maladroit, wrong, and ineffective. The accusation is not so much that the state is dangerous in principle but that it has acted dangerously in practice. Civil servants are too cut off from the society they govern. Decentralization will help put things right. The argument is more empirical in spirit than theoretically based: it refuses either Marxism or Tocquevillianism as a ground for critique, but turns rather to a popular

13. French business has never been as antistatist as its American and British counterparts. The state has been too useful, first in ripping down the Old Regime, then in supporting business against foreign competition, and in containing working class pressures. On French business attitudes see David Landes and John E. Sawyer, in *Modern France*, ed. E. M. Earle (Princeton: Princeton University Press, 1951); Charles Kindleberger, "The Postwar Resurgence of the French Economy," in *In Search of France*, ed. Hoffmann et al. On the role of the state in late development, see Alexander Gershenkron, *Economic Backwardness in Historical Perspective* (Cambridge, Mass.: Harvard University Press, 1962). Also David Landes, *The Unbound Prometheus* (Cambridge: Cambridge University Press, 1969).

tradition of anti-Parisian sentiment. Jean-Jacques Servan-Schreiber is perhaps the most well-known practitioner of this kind of "pragmatic eclecticism."[14] He has been the only prominent politician to make decentralization the centerpiece of his political program. As with the Tocquevillians, the policy specificity of this school is not clear, and for the same reasons, its following is in the center.

F. Cultural Pluralism and Ethnic Nationalism

France has long enjoyed a reputation for being culturally "uniform," in aspiration at least, if not in reality. The conception of being French was unitary, not plural. Several incipient states were destroyed in the forging of French nationhood. That fact was generally celebrated among the bearers of the culture of the *langue d'oeil*, and acquiesced to by the rest.[15]

In the postwar period, this understanding of French national unity has been challenged, both by those at the core of French culture, and those in the periphery of it. The old submerged national fragments have revived; in Brittany, Alsace, Provence, and Occitania there has been a burst of self-awareness and discovery. People are relearning language, the arts, history, dress. The traditional policies imposed by Paris, which sought extinction of these traditions, are now challenged.

14. Jean-Jacques Servan-Schreiber, *Le Pouvoir régional* (Paris: Editions Bernard Grasset, 1971). Also Servan-Schreiber and Michel Hebert, *Ciel et terre: Le Manifest radical* (Paris: Editions Denoel, 1970).
15. Recent scholarship on France has emphasized the diversity which lies beneath the surface of most categories used to generalize about the French, including that of "France" itself. See Theodore Zeldin, *France: 1848-1945*, 2 vols. (London: Oxford University Press, 1973-1977); and Eugen Weber, *Peasants into Frenchmen* (Stanford: Stanford University Press, 1976). Among the French writers who have helped increase public consciousness of the submerged "ethnies," see Morvan Levesque, *Comment peut-on être breton?* (Paris: Le Seuil, 1970); and Robert Lafont, *La Révolution régionaliste* (Paris: Gallimard, 1967); and Lafont, *Décoloniser la France*. On the problem of peripheral nationalisms generally, see Milton Esman, *Ethnic Conflict in the Western World* (Ithaca: Cornell University Press, 1977); Michael Hechter, *Internal Colonialism* (Berkeley and Los Angeles: University of California Press, 1975); and Peter Gourevitch, "State-building, Industrialization, and the Reemergence of 'Peripheral Nationalisms': Some Comparative Speculations," *Comparative Studies in Society and History* (July 1979).

At the same time, in the core itself, many of the bearers of the grand tradition themselves take a somewhat more pluralist view of that culture and how it relates to other influences. France is seen as just a bit less universal, less basic, less original. It is part of a larger whole (Europe) and is comprised of components (Latin, German, Celtic). Cultural diversity thus becomes a value to be cherished.

Both the rediscovery of non-French elements and the changing conception of French elements have supported the quest for new patterns of center-local linkages, ones which would be less suffocating of local differences.

2. Political Control

A second major family of criticism of the traditional French model of centralization comprises those interested less in liberty and human development than in political control. The distribution of power among territorial units and the administrative mechanisms connecting them clearly affects the capacity of those in power at the center to maintain their grip on the state. The relationships are complex and less obvious than may seem apparent. French thinkers, and those in other European countries, developed theories about the proper ordering of the relationship between center and periphery which were quite different from the libertarian tradition. For them, the problem has been to insure the ability of the center to direct the affairs of society. For conservatives, local government is not an arena of participation, or training in liberty, but an instrument of administration and a training ground for discipline and obedience. Local institutions should encourage not political consciousness and conflict, but consensus and acceptance. Power must therefore be in the hands of local elites and the representatives of the central government. French conservatives found these doctrines attractive, as did Napoleon. Similar reasoning was taken by German theorists to Japan, producing some very interesting parallels with French as well as Prussian practices.[16]

16. Kurt Steiner, *Local Government in Japan* (Stanford: Stanford University Press, 1965).

For the left, the problem of control has also been a major pre-occupation. Before the Revolution, progressives suspected local autonomy because conservatives championed it. During the long period in opposition from 1815–1870, the left's interest in decentralization reawakened, but with the Third Republic, the balance shifted back to suspicion. Centralized rule seemed the more necessary because the Republic's control was precarious. Monarchists, reactionaries, enemies of the Republic—these were stronger at the local level than in Paris, hence decentralization could only menace the regime. The *instituteur* and the prefect were the agents par excellence of a state worried about its survival.

Thus, all sides assumed that remaining in power required centralization. In the postwar period this equation between centralization and control is no longer taken for granted. To those in power, it is no longer so obvious that the best way to maintain governmental authority, in general, and the interests of the majority coalition, in particular, is through the Jacobin model. They have come to suspect that the greater dispersion of decision-making away from Paris would have the effect of *improving* control from the center, rather than weakening it. For them, there is at present "surplus" centralization which is counterproductive. For those in the opposition, decentralization appears to offer certain advantages even for the traditional goal of conquering the center and keeping it.

A. Decentralization in the Service of Holding Power

The statist critics of the present system fear that centralization paralyzes government. The concentration of power in Paris means that everything gets referred back to the capital. The political system in general, the bureaucracy and the government in particular, are forced to deal with an incredible range of problems, from "high policy" (foreign affairs, defense, the economy) to the tiniest detail (repairing bridges, painting schoolrooms). Under this overload, the system is choked. It cannot deal with those matters which really count because the machinery is clogged with detail. The problem is not only one of administrative efficiency, but also of politics. When the central government has such vast powers, people hold it responsible for everything. They make endless demands on it. The state becomes sharply constrained by such pressures, losing the freedom to take action in the national interest. In other words, centralization undermines both the legitimacy and the efficiency of the state.

The solution to this situation lies in some kind of dispersal of power out of the capital, and the construction of new "transmission belts" to society.[17] As we shall see, a variety of schemes could work—consolidated departments (proposed by Michel Debré in the late forties), regions, corporate representation, deconcentration, perhaps decentralization, though few of these theorists would go so far.

Such arguments made headway in the postwar years among some Gaullists, including Michel Debré and Charles de Gaulle himself,[18] whose support was of course decisive (see Chapters 4-7). It is they who combined concern, if not reverence, for the authority of state with the sense that preservation required reform. In so doing, they fought against their own statist proclivities and the more cautious outlook of the Jacobins among their own followers.

B. Decentralization in the Service of Gaining Power

The existence of a strong central government reinforces itself in that politicians and citizens have considerable incentive to focus their energies on capturing it. When the local governments are weak, there is little reward in worrying about local politics.

To opposition parties, however, local governments, even

17. Stanley Hoffmann uses this term in his essay "Paradoxes" from *In Search of France.*
18. Michel Debré, *La Mort de l'état républicain* (Paris: Gallimard, 1947); Nicholas Wahl, "The Constitutional Ideas of Michel Debré," in *Theory and Practice: Festschrift for Carl Friedrich*, ed. Klaus von Beyme (The Hague: Martinus Nijhoff, 1972); Nicholas Wahl and Stanley Hoffmann, "The French Constitution of 1958," *American Political Science Review* 53 (June 1959). For de Gaulle's ideas see his *Memoires* and the interpretive writings by Stanley Hoffmann in *Decline and Renewal.*

weak ones, can provide a variety of advantages which have become increasingly attractive in recent years to parties on the left. First, local government offers an organizational base. When there are no ministries, favors, and patronage to be had from the national government, local positions can be very helpful in keeping parties alive. Elective offices, such as mayor and president of the departmental council, maintain party leaders in the public eye; the presidency of the regional council is an even more visible post. Even with limited powers, local structures afford at least some opportunities to attract a clientele via patronage of various kinds.

Another service local government offers the opposition is an arena in which to prepare the terrain for gaining power in the center. Parties may experiment with alliances to other political formations, social groups, and associations. This has been especially important in recent years to the Socialists and Communists. The opportunity to work together at lower levels helped forge bonds of knowledge, experience, and interest after years of distrust. Many hoped that cooperation would strengthen the alliance enough to survive the strains of holding power at the national level. The demonstration of an ability to cooperate would help the coalition reach outward by reassuring skeptical and fearful sectors of the electorate.[19] These local efforts did not, of course, in the end by themselves prevent friction and fractures in the alliance of the left. Nonetheless, the move toward such coalitions spurred interest in local government.

In the postwar period, then, both politicians who were in power and politicians who were out came to support a redistribution of authority between Paris and the countryside. Those primarily interested in control from the center found reasons to think a wider dispersal of power might actually help do that by shielding the center from certain pressures and demands. Those

19. On PCF and Italian Communist Party (PCI) alliance strategies, see Don Blackmer and Sidney Tarrow, *Communism in Italy and France* (Princeton: Princeton University Press, 1975).

in the opposition looked to local government as a staging ground for assault on the capital itself.

From a historical perspective, the attitude of the opposition follows an older pattern, while that of the governmental reformers is somewhat new or more unusual. Since the Revolution, it has been generally true that the forces which dominate national politics in given periods are suspicious of decentralization, while the forces in quasi-permanent opposition tend to find it more attractive. When these positions reverse (when the opposition becomes dominant, and vice versa), so do the attitudes toward areal reform. Thus the present interest in areal reform on the part of the left fits what we expect of the opposition. For the government also to become interested in such changes is somewhat newer.

3. Rationality

A third family of criticism of the traditional areal division of powers in France is concerned primarily with "rationality." The Jacobin model has been admired precisely for having this characteristic in a very obvious way: politico-administrative districts are of uniform size; its chief officers are appointed by a single authority according to impersonal rules of merit; command flows along a pyramid, from the top down through a clear chain of command; this mechanism cannot be *détourné* by particularistic interests. Such a structure seemed ideally suited to a model of political administration based upon the application of centrally determined rules to particular situations.

What has in recent years been challenged is not the value of rationality, but how to get it. Critics argue that French society has changed dramatically since the old structures were set up; therefore, present structures are poorly suited to the nature of contemporary problems.

Departmental boundaries, it is said, were drawn in such a way that no one would be farther than a day's horseback ride from *chef-lieu*. Since then, of course, the population has shifted from agriculture to industry, from the countryside to the city. The departments no longer contain anything remotely like rough parity of numbers. In many places, communes are depopulated; in others, cities and suburbs sprawl over political lines. The economy no longer consists of semiautarchic market towns, but rather of enterprises of widely differing sizes enmeshed in a national and international economy. Much is expected of the government: industrial modernization, full employment, the control of competition, housing, health, transport, schools, culture, and so on. These policy matters are fantastically complex and interdependent. They require a very high capacity for analysis and an extraordinary amount of coordination among civil servants, local officials, and private actors. By their nature, these problems spill over, indeed, flood the old jurisdictions.

Society has changed, the economy has changed, the world has changed; it is not surprising, argue the rationalizers, that the structures fashioned in 1789 should no longer be adequate for managing the nation's business. Old institutions for new conditions is a mix which produces new irrationalities.

First, the lines of command become terribly confused. To cope with new problems, the ministries in Paris rapidly developed their field services in the departments. These have sprung up ad hoc, following the priorities of the individual ministries so that each used a different geographical *découpage*; any given department might, therefore, have found itself in differing jurisdictions from one ministry to another. The development of field services also contributed to confusion by undermining the authority of the prefect as the principal delegate of the government in each department. The various ministerial representatives reported back to their own chiefs in Paris directly, not via the prefect. Quarrels among different field services thus produced unending conflict in the field, and required constant arbitration by the highest levels of government.

A second threat to rationality came from the changing scope of new problems. Since economies were no longer local, a variety of tasks for which governments were increasingly held responsible could not be handled through communes and departments which were simply too small. Many of these tasks were national in scale—monetary, fiscal, and commercial policy. Some tasks had local dimensions but related to a larger locality than before. When better medical care came to require extremely expensive equipment, for example, the state could no longer contemplate furnishing each department or city with the whole panoply of modern machinery. As labor markets became larger, such problems as housing, employment, education, and transportation could no longer be dealt with in relation simply to the old units.

If communes and departments were too small for many of the new problems, the nation, it was argued, was too large. National planning ignored the question of how various activities were distributed geographically across the national territory. Location entailed costs and benefits of its own, so that there existed better and poorer ways of allocating resources within the nation. Local interests, for example, were not necessarily served by focusing on national ones; lowering tariffs might make the economy as a whole more competitive, but could wipe out local industries. National interests might be damaged by allowing overconcentration in one part of the country and underdevelopment in another; these costs might not show up fully in the market, so that private locational decisions might be irrational. The government should therefore worry about "subnational rationality" for itself and for its contribution to national efficiency.

These arguments were sustained by the development among social scientists of a new emphasis on regional economics and geography. Jean-François Gravier's *Paris et le désert français*,[20] published in 1947, caused something of a sensation. Many economists, historians, sociologists, and geographers helped spawn a variety of concepts which provided the intellectual superstructure for these new ways of thinking about rationality.

20. Jean-François Gravier, *Paris et le désert français*, 2d ed. (Paris: Flammarion, 1972). Among the important developers of regional economics were François Perroux and J.-R. Boudeville. See the *Cahiers de l'Institut de Science Economique Appliqué*, ser. L, *Economies régionales*.

The analyses of those interested in rationality were techno-cratic. Their thinking was not concerned primarily with repre-sentation of different political interests or with participation as an end in itself. Rather, they wanted "better" decision-mak-ing, understood as the more appropriate calculation of means to ends by informed decision-makers. The prescriptions varied, depending on which aspect of the problem drew attention: some supported scrapping departments altogether in favor of regions; some wanted simply to clarify the lines of authority among different branches of the civil service. Politically, "ra-tionality" arguments were most popular among some Gaullists, some centrists, some socialists, and some conservatives. It was too apolitical a type of reasoning to interest the left very much, although many elements of the left thought in similar terms of the technical problems which would confront a government it controlled.

CONCLUSION

In the postwar period, several currents of through have con-tributed to an extensive questioning of the traditional Jacobin model of the areal distribution of powers in France. The starting points, the reasoning, and the goals of these critics are quite varied and often contradict one another. Nonetheless, within each of the main political "families" in France can now be found an understanding of political purposes for which loosen-ing and reshaping the links between Paris and the countryside are considered indispensable. Many Marxists, liberals, Catho-lics, nationalists, Tocquevillians, and conservatives assert the need for greater participation of individuals and groups in deci-sion-making, and for greater pluralism in society. Rationalists of various political persuasions want to release the state from the paralyzing effects of irrelevant administrative structures and sterile political categories. Politicians, both those in power and those out, see various advantages in stronger local government.

These goals support the search for new links between Paris and the countryside. If traditional conceptions of the public

good and national unity inhibited change, the new lines of
analysis, or more precisely, in some cases, the reemergence of
older currents of thought, now provide the intellectual rationale
for new policy directions. For the first time in several generations, the need for thorough restructuring of French administrative and political scaffolding became an important matter of
interest to a wide range of groups. Numerous schemes were put
forth, some of which were taken very seriously indeed. At
times, the issue of areal reform held center stage in French
politics. The process and the outcome can be understood in a
variety of ways. These will be explored in the next chapter.

CHAPTER 2

ALTERNATIVE EXPLANATIONS
The Importance of Politics

Why has reform of the French system of local government and administration remained limited? What explains the nature and scope of those reforms which have come about? In this book, I wish to stress those causes that are political, in the most common-sense meaning of that word—those causes having to do with the struggle for control of government among rival political leaders and political parties. Local government is of most immediate interest to the people whose careers depend on it, the politicians. It is also the politicians who in the end must approve or disapprove any changes; legislation must be voted and even a referendum question cannot be posed unless some politicians choose to do so.

Certainly politicians do not operate in a vacuum. There are other forces at work, and there exist therefore other types of explanations to account for the policy outcome in this field. These alternative modes of reasoning include: the nature of French authority relations, the economic interests of significant social forces, the requirements of a mixed capitalist economy, regional imbalances in wealth and population, cultural diversity, the strains of modernization, political culture and political thought, the nature of the state itself, specific personalities, specific events. We can find literature on local government emphasizing one or more of these factors.[1] This abundance of in-

1. A very useful English-language guide to the main events in the regionalism controversy can be found in William C. Andrews, "The Politics of Regionalization in France," in *Politics in Europe*, ed. Martin O. Heisler (New

terpretations is not surprising. It arises quite naturally from the multiplicity of goals sought through local government. Each value sought, each function to be served through local government suggests a different standard of evaluation, a different mode of interpretation, a different reference point for explanation.[2]

In this book, these other modes of interpretation are deliberately slighted in favor of the political for two reasons: one contextual, the other more properly intellectual. The contextual reason is that the present literature on local government reform rather neglects the political line of inquiry. While other arguments have been searchingly explored, the political dimensions of areal reform have not. As a result, discussions of the subject are skewed. Interpretations which can be quite powerful when situated in relation to politics distort our understanding through neglect of that dimension. Hence the present work is both compensation for neglect and an effort to specify the political factors to which other arguments should be related.

A second reason for stressing the political dimension here is that the other traditions of interpretation are in a sense too strong. They account for change, or its absence, in such broad general ways as to be unable to distinguish among *types* of change or *degrees* of change. By predicting either considerable change, or no change at all, these arguments do not help explain the choice among a variety of alternative schemes, each of which would have been compatible with the particular factor in question. The contention here is that political considerations

---

York: McKay, 1974). Some very pertinent comparative observations are in Sidney Tarrow, *Between Center and Periphery: Grassroots Politicians in Italy and France* (New Haven: Yale University Press, 1977). In French, see particularly Pierre Grémion, *Le Pouvoir péripherique: Bureaucrats et notables dans le système politique français* (Paris: Le Seuil, 1976); and Yves Mény, *Centralisation et décentralisation dans le débat politique français, 1945-1969* (Paris: Librairie Générale de Droit et de Jurisprudence, 1974).

2. On the functions of local government, see Arthur Maass, "The Division of Powers, An Areal Analysis," and Paul Ylvisaker, "Some Criteria for a 'Proper' Areal Division of Government," in *Area and Power*, ed. Arthur Maass (Glencoe: Free Press, 1959).

tailor the effects of broader, "systemic" forces to cut out garments of particular shapes and sizes.[3]

TRADITIONS OF INTERPRETATION

The argument on behalf of a political interpretation is developed in this chapter by contrasting it with other types of reasoning about local government reform. These can be classified into three families: the *socio-psychological and cultural;* the *socio-economic;* and the partisan political.

1. The Social-Psychological and Cultural Family of Interpretation

In one way or another, most of the members of this branch can be traced back to Tocqueville.

THE AUTHORITY RELATIONS INTERPRETATION: This argument, associated most closely with Crozier's formulation in *The Bureaucratic Phenomenon*,[4] accounts for the limited nature of reform by suggesting a kind of psychological resistance to decentralization. For Crozier, vibrant local government, citizen involvement, and pluralist give-and-take have socio-psychological requisites: an ability to cooperate, to take orders and give them, to work easily with those above and below. These qualities the French lack: they combine together a horror of face-to-face relations, a jealous egalitarianism, and a suspicion of authority along with a dependence on it, all of which are inimical to a decentralized system. Hence the French resist changes which would force them into a different mode of human interaction.

This may indeed be a plausible rendering of certain characteristics of the French people. As such it helps account for a

3. On the problem of alternative explanations of a given phenomenon, see James Kurth, "The Widening Gyre: The Logic of American Weapons Procurement," *Public Policy* 19 (Summer 1971): 373–404; and Arend Lijphart, "Comparative Politics and the Comparative Method," *American Political Science Review* 65 (September 1971): 682–693.

4. Michel Crozier, *The Bureaucratic Phenomenon* (Chicago: University of Chicago Press, 1964).

generalized resistance to extensive localization and decentralization of political life. The argument is, however, both too broad and too narrow. First, not all French people oppose such changes. There is disagreement. Some do desire decentralization in one version or another. That which is common to *all* Frenchmen cannot account for differences among them.

Change, furthermore, does occur. The blockages are not so strong as to make a perfectly static society. France has altered dramatically in the past thirty years—birth rates, economic growth rates, urbanization, schooling, ideology, even local government structures have all changed. Do these contradict the *société bloquée* reasoning? Or is that an argument less about the content of *change* than about *style*, in which the style becomes the important value sought through reform? Or is it an argument that style *affects* content? Is it centralization and French authority relations which prevent redistribution of income, better hospitals, cleaner factories, the socialization of investment, competitive industries, lower unemployment rates, autogestion, and so on? If so, why do other countries, less centralized and with different authority patterns, have similar problems? Crozier and the other proponents of socio-psychological interpretation have not been clear as to which substantive changes are rendered impossible by the system of authority relations and which substantive changes are not.[5] We can never be sure, therefore, whether any particular changes which do occur are or are not in contradiction with Crozier's line of analysis.

Yet a third problem with the authority relations school has to do with timing. Social psychology and culture change only slowly. That is, after all, their value as variables: they are more enduring than the pell-mell political hurly-burly of parties and labels. But, as persistent features of the political landscape, slow to change, these variables do poorly at accounting for shorter oscillations in policy, which do occur. In the fifties, the Gaullists were ardent Jacobins who interpreted any reform of local struc-

5. For an excellent exploration of the applicability of Crozier's model to a substantive policy issue, see John Zysman, *Political Strategies for Industrial Order: State, Market, and Industry in France* (Berkeley and Los Angeles: University of California Press, 1977).

tures as weakening the state. In the sixties, de Gaulle and Debré supported a set of moderate changes, including regionalization, which many members of the majority opposed; in the seventies, interest in such changes among what remains of the Gaullists has dried up. Comparable shifts can be noted on the left: the Communists and Socialists have moved from extreme wariness and scepticism of areal reform to strong advocacy of certain projects. The center has always been rather sympathetic to changes, but was much more vocal about being so before 1974 than it has been since joining the government. We need therefore to find factors which account for swings of the pendulum, which explain why the very same people are sometimes more enthusiastic about particular proposals, at other times less so, and why some proposals rather than others succeed or fail.

THE POLITICAL CULTURE INTERPRETATION: A second variant among this family of interpretations stresses French political thinking about the state. French political culture is seen as committed to the Jacobin model and suspicious of both pluralism and decentralization. Most groups in France have felt that their goals—be these equality before the law, or equality of condition, or freedom, or national unity, or economic development—require a strong central authority capable of identifying the national interest and working toward its realization without having to negotiate with, or be checked constantly by, local forces. Partial interests, of which local interests are one type, have dubious legitimacy even to conservatives. Hence, according to this argument, the French prefer unitary governments which at least treat *all* parts of the country heavy handedly, rather than allow the divergences and internal differentiation which local autonomy would produce.[6]

As with the authority relations argument, the political culture argument certainly has some force. Nonetheless, *by itself*, the political culture argument has flaws similar to those of the

6. On French political theory concerning the geographical distribution of power, see Stanley Hoffmann, "The Areal Distribution of Powers in the Writings of French Political Thinkers," in Maass, *Area and Power*. Also Ralph Nelson, "The Federal Idea in French Political Thought," *Publius* 5 (Summer 1975).

authority relations school. French philosophers, elites, and masses have disagreed about these matters. Change has occurred. Arguments which assume uniformity and constancy cannot explain either the disagreements or the changes. We still need finer-tuned arguments.

"PERIPHERAL" NATIONALISMS: In several European countries pressure for areal reform has come from the demands of reawakened *ethnies* subordinated during the construction of the nation-state. In France as well there has been some *prise de conscience* among Basques, Catalans, Bretons, and Alsatians, who have raised public awareness of the price paid in building France. Decentralization can be interpreted as a response and a solution to such pressures.

While the argument has some force, it also has several flaws. First, in France these movements have been quite weak in comparison to comparable ones in other countries. The Scots, the Catalans and Basques in Spain, the Flemish in Belgium, the Quebecois in Canada—these groups have been able to translate cultural identity into votes, organization, money, and in some cases the capacity to undertake violence. In France, nationalist movements have not broken out of a kind of folkloric appeal to an effective political one. Corsica is the partial exception, and even there sporadic acts of violence have not led to mass mobilization on the basis of a cultural appeal.[7]

Second, instead of a loosening of the system, strong demands for autonomy may elicit contrary repressive tendencies from the center. In Spain, Franco restricted the regions far more severely than his somewhat more liberal successors appear to be doing; in Yugoslavia, Tito has felt compelled to crack down on nationalist dissidence in Croatia and elsewhere.

Third, these nationalist movements cannot be understood purely in cultural terms. Generally, they also involve economic grievances of certain kinds. Regions with strong nationalist sentiment tend to be those which are economically more dynamic or have a hope of being more dynamic, in comparison to

7. On cultural nationalism in France, see Robert Lafont, *Décoloniser la France* (Paris: Gallimard, 1971); and idem, *La Révolution régionaliste* (Paris: Gallimard, 1967).

a relatively stagnant political center. Conversely, regions which are economically stagnant in relation to an economically dynamic political center tend to be politically quiescent. The French case falls into the second category. In comparative terms, this may help account for the more limited scope of reforms in France than in other countries. Chapter 10 explores further this problem of peripheral nationalism in comparative perspective.

In the French case at least, peripheral nationalism has not been central to the discussion of areal reform. The argument has been concerned with how government should be organized territorially over what is taken to be a more or less culturally homogenous area. Significant pressures both for and against change come from areas with ethnic distinctiveness and from those without it.

2. The Socio-Economic Family of Interpretations

The psychological-cultural interpretations were criticized here for having a poor capacity to handle short-range and middle-range variations over time. Socio-economic interpretations appear to offer some help in this respect because they deal with factors which by their nature change more rapidly: supply and demand, demography, urbanization. Most arguments of this broad type are modernization arguments. They postulate a set of stages in the development of society. For each stage of development there exists a corresponding set of institutional "needs" which must be met, and a pattern of arrangements which is optimal for the satisfaction of those needs. Change in society induces pressures for change in the institutional structure. To understand the type of institutional reform we must understand more closely the social pressure producing it. As a result, the analysis of the quarrel over institutional change turns into the analysis of some other process. Some of these arguments claim inspiration from economic liberalism, others from a certain type of Marxism.

SOCIO-ECONOMIC MODERNIZATION: Over the past decades, many aspects of French life have been changing dramatically. We have seen rapid urbanization, depopulation of the countryside, a sharply shrinking agricultural sector and expanding industrial and tertiary ones, a rising birth rate, mass education, and so on. These new conditions produce new demands on the state which is pushed into decision-making of a kind also new in its range, scope, complexity, interconnectedness, particularity, technicality, and expense. To handle these tasks, the old structures are no longer adequate. They are poorly matched to the new content of government activity. It is not surprising, therefore, that there develops considerable pressure to modernize the system.[8]

This reasoning has, certainly, considerable force. It accounts in a broad way for a generalized pressure for change. It does not, however, provide much help in accounting for the choice of a *particular* type of reform. Several different schemes could each be plausibly shown to fit the needs of the new society. These needs are, moreover, diverse; each has its own institutional imperatives, each of which may conflict with the imperatives of other policy areas. It is hard to show that the nature of the tasks compels one type of reform over another. In the sixties, for example, it could be argued that something *had* to be done about the administrative mess produced by a great postwar social and economic change. Several *different* reforms, however, could have fit that particular bill: the Decrees of 1964, which were implemented, or the Referendum of 1969, which failed, or the *loi Frey* of 1972, which passed, or the elimination of departments, which was not done, or the direct election of regional councilors, which also did not pass—all of these could quite plausibly have met the functional need for new institutional arrangements. The "social change" reasoning fails, therefore, to discriminate among solutions which are equally possible from its point of view. In a sense, this is again the "timing" problem: the pressures which are emphasized turn out to be quite broad; within the period during which these pressures are unfolding, shifts and turns in policy occur which cannot plausibly be linked to microshifts in the pressures. Other

8. Jacques de Lanversin, *L'Aménagement du térritoire et la régionalisation en France* (Paris: Librairies Techniques, 1965).

modes of interpretation must therefore be brought into play.

THE INTERESTS OF MAJOR SOCIAL FORCES: Groups have needs. They want things from politics. Since institutional structures are not neutral, some arrangements fit the needs of a particular group better than others. Proposals for change emanate from the needs of such groups, and are judged by them according to how well they will promote the realization of their ends. The strongest groups prevail. To explain the choice of policy among alternative policies toward the areal distribution of power, this line of reasoning suggests, therefore, that we should explore the interests of major economic actors.[9]

There are several versions of this sort of thinking. Big business, for example, is held to require a strong (Jacobin) state in France. Conversely, it is argued that big business requires an effective state, one unburdened by a mass of petty problems, capable of focusing on "high policy" and able to elicit considerable mass legitimacy. Some kind of decentralization could help do this. Both propositions seem quite plausible, and are in complete contradiction with one another. Each imputes a different calculation from the same starting point.

The same divergence can be repeated for other social groups. If big business needs a Jacobin state, do unions need a Girondin one? Perhaps, but unions could also rationally support a Jacobin model as best for controlling the economy. Small business may turn to the state for aid, or may attack the state as a tool in the hands of big capital.

What this suggests is that the concrete interests of different economic and social groups do not discriminate in any very obvious way among different schemes for reforming the areal distribution of powers. The ambiguities contained within many of the alternative proposals are great enough to render problematic any strong inference of group positions on areal reform from their specific economic situation. Often groups will in fact

9. For discussion of the PCF and local government see Mény, *Centralisation et décentralisation*; and the essays by Sidney Tarrow, Robert Putnam, Alan Stern, Peter Lange, Denis Lacorne, and Jerome Milch in *Communism in Italy and France*, ed. Donald Blackmer and Sidney Tarrow (Princeton: Princeton University Press, 1975).

have no particular position at all on a given reform. If they have a position, it is more likely to derive from a broader analysis of general *political* needs than from a precise calculation of specific needs arising out of an economic or social situation. Thus, a labor union's position on the *loi Frey* would come less from a judgment on how this bill would affect wages or labor legislation or collective bargaining in general, than from an evaluation of what impact the changes would have on the strength of its partisan allies, the Communists or Socialists. The union's fundamental interest doubtless lies in the policy issues, but the way of reasoning about it passes through political calculations.

REGIONAL IMBALANCES: Another variant of the socio-economic family of interpretations looks to the regional disparities of wealth, population, economic dynamism, and so on. Here again there are several sides to the argument, which reach conflicting conclusions. Dynamic regions, for example, may feel shackled by a central government which siphons off money, takes a long time to make decisions, blocks projects of local importance, and imposes different priorities. Rhone-Alpes is a frequently cited example.[10] Conversely, dynamic regions may oppose decentralization, reasoning that, since they tend to dominate the national system as a whole, they have every interest in preserving the state's powers and integrity.

Poor regions may clamor for more autonomy on the grounds that it is their membership in the national political economy which causes their imporverishment. This argument is made in Brittany, and to some extent in a region like the Nord, once dynamic, now stagnant, looking to the Benelux countries and Germany for stimulus. Conversely, poor regions may oppose a decrease in state control; they reason that the richer regions may thereby escape their obligations to contribute transfer payments in aid of their less fortunate fellow citizens. Helping backward regions is, moreover, not at all the same as dispersing power; if the distribution of funds is done by agents of the center located in the periphery, either directly or via patronage, it strengthens the grip of the center, rather than weakening it.

10. Claude Glayman, *Liberté pour les régions* (Paris: Fayard, 1971).

These arguments are all plausible. They suggest connections between regional situations and attitudes toward institutional reform which are worth exploring. But, as with the economic interests argument, the interests of the regions in any specific formal distribution of power appear to be ambiguous. As a result, judgments about the desirability of alternative schemes are likely to be affected by other factors.

Each type of socio-economic explanation has brought us to the same problem, posing an important choice in research strategy. In each case, some relationship between the *substance* of pressures for change and the *type* of change appears to be plausible, but not obviously demonstrable from any gross correlations of interest and attitude. It is always possible that greater explanatory leverage could be attained with finer tuning. That is, the situation may not be that there is no relationship, but that the categories being used are too crude to show what relationship exists. Better categories might yield better results. Certainly, very interesting work of this kind has been done for other countries: Samuel Beer has shown that changes in the American federal system can be linked to changes in the policy content of group needs.[11] Different types of policy make use of different levels of government. As these change over long periods of time, Beer suggests, the relationship between Washington and local governments changes. Similarly Martin Shefter has demonstrated that the type of party organization which developed in various American cities and states can be plausibly related to certain characteristics of the dominant economic groups in each locality.[12] Similar research might fruitfully be done for France.[13]

11. Samuel Beer, "The Modernization of American Federalism," *Publius* 3 (1973): 49–95; and idem, "Federalism, Nationalism, and Democracy in America," *American Political Science Review* 72 (March 1978): 9–21.
12. Martin Shefter, *Patronage and Party in America* (New York: Basic Books, forthcoming).
13. Two recent Ph.D. dissertations offer some help along these lines: Robert Berrier, "The Politics of Industrial Survival: The French Textile Industry," (Ph.D. Diss., Massachusetts Institute of Technology, 1977); Gail Russell, "The Politics of Industrial Conversion: The Case of the North of France" (Ph.D. Diss., Princeton University, 1979).

Even if one were to do such research, however, two problems would remain. First, the broad historical arguments would not resolve the issues of short-term timing and shifts of position by a particular group. Second, it would leave certain political dimensions unexplored, dimensions which offer some promise of help. The "finer tuning" strategy is also quite expensive; it requires the very thorough exploration of numerous policy areas and the substantive interests of many different groups—no small task, even for a region. For these reasons, a choice was made here. The socio-economic and the cultural explanations were both considered to be useful but not conclusive. While further refinement of each would quite probably be useful, it was deliberately decided not to pursue either path. Instead, it was assumed that these types of reasoning do not discriminate among different solutions to the problem of territorial reform in France, and that one must therefore explore the third group of interpretations, which focus more exclusively on politics.

3. The Partisan Political Family of Interpretations

It is politicians who ultimately must ratify or refuse changes of policy. Institutional change is a type of policy of special importance to *la classe politique*. Elected office holders, party leaders, and civil servants are the special clientele, the interest group, most directly affected by these structures, which shape jobs, security, power, and other gratifications. Any alteration of politico-administrative boundaries, functions, or modes of representation threaten existing power relationships. Change may offer new opportunities for patronage, new instruments for social transformation (or obstruction), new positions of prestige. Change may also menace these, or at least create uncertainty. Politicians are likely to support such reforms only if they feel able to manage the transformation such that it is *they*, rather than their rivals, who occupy the new posts.

In explaining reform, we must look to factors which shape politicians' evaluation of the costs and benefits different schemes would bring. We may sort such factors out into two categories: those which are general, or systemic, affecting all political parties and elites; and those which are specific, influencing disproportionately certain parties and individuals.

A. General Factors

The most important of the general causes of the persistence of centralization is the persistence of sharp political divisions in France. Whatever coalition of forces dominates the central government, it feels insecure, constantly under attack, besieged by a powerful enemy. The opposition is seen, moreover, not merely as an alternative government, but as a countersociety, whose victory would be a disaster. These characteristics of polarized politics are familiar enough.[14] Their effect on the areal distribution of power is to increase the attractiveness of the existing centralized model, and to undermine the appeal of any experimentation. Centralization puts command of key instruments of power in the hands of the government in Paris: policy, schools, the media, economic policy. Decentralization means sharing some of that power with the opposition. If the opposition is too dangerous, such sharing is unimaginable.

Intense internal division has indeed been one of the two principal driving forces behind the creation and maintenance of centralization in France. The other force is war. Prior to the modern period, the Capetian kings strengthened their direct rule over the royal domain around Paris in order to create a secure base of activity. The first major initiatives for extending centralization over the whole of France arose from the effort by the early Bourbon kings and their ministers to eliminate the power bases of those who had contested royal authority during the Wars of Religion and the Fronde.[15] The need to do so was

14. Giovanni Sartori, "European Political Parties: The Case of Polarized Pluralism," in *Political Parties and Political Development*, ed. Joseph LaPalombara and Myron Weiner (Princeton: Princeton University Press, 1966).
15. Robert Fawtier, *The Capetian Kings of France: Monarch and Nation, 987–1328* [*Les Capétiens et la France*] (London: Macmillan, 1964); Roland Mousnier, *La Venalité des offices sous Henry IV et Louis XIII*, 2d ed. (Paris: Presses Universitaires de France, 1971).

strongly reinforced by the pressure imposed by constant warfare to mobilize national resources more effectively.[16]

At the time of the Revolution, experimentation with decentralized forms crumbled before the advance of foreign armies and constant internal dissension.[17] The Restoration governments, despite their criticism of revolutionary reforms, proved unwilling to give up the instruments of political control now in their own hands; their position was not secure enough to permit implementation of their professed ideals. During the long period of conservative domination of politics (1815–1875), interest in decentralization shifted to the left. Hitherto, local government had been fatally tainted for the left by association with the particularisms and aristocratic reaction of the Old Regime. With a partially modernized state now in conservative hands, some progressives developed a critique of centralized power itself—Proudhon is the most celebrated example.[18]

After 1870, left and right switched sides again. In the battle to defend the Republic against various enemies, control of the schools and the police could simply not be given up. At the same time, the left carried out one aspect of its early program which did alter center-periphery relations: democratization of the suffrage, including the direct election of town and departmental councilors. This made such bodies more responsive to local forces and harder to manipulate from Paris. Parliamentary government in Paris lessened the autonomy of the executive, forcing it to bid for the support of deputies. In the absence of disciplined parties, this gave some leverage at the national level to local interests. Thus, while the formal model of Jacobin control was not changed, the electoral mechanisms and party rela-

16. On the role of war in shaping political regimes, see Peter Gourevitch, "The Second Image Reversed: The International Sources of Domestic Politics," *International Organization* 32 (Autumn 1978): 881–912.

17. François Furet, "Tocqueville and the Old Regime," Lecture at Center for European Studies, Harvard University, 2 December 1976; François Furet, *Penser la Révolution française* (Paris: Gallimard, 1978).

18. On Proudhon's ideas about the distribution of power, see Hoffmann, "The Areal Distribution of Powers."

tions altered the effective distribution of power. During this same period, part of the right, frozen out of power in Paris, reverted to its earlier nostalgia for an idealized past of a free, flourishing, vital, provincial society governed by natural elites. When Vichy gave these forces a chance to govern after 1940, the combination of internal dissent and international pressure once again forced the right to abandon this decentralized vision.[19]

Since 1945, the pattern has continued. The parties of the right, the center, and until recently the Socialist left cannot imagine sharing power with the Communists, at any level. And the left's analysis of the hostility its government would face in changing a capitalist economy hardly encourages the loosening of controls from Paris.

In short, the nature of political cleavages in France seems to inhibit reform of the system of center-local linkages in the direction of greater decentralization. The hostility among political formations is so deep, and the balance of forces sufficiently even, that no group or combination of groups ever feels either secure in office or able to trust the opposition. As a consequence, political polarization appears to induce the following decision-rule among French politicians: *when in the opposition, support decentralization; when in power, hang on to all the instruments centralization provides.*

Thus, policy toward centralization is derived from the party system. It may be, as Crozier suggests, that over the long run the causality is reversed: the institutional framework shapes the party system. Decentralization, Crozier implies, would alter human relations, shift politics to more realistic issues, and moderate political hostilities. Perhaps, but in the shorter run, intense partisan conflict inhibits risk-taking.

THE EFFICACY OF PRESENT INSTITUTIONS: However much French local elites complain of their dependence on Paris, French centralization does give them certain benefits. Because

19. Pierre Barral, "Idéal et practique du régionalisme dans le régime de Vichy," *Revue Française de Science Politique* 24 (October 1974): 911–939; Stanley Hoffmann, "The Vichy Circle of Conservatives," *Decline or Renewal?: France since the 1930s* (New York: Viking Press, 1974), pp. 3–25.

of it, they are the privileged intermediaries between their constituents and the state apparatus. Jean-Pierre Worms and Pierre
Grémion have written convincingly of the complicity that grows
up among civil servants and local officials.[20] Each derives advantages from cooperation with the other. The *fonctionnaire* gets
credit from his superiors for having a cooperative local population; the politician gets credit from his constituents for showing that he knows how to deal with the bureaucracy. Over time,
such ties strengthen. Change, even that which in principle
might mean more powers to the locality, provokes unease because it menaces these relationships. Sidney Tarrow's comparisons of French and Italian politics are revealing. Since the
Italian state apparatus functions less effectively than the French,
the benefits to be obtained through established positions in it
are correspondingly smaller. Italian politicians are therefore
more likely than their French counterparts to see a balance on
the account sheets of the system in favor of change.[21]

B. Particular Factors
The second set of factors shaping the receptiveness of the
French political system to reform of the areal division of powers
consists of those which affect political formations differently.
    THE PARTY SYSTEM: Some aspects of the party system affect
all parties alike: sharp polarization is both an opportunity and a
constraint, something no group can avoid, however much it
may wish to. Other aspects of the system shape the calculations
of politicians asymmetrically. That is, they mean different
things for different parties. Some features of the French party
system which affect evaluations of proposals for areal reform
include:
    Strength of local implantation. Local governments provide
institutional bases for party organization. Positions such as
mayor or departmental councilor give visibility to party leaders,
some opportunity for patronage, an instrument for leadership
training, an activity for militants, and a locale for demon-

---

20. Jean-Pierre Worms, "Le Préfet et ses notables," *Sociologie du Travail*
(July–September 1966); Pierre Grémion, *Le Pouvoir péripherique*.
    21. Tarrow, *Between Center and Periphery*.

strating the capacity to govern. As noted earlier, these rewards are likely to be especially attractive to parties out of power at the national level. If such parties are well entrenched in the *existing* structure, however, they may be suspicious of proposals for change, even those which promise more power to local governments. Conversely, parties with poor local implantation are likely to feel they have less to lose and will be more open to experimentation. Similarly, new parties are likely to have a weaker commitment to existing structures than do older ones. The former are less likely to have much of a local infrastructure than the latter, and the older organization is likely to contain established interests threatened by change.

These expectations are borne out by French experience. The most poorly implanted party was the new Union pour la Nouvelle République (UNR, later UDR) during the first decade or so of the Fifth Republic. It was precisely during that period that Gaullist interest in changing local government reached its height. The other parties of left, center, and right interpreted the Gaullist proposals as attempts to destroy their existing power bases. As the Gaullist party organization has become more secure, its willingness to experiment has decreased. As government policy has become more cautious, the parties on the left feel less threatened; as the opposition, they are able to increase their interest in stronger local government.

Party alliance strategies in a fragmented party system. Since reform of the areal distribution of powers alters the relationships among and within party formations, the process of change will naturally be powerfully influenced by the character of party relationships. In a two party or bipolar party system of some stability, the governing party or coalition may feel strong enough to manage the disruptions caused by reform—hence, perhaps, the willingness of the Swedish Social Democrats and the British Labour party to support extensive reorganization of local government.[22]

22. Thomas Julius Anton, *Governing Greater Stockholm: A Study of Policy Development and System Change* (Berkeley and Los Angeles: University of California Press, 1975). On Britain see the Royal Commission on the

That fragmented, conflict-ridden party systems have a propensity to immobilism is well known. The problem may be especially acute for areal reform. In such a system, political office can be captured only by cooperation between parties. When such cooperation is not forthcoming, the chances that any given party will capture political offices diminishes, and so, therefore, interest in local government also lessens. If party relationships improve, the prospects of electoral victory improve, leading individual parties to evaluate the rewards from change more positively.

In the postwar period, the interest of the Communists and the Socialists in areal reforms rises and falls with the state of their relations with each other: favorable in periods of collaboration, unfavorable in periods of open conflict. Thus, in the fifties and sixties, local government was simply another terrain for conflict between the two Marxist organizations. After 1969, when both changed their strategies to cautious cooperation, they found that local government offered certain advantages for trying this strategy. Local government could provide the framework at the micro level for the alliance which would bid to take power at the national level. Through constructive local action, the partners hoped to demonstrate their reliability to social groups and political parties who doubted it.[23] The demonstration would also be valuable for militants and voters within the left's formations. After years of conflict, the mutual distrust of Socialists and Communists runs deep. The experience of working together in towns and departments would allow both sides to learn, and internalize, new patterns of behavior. Thus, the alliance strategy which led to the Common Program led also to joint interest in local government reforms which would strengthen local government. Following March 1978 if the strains between the PCF (Parti Communiste Française) and the PSF (Parti Socialiste Française) continue, one

---

Constitution, 1969–1973, *Report*, vols. 1 and 2 (London HMSO, 1973).
    23. Blackmer and Tarrow, *Communism in Italy and France*.

might expect a decline in the importance of local government reforms for each group.

Relations among party formations of the center and right affect their evaluation of local government reforms as well. The various strengths and weaknesses of the Gaullist party and the policies of its leadership have both strengthened and weakened the cause of institutional reform at different moments. Gaullist strength at the national level has undermined reform by weakening those political parties which have been the most consistently interested in it—the center, in particular, the Catholic center. Conversely, Gaullist weakness at the local level, combined with hostility toward the existing elites represented in local structures, tempted the Gaullists for a time to shake up the whole structure of local government as a way of loosening the grip of their enemies and opening the way to their friends. The shift after 1969 toward a more cooperative relationship between the Gaullists and the other parties of center and right has led to ample control of that temptation.

Interparty cooperation has thus had contrary implications for reform within the two poles of the French party system: on the left, it has increased interest in reform; on the center and right, it has decreased it. This is not inherent to the parties, but is rather a product of connection between this issue and party needs at particular moments. These can, of course, change.

The distribution of voting strength. For the French left, the incentive to be interested in one type of reform—regionalization—is diminished by the geographical distribution of its voting strength. Though twenty percent of the French electorate lives around Paris, the capital district has been excluded from all regional reform projects (and did not receive its own structures until 1975–1976). A large part of the left vote lives, of course, in the Red Belt around Paris, and is therefore lost to the left in contests for control of regions. In Italy, by contrast, the Red Belt is located outside Rome so the left there has a greater incentive to be interested in the regional form of decentralization. (See Chapter 9 for the Italian case.)

The political context of reform proposals. Frequently the political meaning of a particular proposal was judged less according to an evaluation of its content than by the identity of
those who proposed it. Throughout this period, politicians felt
confused about the political meaning of different schemes. The
areal distribution of power did not fit easily into traditional
categories of evaluation, which were themselves increasingly
subject to question.[24] Politicians were not sure whether greater
diffusion of power was progressive or reactionary, left or right,
good for the masses or bad for them, helpful to big business or
harmful to it, useful to the party or dangerous. As a result, the
context in which a particular proposal was presented had a considerable impact upon reactions to it. In the early sixties, for example, territorial reform was pushed by the Gaullists; the left
responded negatively, partly because of actual content (corporatism, elitism) but also because anything proposed by the Gaullists aroused suspicion as to the political meaning of the changes
in question. If the Gaullists want it, the left reasoned, it must
be bad. In the seventies, the situation is reversed: the center
and the right fear decentralization because it is pushed by the
left.

Personality. At critical moments, the fate of institutional
reform has been bound up with the needs and actions of particular individuals. The most spectacular example is de Gaulle,
whose political requirements were frequently the stop–go mechanism of regional reform, shaping when reform would be pro-
moted and what would be proposed.

Other political issues. Reform of the areal distribution of
power in France has never been the paramount issue, even
when it is the ostensible subject of debate. Alignments around
given options have not been formed around the reform proposals alone—it is not a cleavage-determining issue. Rather,
other basic cleavage lines spill over into this issue area. Positions
on reform derive from positions on other issues. The most spectacular of these has been foreign policy, somewhat paradoxically

24. Suzanne Berger et al., "The Problem of Reform in France: The Political Ideas of Local Elites," *Political Science Quarterly* 54 (September 1969).

since this issue seems to be internal and domestic in essence. International tensions have had a profound effect on French party relations, shaping the pattern and possibilities of coalitions among voters and politicians. The emergence of the Cold War, and its relative softening, the antisuperpower stance of de Gaulle, and its modification by his successors served to make and unmake various alliances. In synchronization with these changes, the fate of territorial reform has bobbed up and down.

CONCLUSION

There are, then, a variety of ways of understanding the nature and scope of the reform of territorial distribution of powers in postwar France. Three traditions of interpretation have been identified, each focusing on a different type of "interest."[25] The social psychology-culture school stresses "ideal" needs, in the language of Max Weber: thought and culture interacting with personality and concrete historical situations to produce patterned behavior.[26] The socio-economic school pays close attention to "material" needs: the institutional requirements arising out of the economic compulsions of various organizations. The third type of interpretation looks at "political" interests:[27] the imperatives arising out of the struggle over political office from calculations of politicians worried about partisan and personal advantage understood in a variety of ways.

Each school of interpretation locates the obstacles to change in a different place; therefore, each interpretation implies that change in the areal distribution of power must await change in that other domain. Thus, the argument of the cultural school suggests that areal reform cannot occur unless French culture

25. Max Weber, "The Social Psychology of World Religion," in *From Max Weber*, ed. Hans Gerth and C. W. Mills (New York: Oxford University Press, 1946).
26. Clifford Geertz, "Ideology as a Cultural System," in *Ideology and Discontent*, ed. David Apter (New York: Free Press, 1964).
27. For an analysis of political interests in this sense, see Michael Walzer, *Revolution of the Saints* (Cambridge, Mass.: Harvard University Press, 1965).

and psychological attributes change; the economic arguments make the process dependent on transformations in that sphere; and the political argument looks to changes in political relationships. In this book, I give primary emphasis to the third type of reasoning. The case for doing so is, I believe, strong but by no means exclusive of other arguments. I shall reserve for the final chapter of this book further speculation on the connections among the different arguments.

PART TWO

THE DEBATE

The regions and departments of France.

CHAPTER 3

WHAT SOLUTIONS?

In order to explain a policy outcome, it is necessary to define it in relation to other possibilities. This chapter offers such a typology of outcomes by constructing a set of four policy options concerning the areal distribution of power from which the French public and politicians may be said to have chosen. Having defined the options, the actual outcomes in the period 1944–1978 are presented. Finally, the political developments which shaped this sequence of outcomes are laid out. This material is presented here in schematic, summary form for those who may wish to have a frame of reference for the subsequent analysis. Those who dislike this degree of condensation are urged to move directly to the more straightforward presentation in the chapters which follow.

In postwar France, reform of the structures which link Paris to the countryside became an increasingly important objective to large numbers of people. Between a general sense of the "need for change" and any specific project, though, lies a rather vast terrain. The areal distribution of powers is frightfully complex. Should the units be large or small? Should the executive be named by the government or by the local population, directly or indirectly? Should members of the local assembly be elected by the population, or by public bodies such as town councils? What powers should the central government have over the local ones? and so on. For each question, several answers can be imagined. The number of possible "solutions" to the problems posed by the distribution of powers is therefore immense.

A major consequence of this complexity is that the areal distribution of powers becomes an issue of great political "plasticity." That is, it is an issue to which a great range of meanings can be attached. By stressing this or that aspect of change, a particular political coloration can be given to the whole; it can be located as left, right, progressive, or reactionary. For the left, for example, a given proposal could be interpreted as progressive because it called for an important distribution of powers away from Paris, or it could be called reactionary because these powers would be vested in persons not subject to control by directly elected representatives.

The complexity of the combinations of the confusion in political analysis has given great leverage to those in a position to define which project could be considered at any given moment. Generally, this meant the government, though at times, when the government wished to take no action at all, initiative passed to the opposition. Some simplification is indispensable to political discourse. As in all situations, those who do the simplifying have considerable leverage over the debate and its outcome.

THE OPTIONS

Simplification is also necessary to the task of explanation. To interpret what happened in France, we must construct a range of alternatives, from which specific policy choices were made. A typology of possible reforms is therefore presented below. While the number of dimensions along which proposals for reforms of the areal distribution of powers could vary is quite large (the number of units, the mode of selecting representatives to the assembly, the type of executive, powers, finances, central supervision; and "topocratic"[1] representation, or the

---

1. The label "topocratic" is taken from Samuel Beer, "Federalism, Nationalism, and Democracy in America," *American Political Science Review* 72 (March 1978): 9–21.

position of local units in the national system), the arguments in France revolved principally around three sets of issues: (*a*) The appropriate unit—should powers be devolved onto existing units of local government, the department, and the commune, or onto new units, the region? (*b*) The nature of representation—should representatives be elected directly or indirectly, and on the basis of territory or functions (professional associations)? This we may label as democratic versus elitist, territorial versus functionalist. (*c*) The type of institution receiving devolved powers—should power go to the agents of the central government located in the field (deconcentration), or to personnel responsible to locally chosen populations (decentralization)? While these dimensions are analytically quite distinct and have limited logical transitivity, empirically some blurring took place. That is, decentralizers tend to oppose functional representation, while deconcentrators tend to support it. We may therefore combine *b* and *c* into a composite dimension and present four options, which are depicted graphically in Table 1. The option of doing nothing at all is not listed. Verbally at least, everyone accepted the need for some change.

Option A: Hardline Jacobinism. The traditional framework of departments and communes are retained. Bureaucratic dysfunctions can be corrected by transferring some decision-making from the capital to the field, and by lightening the *tutelle*

TABLE 1
The Options

| | | UNIT OF LOCAL GOVERNMENT | |
		Department / Commune	*Region*
CHARACTER OF DISTRIBUTION OF POWERS AND REPRESENTATION	*Deconcentration* Elitist and Functional	Option A	Option B
	Decentralization Democratic and Territorial	Option C	Option D

over towns and departments. The existing mechanisms for consulting society are deemed adequate. Representation remains as at present in the hands of territorially elected officials, with no formal place being given to functional groups. Local governments may be given some sharply limited new powers and funds, subject always to supervision from the center. Administration remains centrally controlled, hierarchically organized, tightly coordinated, with uniform boundaries and limited transfer to the field. The advocates of this option tended to be elitists. Those who wanted greater democratization gravitated toward some version of options C or D.

Option B: Modernized Jacobinism. The traditional division into departments is inadequate. A new larger level is required—the regions. These are to have some representative functions, even allowing for a new type of representation, functional. Primarily, they are instruments of deconcentration; power is delegated to agents of the central government in the field. At the same time, the lines of authority between Paris and its field offices are streamlined: boundaries are made uniform, the powers of the prefect clarified and reinforced. Competences and funds are provided the units, but under strict central supervision. One version of this option goes so far as to replace the departments by regions; in most discussions, the regions are simply added on. Option B is also elitist, though there is some disagreement over the desirability of functional representation. Those who advocate local control move to options C or D.

Option C: Participatory Decentralization—Departmental or Communal. Deconcentration is both inadequate and undemocratic. The power given local bodies must be accountable to locally chosen representatives. The local executives must be chosen via election, not appointed by the national government. Legislation, budgets, and the like should be in the hands of an elected assembly. Local units would have wide powers, ample means of funding, an ability to organize their own administrations, absence of an onerous *tutelle*. Functionalists would add representatives of socio-professional groups or colleges. Generally, those who stress decentralization also support democratic rather than elitist modes of selection. However, the supporters of participatory decentralization have been sharply split by the choice between departments and regions.

Option D: Participatory Decentralization—Regional. Here regions replace departments as the basis of local government. Regional executives are accountable to local populations, either directly or via elected representatives. Functionalists want socio-professional representation; others do not. Some of these regionalists want to replace the department; most do not.

It is interesting to note which possible reforms never got serious attention.[2] Federalism, for one.[3] Some enthusiasts of regionalism had the German, the American, or even the Britain-Scotland example as models (subnational units with constitutionally defined autonomous domains and partial sovereignty), but no major political figure or formation ever took it up. Conversely, while some advocates of regionalism accept that in the long run, strong regions render the departments irrelevant, politicians have avoided calling openly for abolition of the departmental level. While almost everyone can find some fault with the system of *Grands Corps,* and some suggest eliminating the prefect as the effective executive of the department of region, there has been no serious consideration of breaking up the hold that the *Grands Corps* have over the bureaucracy as a way of permitting greater pluralism and local autonomy.

2. For an analytic presentation of various proposals put forward in the past three decades, see Yves Mény, *Centralisation et décentralisation dans le débat politique français, 1945–1969* (Paris: Librairie Générale de Droit et de Jurisprudence, 1974). For periods see Maurice Bourjol, *Les Institutions régionales de 1789 à nos jours* (Paris: Berger-Levrault, 1969), and Christian Gras and Georges Livet, *Régions et régionalism en France du XVIII'e siècle à nos jours* (Paris: Presses Universitaires de France, 1976).

3. Some federalists were involved in the *Mouvement National pour la Décentralisation et la Réforme Régionale,* a lobbying group of centrists and Gaullists, but their federalist arguments were never taken seriously, even in the Movement.

THE OUTCOMES

Using this typology of options, the postwar debate over the areal distribution of powers in France can be described as follows:

1945-1947: Constitution-making. Retention of the Third Republic's system emphasizing communes and departments. Some clauses of the new constitution call for democratization of the departmental executive. Some aspects of regional structures retained from Vichy and Liberation period (limited C and D).

1947-1958: Clauses of the constitution concerned with departmental democracy not implemented (abandonment of limited C). Some cautious movement, via administrative decree, toward administrative deconcentration, and toward regional planning bodies (partial B).

1958-1964: Reform of departmental administration to improve central coordination (option A) and further development of regional structures, with a large component of functionalist, elitist representation and deconcentration (option B).

1964-1969: Regional *prise de conscience*. Emergence of interest in decentralization on the left, both C and D. Proposal, via referendum, of a blend of B and D defeated.

1969-1974: Shift away from regions back toward departments and communes (from B and D to A and C). Georges Pompidou seeks to end regional agitation with *loi Frey*, a version of option B. Other measures emphasize towns, departments, and deconcentration to both departments and regions. Left becomes increasingly proregional and prodecentralization.

1974 to present: Giscard moves from mild proregionalism toward Pompidou's caution. Maintenance of *loi Frey*. Continued discussion of limited reforms falling largely within framework of option A.

It is obvious enough that French policy toward local government has not been uniform. The amplitude of the oscillation is not massive, but it is discernible and important enough to be worth examining.

THE PATTERN OF POLITICS

The phases of political life in the postwar period were not primarily shaped by the issue of the areal distribution of power. Rather, this policy domain has been heavily dependent on other issues. In his book on the foreign policy of the Fourth Republic,[4] Alfred Grosser notes three main cleavage issues in French political life: foreign policy, colonial policy, and socio-economic policy. It was constant conflict over what to do in these areas which shaped the formation and the disintegration of governing coalitions, as well as mass electoral behavior. While colonial questions have diminished in significance, the memory of quarrels about it continues to affect political alliances, while both foreign policy and socio-economic policy retain their primordial importance. The events which mark different eras in postwar political alignments all have to do with these policy eras. Since our primary concern has to do with those alignments, the periods have been divided according to shifts in alliance patterns.[5]

1944-1947: The Liberation Coalition. Period of flux, discussion, interest in new departures and experimentation. The anti-Fascist resistance dominates political scene. Constitution-writing shaped by quarrel between Gaullists and other parties.

1947-1958: Third Force Governments. Expulsion of the Communists in 1947 and isolation of the Gaullists lead to multicolor governments and immobilism. Partial breaking of logjam with integration of some Gaullists after 1952. Increasing paralysis over Algeria.

1958-1962: Gaullist Coalition, Phase 1. Moratorium on political fighting during the Algerian crisis in order to save repub-

4. Alfred Grosser, *La Quatrième République et sa politique extérieure* (Paris: Armand Colin, 1961).
5. This applies both to the substantive content of the alliance (what was the nature of the groups who used a particular banner) and its nominal content (the combination of etiquettes supporting a government or group of governments).

licanism. Thaw in Cold War, plus de Gaulle's antisuperpower and anti-Common Market stance, contribute to partial integration of the left. Confusion of class and other political demarcations.

1962-1969: Gaullism, Phase 2. Revival of partisan political conflict. Open conflict between Gaullists and other parties. Increasing critique by left of economic policies. Foreign policy continues to maintain broad support for the government.

1969-1974: Gaullism, Phase 3. Following *les événements*, shift by Pompidou toward more conservative social policies and more conservative bases of support. Increasing polarization along left, right, and class lines. Formation of left alliances.

1974-1978: After Gaullism. Continuation of left-right polarization, very closely balanced. Giscard's coalition mixes conservatism and an appeal to the center. Left coalition, begun in aftermath of electoral disasters of 1969, comes unraveled in legislative election of 1978.

These twists and turns in political alignments over the past three decades largely governed policy toward reform of local government. At every moment, parties and politicians had political problems: how to win elections, mobilize militants, retain control over party organizations, sustain political cohesion, fulfill ideological objectives. Projects for institutional change were judged in part by how they affected the realization of those goals. Changes in party relationships had important consequences for policy positions. This was true in all policy realms, and is therefore true concerning the areal distribution of power as well. We shall try to establish the plausibility of this understanding through an analytic account of the postwar consideration of the reform of linkages between Paris and the countryside.

The succeeding chapters will handle this material as follows: Chapter 4 shows the connections between political change and local government policy from 1944 to 1962, from the Liberation through the writing of two constitutions through the end of the war in Algeria. Chapter 5 stops the chronology temporarily to explicate the political choices facing the parties of the center and right once the weight of the Algerian crisis had been lifted. Chapters 6 and 7 show what choices were made first by de Gaulle, then Pompidou, and then Giscard and Jacques Chirac, and how these choices affected policy. The comparable analysis for the left (political choices and policy implications) is compressed into Chapter 8.

CHAPTER 4

MISSED OPPORTUNITIES
The Founding of Two Republics, 1945–1962

FROM LIBERATION TO COLD WAR, 1944–1947

The aftermath of war is always a propitious moment for the consideration of change. This is especially true after a defeat. France experienced both the ignominy of 1940 and the euphoria of 1944. The "strange defeat" set off, both among the resisters in occupied France and the resisters in exile, a profound self-examination as to the causes of the debacle.[1] Everything associated with the past was questioned, including the spatial organization of powers. With the Liberation came a tremendous explosion of talk, thought, and hope. There was enormous interest in innovation; everyone talked about redesigning the country, tailoring a new suit to fit new proportions. For a time political circumstances favored change. Quite soon, the situation shifted dramatically: the internal disagreements of the Resistance surfaced; politicians and parties struggled for dominance. In the end, the old garment continued to be worn, albeit by a changing body. The principal options concerning local government in this period were limited versions of regionalism and corporate representation (option B), and democratization of departmental and communal government (option C). The Constitution of 1946 contained little of either.

Experimentation with new structures and new forms of representation had already begun before the war. Some professional

1. Marc Bloch, *Strange Defeat*, trans. Gerald Hopkins (New York: Norton, 1968).

associations organized themselves on regional lines, and regions were set up for certain administrative purposes.[2] These remained quite limited, however, until Vichy. The particular type of conservatives who dominated Vichy in its early days sought to recreate the limited state, governing an orderly, hierarchical society. To do so, they thought, required several conditions. First, the functions of the state should be reduced to that minimum compatible with the maintenance of order. Second, as many activities as possible should be transferred from the *pays légal* to the *pays réel*, that is from state to society, from politicians to the leaders of social and economic corporations (peasants, businessmen, workers, families, youth). Third, power should be shifted from Paris, where life is artificial, to the countryside, where community flourishes naturally, and from departments, which are unnatural creations of the Revolution, to provinces, which are older and organic.

These goals clashed with the reality that France was not in 1940 a *tabula rasa*, nor was she free to shape her own destiny. To reverse gears on a society that had been hurtling in a particular direction for decades, even centuries, required vast state intervention, a contradiction with the limited government desired by the Vichyites. And of course the Occupation itself impelled coercion. Reforms were abandoned. Regional prefects were created, but the boundaries of the provinces were never officially mapped out. Decentralization gave way to a municipal law which suppressed the election of mayors in all communes of over two thousand people, and suspended all the *conseils généraux* and *conseils d'arrondisement*. The professional associations were turned into vehicles of state control over people and their activities.[3]

2. Maurice Bourjol, *Les Institutions régionales de 1789 à nos jours* (Paris: Berger-Levrault, 1969); Jean Bancal, *Les Circonscriptions administratives de la France* (Paris: Receuil Sirey, 1945); Christian Gras and Georges Livet, *Régions et régionalisme en France du XVIII'e siècle à nos jours* (Paris: Presses Universitaires de France, 1976); Howard Machin, *The Prefect in French Public Administration* (London: Croom Helm, 1977); Les Cahiers français, *La Région* (Paris: La Documentation Française, 1973); *Le Monde, La Régionalisation*, "Dossiers et Documentation" no. 8, February 1974.
3. Stanley Hoffmann, "Aspects du régime Vichy," *Revue Française de*

These experiments were not, however, without consequence. Many Vichy initiatives survived in "purified" form. The "peak" associations for interest groups were retained and extended; the CNPF *(Conseil National du Patronnat Français)*, FNSEA *(la Fédération Nationale des Syndicats d'Exploitants Agricoles)*, and CGPME *(Confédération Générale des Petites et Moyennes Entreprises)* all derive from that period. Regions remained in the form of special officers, *commissaires de la République*, charged by the provisional government with broad mandates to assure leadership in the midst of considerable disorder and political strife.

In the debate over the new constitution, de Gaulle sought to retain both the regional innovation and the corporatist ones. The famous *discours de Bayeux* of 1946 does not mention the regions, but it does set out much of what did become reality in the Constitution of 1958, the Decrees of 1964, and what was attempted in the Referendum of 1969. In that speech, delivered after he had resigned as head of the provisional government in January, de Gaulle formulated his critique of traditional modes of linking the government with society.

> In sum . . . party rivalries have in France a fundamental character which always challenges and endangers the highest interests of the country. This is a basic fact, deriving from national temperament, the forces of history, and the disturbances of the present. It is indispensable for the future of our country and for democracy that our institutions take note of this fact and defend against it, in order to preserve the credit of our laws, the cohesion of Governments, the efficiency of the administration, the prestige and authority of the state.
>
> It is clear and understood that the definitive vote of laws and budgets falls to an Assembly elected by direct universal suffrage. But the initial impulses of such an Assembly don't necessarily embody complete clairvoyance and serenity. It is therefore necessary to give to a second Assembly, elected and composed in

Science Politique 6 (January–March 1956): 44–69. A translation of this well-known essay was published in Stanley Hoffmann's *Decline or Renewal?: France since the 1930s* (New York: Viking Press, 1977).

another manner, the function of examining publicly what the first Assembly has done, to formulate amendments and to propose projects. Moreover, if the great currents of general political opinion are naturally reproduced in the Chamber of Deputies, local life also has its tendencies and rights.

All this leads us to create a second Chamber to be chosen essentially by the departmental and municipal councils. This Chamber will complete the first one by inducing it, if appropriate, either to revise its projects, or to look at other ones, and in inducing greater appreciation in the formulation of laws of the administrative dimension, which a purely political body had a tendency to neglect.

It would be appropriate to add to this second Chamber, moreover, representatives of economic, familial, and intellectual organizations so that the voice of the grand activities of the country will be heard in the very heart of the State.[4]

Thus, for de Gaulle new modes of representation were essential to a reform of the political system. To shift representation toward local governments and other intermediate bodies carrying on critical social functions would help curtail the abuses inherent in political parties.

At this point, there was as yet no fusion of the corporatist vision with a regionalist one, as there would be in the project of 1969. The commissaires were seen as useful for purposes of control; coordinating ninety prefects was more cumbersome than dealing with a dozen or so handpicked individuals with vast powers over a large territory. In the confusion of setting up government in a country occupied half by the enemy, half by the Allies, wracked with struggles inside the Resistance, beset by immense problems of food, shelter, and clothing, the superprefects would be proconsuls, capable of rapid, authoritative action.

Compared to French republican traditions, de Gaulle's ideas were certainly a departure. Even so, it is hard to know whether the *discours de Bayeux* represented an ideal, or what he

---

4. Charles de Gaulle, "Discours prononcé à Bayeux, le 16 juin 1946," *Discours et messages* (Paris: Berger-Levrault, 1946), pp. 723, 725.

thought it was possible to suggest under the circumstances. Since January 1946, de Gaulle had been locked in a struggle for dominance with the politicians in the Constituent Assembly. He wanted to govern according to his own rules, not those of the Third Republic. Earlier, he had been forced to cooperate with the politicians in order to persuade the Allies he had some legitimacy and genuine backing. Now, to win the struggle, he had to mobilize French mass opinion. There were simply limits beyond which such opinion probably could not be taken. Corporate representation was generally tainted by Vichy and Fascism. Departments and communes were sacrosanct cells of French democracy. Hence, de Gaulle had to be cautious, as was the case in 1958 as well. (In 1969, for reasons to be explained, de Gaulle's political need was to be provocative, which is why he came the closest then to proposing his real beliefs.)

The fusion of political ideas and immediate political imperatives was also true among the parties who dominated the Constituent Assembly, the Mouvement Républicain Populaire (MRP), the Socialists, and the Communists. As the conflict with de Gaulle sharpened, the parties abandoned their initial sympathy for institutional reform in favor of retaining the status quo. The two Marxist parties certainly abhorred corporatism, while the MRP, though ideologically more attuned to it, could not, in the logic of the Assembly's fight with de Gaulle, propose it.

The inclination to defend republican traditions, which at the local level meant departments and communes, was strongly reinforced by organizational and positional interests. The first elections (in 1945) after the Liberation had been for departmental and municipal councils. The parties of the Constituent Assembly did well in those elections; de Gaulle presented no candidates as Gaullists, hence had no formal strength at that level. As a result, de Gaulle's effort to give power to special administrators, such as the *commissaires de la République*, looked to the parties like a move to undermine institutions where they were strong in favor of ones directly under de Gaulles's thumb.

Toward the end of 1945, the Constituent Assembly voted a fifty percent reduction in the credits allocated to the *commissaires*. The following March it voted to abolish them altogether. Instead of de Gaulle's proposed innovations in new levels of government and types of representation, the parties proposed democratization of existing structures. Their suggestions included recall of deputies by electors, election of judges, the transfer of departmental executive power from prefects to the presidents of the departmental councils, suppressing prefects altogether, and instituting local referenda. As the struggle with de Gaulle and with each other sharpened, the parties gradually abandoned most of these schemes.[5]

In the Constitution of 27 October 1946, article 88 requires that administration be based on departments. Article 88, phrase 2 specifies that the presidents of the municipal and departmental councils "shall be responsible for carrying out the decisions of these councils." Only this remained of all the earlier fervor for change.

More extensive reform had become politically impossible because of the struggle between de Gaulle and the parties. Implementation of even this degree of change was stifled by the new political conditions of the Cold War. Title 10 fell victim to the Prague coup, much as decentralization had crumbled under the pressure of the Austrian invasion in 1792. In the spring of 1947, two decisions, one by the Communist party to oppose the policies of the government of which it was still a member, and the second by the remaining parties to eject the Communists

5. On the questioning born of the Resistance see P. Coste-Floret, "Quelques Idées sur la Constitution de demain," Henri Michel and Moris Mirkine-Guetzevitch, eds., *Les Idées politiques et sociales de la Résistance* (Paris: Presses Universitaires de France, 1954), p. 281. On the immediate postwar years, see Gordon Wright, *The Reshaping of French Democracy* (Boston: Beacon Press, 1948); François Rétournard, *L'Assemblée des présidents des conseils généraux dans la vie publique française depuis 1945*, Serie recherches, no. 2 (Paris: Fondation Nationale des Sciences Politiques, 1964); Philip Williams, *Crisis and Compromise* (London: Longmans, 1964); Charles-Louis Foulon, *Le Pouvoir en province à la liberation: Les Commissaires de la République, 1943-1946* (Paris: Armand Colin, 1975).

from the Cabinet, led to a period of great strikes, economic
dislocation, and political tension. About the same time, de
Gaulle reentered public life with formation of the *Rassemblement du Peuple Français* (RPF). Fearful of both the Communists and the Gaullists, the government became unwilling to
give up the traditional instruments of control provided by centralization. Indeed, it even found useful the relatively new
device of "superprefect." The Vichy regional prefects and the
commissaires were revived in the form of eight IGAMES, or
*Inspecteurs-Généraux de l'Administration en Mission Extraor-
dinaire*. Their job was to coordinate police and other civil opera-
tions across departmental boundaries, and to assure liaison with
the military's regional divisions, to which their districts corresponded. Created to meet a crisis, the importance of the
IGAMES declined when it ended, but they remained in existence throughout the Fourth Republic as a sort of regional super
police chief.

Thus the clause of the constitution requiring administration
to be based on departments was bent by the crisis. The clause
calling for democratization of local executives was broken altogether. A bill to implement it was introduced in May 1947,
but the debate was delayed two years. The following year, the
government proposed a bill to reinforce the position of the prefects in the departments in relation to the field representatives
of the various ministries; by referring to their own bosses in
Paris rather than to the prefect, their ostensible superior in the
department, the field representatives were undermining the
prefect's position as *seul délégué du gouvernement*. Note that
both measures sought to solve major problems—local control,
participation, administrative efficiency, and smoother lines of
command—in the context of departments. Both bills were
returned to committee by the same vote in 1949. The minor
reason for their defeat was the cancelling effect of two conflicting interest groups: the departmental councilors who
favored democratization of local executives, and opposed
strengthening the prefects and the prefectoral corps which
wanted just the reverse. The major reason for their defeat was

the caution induced by sharp political conflict, and the renewed appreciation it brought in the government for the traditional levers of command.

THE COLD WAR AND IMMOBILISM, 1947–1958

The fall of the Iron Curtain brought to an end the openness to experimentation which had been so characteristic of the Liberation period. In the long run, the failure of thoroughgoing departmental reform in the 1940s—be it the left version of direct departmental democracy, or Michel Debré's *grands départements*—probably contributed to greater experimentation later on, particularly concerning regions. The decision to maintain the system *tel quel* did not satisfy a whole range of pressures for larger units, administrative efficiency, more participation, and democracy. Continuity tapped a historical legitimacy, but failed to lay the groundwork for a newer one, seen as usefully linking social needs and institutional structure. Over the next twenty years, this pressure for change pushed at the settlement of 1947, chipping away at it, laying the basis for another attempt at basic reform. Throughout the period, the political situation remained hostile to any major projects touching local structures.

Blocked by politics, administrative reform in France went underground, as it were. It moved out of the public arena dominated by parties, to the less visible meeting rooms of interest groups, notables, and high civil servants. Dissatisfied with the maintenance of the status quo, these actors labored to create a tissue of institutions and ideas which would be ready for such time as the political situation became more receptive to structural reforms.

One source of continued pressure came from the grassroots, out in the provinces. In various parts of the country, small groups of local leaders developed an understanding of their problems which required solutions conceived not in a departmental or communal framework, but in a regional one. The precise arguments varied. All had in common the notion that modern problems affected whole areas, spilling way beyond the traditional boundaries. This was most evident for the economy. Investment decisions took place increasingly in Paris, as industrial concentration increased, or outside France altogether, as France opened her borders. Levels of employment, income, infrastructure, and the like were therefore no longer under any reasonable degree of local control. While such trends had been developing for some time, they could only intensify, particularly as government policy seemed to encourage them.

Worse, some parts of the country faced structural problems of a special sort. In the Nord, for example, the principal industries, coal and textiles, were losing their centrality to the French economy and their competitiveness on international markets. Brittany had too many people engaged in marginal farming without enough industrial expansion to absorb surplus labor. In the Lyon area, things were going well, but prosperity created its own needs, for transport, housing, telephones, and the like.

In some places, this regional economic analysis intersected with a cultural one. In regions with an existing cultural identity, such as Brittany, leaders argued that the culture was itself menaced by economic decline. The absolute number of Bretons would be diminished by emigration, and those who stayed would lose the ability to retain their distinctiveness. Where such consciousness existed, it doubtless helped the formation of a regionalist analysis and critique of the old structures. However, even in other areas, which lacked a cultural identity, regionalist arguments made some progress.

The most conspicuous evidence of the regionalist argument in the early fifties was the formation of *Comités d'Expansion Régionale* (CER) or the *Comités Régionaux de Coordination*. Of these the most important and famous was the CELIB—the *Comité d'Etudes et de Liaison des Intérêts Bretons*, formed in 1950.[6] The CELIB was set up as an association of cadres, not a

6. On the CELIB, see J.E.S. Hayward, "Functional Representation and Group Politics," *Political Studies* 17 (March 1969): 48–75; Joseph Martray, *La Région: Pour un état moderne* (Paris: Editions France Empire, 1970); Michel

mass movement; its members came from a wide variety of associations, from businesses, professional corporations, trade unions, chambers of commerce, local governments—the typical list of intermediate groups. Its goal was to multiply the leverage of Brittany in the national system by fusing together the pieces of influence spread among its hundreds of member organizations. The CELIB sought deliberately to be nonpartisan by including all political party affiliations. Had it not done so, it would have become the instrument of one political grouping or another. This way it could claim to be more representative. The cost, of course, was that paid by all such groups: it had to avoid taking positions on partisan issues which divided its members.[7]

Similar associations were formed in other regions. In some cases the impetus came from below, as with the CELIB, and the counterpart organizations in the Nord and in Bordeaux. In others, the CER was set up by the central government, via decrees. The arguments developed by the *comités* were similar on some points, different on others. All of them wanted some kind of regional economic planning. As with the national plan, which was coming into existence at this time, the life of each region would be "modeled": demographic trends, employment needs, investment prospects. From this, targets would be established, in relation to which a whole variety of needs could be determined. This regional plan would then provide a benchmark for public and private investment.

The differences over what regional economic planning meant surfaced in disagreement as to what institutions such a process would require. Those concerned with participation wanted new local governments, directly elected with the money and power

---

Philipponeau, *La Gauche et les régions* (Paris: Calmann-Lévy, 1967); and on the Breton reawakening, Morvan Levesque, *Comment peut-on être breton?* (Paris: Le Seuil, 1970); Joseph Lajugie, "Aménagement du térritoire et développement économique régionale en France (1945–1964)," *Revue d'Economie Politique* 74 (January–February 1964).

7. On stalemate within broad peak associations, see among other works, Raymond Bauer, Ithiel Pool, Lewis A. Dexter, *American Business and Public Policy* (New York: Atherton, 1967).

to pursue regional needs, in case the central government proved
unresponsive. Others understood regional planning in far more
technical and administrative terms. They wanted information
and advice from local communities; command would rest with
the center.[8]

Parallel to this grassroots, regional *prise de conscience*, and
working with it, was the development of regionalist analysis inside the bureaucracy of the central government. When national
planning was first launched in the late forties, no attention was
paid to the subnational dimension. Targets were formulated in
aggregate terms—so much steel, so much electricity, so much
housing for the nation as a whole. In some ministries, though,
some civil servants found it useful to break these analyses down
into geographical as well as sectoral components. For them,
other kinds of rationalities existed. The cost of a project varied
with the location. Overcrowding around Paris made anything
put there considerably more expensive than it would be in a region where people were leaving, or whose economy was stag-
nating. The social cost of an industrial factory included not only
the marketability of its products, but the costs of housing,
transport, and education of its labor force or, conversely, the
costs of *not* hiring labor in depressed areas. Certain social investments demanded large scale: every department could not
have its own supermodern hospital, nor could it have its own
superlative sports complex. In short, these civil servants were
making arguments analogous to that of the regional activists.
While the latter sometimes saw the nation benefiting at the expense of the region, the former thought both levels would be
aided by this kind of calculation. Improving national GNP and
efficiency of resource allocation required both a national plan
and consideration of the spatial distribution activities within
it.[9]

8. Jacques de Lanversin, *L'Aménagement du térritoire et la régionalisation
en France* (Paris: Librairies Techniques, 1965); Kevin Allen and M.C.
MacLennan, *Regional Problems and Policies in Italy and France* (London:
Allen and Unwin, 1970); Niles M. Hansen, *French Regional Planning*
(Bloomington: Indiana University Press, 1968).

9. Pierre Bauchet, *La Planification française*, 5th ed. (Paris: Le Seuil, 1966);

Over the two decades, between the late forties and the early sixties, the bureaucracy, interacting with locally based elites, produced a series of small measures which cumulatively modified the administration of localities. In 1950, the Ministry of Reconstruction and Urbanism published the first effort at subnational spatial planning. In 1952, the Planning Commission accepted an invitation from the CELIB to help prepare a Breton regional blueprint in time for the Second Plan. In those regions which had not spontaneously created *Comités d'Expansion Régionale*, the government established them by decree. A decree of 5 January 1955 restricted industrial location in Paris. A set of decrees in June 1955 created semipublic, regional development societies, set up the *Fonds de Développement Economique et Sociale* to promote regional expansion, and required the dispersal of governmental agencies away from Paris. A major step in this process of ad hoc institutional creation was the promulgation in 1956 of the *régions de programme* (planning regions). Departments were grouped into twenty-one regions, which would become the framework for planning, coordination, and administration. The boundaries delimiting these districts proved durable; except for the naming of Corsica as the twenty-second region, they remain those of the regions today.[10] These regions were the dependents of the state: they had no autonomous legislature or executive or civil servants. At this stage they were entirely creatures of the central government. They modified the state's internal procedures, not the formal mechanisms of representation and legislation. Nonetheless, the new measures reinforced the efforts of those who were

---

John and Anne-Marie Hackett, *Economic Planning in France* (London: Allen and Unwin, 1963); Stephen Cohen, *Modern Capitalist Planning* (Cambridge, Mass.: Harvard University Press, 1970); John McArthur and Bruce Scott, *Industrial Planning in France* (Cambridge, Mass.: Harvard University Press, 1969).

10. Serge Antoine and Jean Vergeot, "Les Régions de programme," *Les Cahiers français* 35 (December 1958); Serge Antoine, "Réformes administratives et régions économiques," *Economie et Humanisme* 118 (May–June 1959); René Monier, *Région et économie régionale* (Paris: Berger-Levrault, 1965).

trying to mobilize regional sentiments by increasing the incentives to do so; there would now be somebody or something regional worth lobbying.

These changes were controversial. Inside the bureaucracy,
they provoked strong opposition from members of the *Grands
Corps* and other civil servants, who feared disruption of the
traditional hierarchy and infringement on their jurisdictions. It
is not clear exactly what sorts of civil servants supported these
decrees, and what sorts opposed. In some cases, the nature of
the job induced reformist consciousness—the *Ministère de
L'Equipment*, for example, had to come up quickly with ways
of analyzing the immense range of new projects demanded of
it. New structures, new criteria always alter power relations, in
addition to other things. Intellectual and situational factors
doubtless combined to produce a very complicated struggle. In
each branch the reformers were probably a minority. That they
got anywhere at all is due to the limited backing given by prime
ministers at key moments (moments when political developments permitted some action), in particular, by Pierre Mendès-
France and Edgar Faure.

In the country as a whole, these changes were not closely followed. Everyone complained of inefficiency and overcentrali-
zation, but there was little agreement as to what should be
done, and attention was focused elsewhere. The Communists
continued to advocate greater departmental democratization,
calling for suppression of the prefect, greater financial powers,
and a democratic executive. The governing parties were much
too worried about surviving to experiment in this way. The
Gaullists wanted to defend the state and saw any reform of this
kind as a menace to its integrity.

Over a fifteen year period, in sum, a series of decrees stitched
together a patchwork of institutions and procedures. Certain
features of the politics of local government reform were already
evident. Some civil servants, some politicians, and some "social
force" activists were interested generally in change. They did
not agree, though, as to which structures would be best. Other
members of each category opposed such changes, or some of

them. The characteristics of each group are far from clear. Each side blocked the other, leading to stalemate, or very limited change. To end the stalemate, or push the situation in favor of greater change, required "outside" intervention by politicians able to overcome internal lobbies. In this period, such support was either not forthcoming, or at best very limited. The parties upon whom the government relied were in no mood to play around with republican institutions. They had no desire to take such risks as sharing power at the local level with Communists, already excluded at the national level. Fearful of the Gaullists as well, Third Force governments derived reassurance from the machinery at their command.

At a couple of moments, politics in the Fourth Republic did become more favorable to reforms. Such change as did go forward happened during those brief moments when the system became relatively unblocked—the Dienbienphu disaster gave Mendès-France the leverage to achieve several reforms, among them the decrees mentioned above; Edgar Faure continued, though with diminishing room for maneuver. More extensive reform, towards fuller versions of options A or B, or going even further toward C and D, would require shifts in the political situation. Some significant political force would have to find more reform useful to it, and take it up. This was not to happen until after the Algerian War ended.

THE FIFTH REPUBLIC, 1958-1962

The collapse of one republic and the creation of another would certainly appear to have been an auspicious moment for institutional innovation. This proved to be the case with the *capital* division of powers, but not the *areal* one.

De Gaulle had considerable leverage in 1958. Fear of the military, political fragmentation, a sense of helplessness in the face of the Algerian problem all allowed him to impose a new constitution as a condition of his takeover. We know that this constitution represented a considerable shift away from traditional republican doctrines about the proper distribution of authority.

The strong executive, the presidency, the restrictions on the National Assembly, the referendum provisions, and the emergency clause were all points that most politicians found hard to swallow. They were all matters over which de Gaulle had fought with the very same people in 1946. Nonetheless, given this new change, de Gaulle did not attempt to implement *all* elements of his thinking. The organization of local government was retained intact: departments, communes, and prefects. The new constitution said nothing about regions, nothing about deconcentration, nothing about decentralization. Local governments as such were given some importance: they elected senators to the upper house in Paris, and elected officials constituted the electoral college for the selection of the president of the Republic. The latter was a role to be played only once in seven years, while the former role remained basically advisory, as the Senate had quite limited powers. Nor did the Constitution of 1958 do much to introduce corporatism into the modalities of representation. The electoral law was put back to the Third Republic model, but an Assembly based on universal suffrage, territorially organized, remained the key institution for enacting legislation. Social groups were put into the *Conseil Economique et Social*, a purely consultative body, and one which existed only at the national level. Thus, the constitution made no provision for corporate representation at any subnational level, be it region, department, or commune.

This result appears somewhat paradoxical. De Gaulle is generally thought of as having virtually a blank check in 1958. Why then were new local governments and corporate representation not written in? These were surely lesser matters than the capital division of powers. Opposition to new arrangements would therefore doubtless have focused on the relationship between the president and the Assembly. To the constitution-makers the greatest degree of latitude must surely have been in these less central issues.

How can we explain that the reverse occurred? Largely by seeing the Gaullist problem in 1958 as one of providing the basis for political control in an extremely difficult situation. A regime brought in to forestall a military coup was hardly likely to disperse power. It would be most concerned with maintaining administrative stability. Whatever the long-range problems with local structures, in the short run, these structures were familiar; they responded to direction from above, and they were widely accepted. Changing local government or the administration would have produced, at least at first, massive confusion; for a while the lines of authority would be unclear, contested, ambiguous. Thus, whatever the Gaullist analysis *à la longue* (that reform of these linkages was imperative for the overall health of the system), such changes were not an immediate necessity.

At the national level, however, a new type of executive *was* indispensable. To tackle the immediate problems at hand—Algeria, order, reestablishing civil authority over the military, stabilizing the economy, strengthening French influence in international affairs—required a new institutional base. The old system made the executive too dependent on fragmented parties. De Gaulle needed ways of mobilizing popular pressure directly against various opponents—initially the military, but also the party politicians, and even foreign governments. He needed ways of handling emergencies, controlling the Assembly. Without such instruments he could not even begin.

The constitution-makers understood that, while their leverage was great, it was not unlimited. The public would accept a great deal, but public support, and the support of a significant fraction of the politicians, was indispensable. That support had to be husbanded, at least somewhat. Priorities had to be established as to which innovations were worth battling over, which could be delayed. The structure of local government and the system of representation did, after all, enjoy considerable legitimacy and touched very complicated and deeply rooted interests. There would certainly have been opposition to changing them. In the end, the Gaullist *équipe* decided that reform of local structures was simply not critical enough to warrant the controversy. The constitution-makers behaved as if they had to choose: they could redo either local government and administration, or the capital division of powers. Obviously they chose the latter, and they did so partly because it provided the greatest rewards in terms of power and control.[11]

If the Constitution of 1958 continued the status quo concerning the formal distribution of powers among different levels of government, the policies pursued after 1958 also continued the previous practice of incremental change via decree. In January 1959, the government moved to do something about the confusion stemming from rapid expansion of the administration. It harmonized the administrative districts of the ministries and created a regional prefect who would preside over regional conferences of administrators within each department. Other decrees sought to expand the field of action permitted communes by allowing them to form associations in support of joint projects. Nevertheless, change remained limited.[12]

As so frequently happened in the consideration of the areal distribution of powers, local reforms were subordinated to other goals. Even when political leaders were themselves interested in such changes, they found them less important than other objectives. Situations of political fluidity were often situations of political uncertainty, when a stable structure appeared most useful. Conversely, when the situation was politically fixed, it was often so frozen that nothing could be done. For local reform to succeed required some odd combination of security and fluidity. A significant political force had to find the situation stable enough to risk shaking up the structures. And that situation had to be fluid enough to give that force a chance of success. Too much stability would give no realistic possibility of change; too much fluidity would trigger the caution reflex. Something approaching these twin conditions came into being after 1962.

11. Nicholas Wahl and Stanley Hoffmann, "The French Constitution of 1958," *American Political Science Review* 53 (June 1959); Nicholas Wahl, "The Constitutional Ideas of Michel Debré," in *Theory and Practice: Festshrift for Carl Friedrich*, ed. Klaus von Beyme (The Hague: Martinus Nijhoff, 1972).

12. Bourjol, *Les Institutions régionales*.

CHAPTER 5

WHITHER GAULLISM?
Alternative Coalitions and Strategies

The end of the Algerian War in 1962 released two of the principal constraints on French politics: fear of the military, civil war, chaos; and the bitterness of decolonization. The effects of the new liberty were felt quickly. The National Assembly reasserted itself and brought down the government for the first time under the new constitution. De Gaulle moved at once to demonstrate the superiority of his popular support. Not only did he win the ensuing legislative election, but he called a referendum proposing direct election of the president. This move had two interrelated advantages. First it removed a piece of power from the politicians who had comprised the old electoral college. Second, it undercut the political oppositions to de Gaulle by showing that he could attack them and win.

While the Gaullist victory in 1962 was unambiguous, it did pose quickly enough the long-range political problem of the regime: with the end of the war in Algeria, the governing majority would have to find some more durable base than fear and an individual's charisma. The end of the war also posed a problem for de Gaulle himself: how, in the absence of an overriding national emergency, to obtain the mass backing he needed to govern autonomously from the pressures of any group or organization, including his own party. In the years following the *Accords d'Evian* in 1962, these two goals, the quest for survival by both Gaullists and de Gaulle, provided the impetus for several significant efforts at reforming the structure of local government and administration, most notably the Decrees of

1964 and the Referendum of 1969. To demonstrate this, it is necessary to analyze the Gaullist movement, its composition, its goals, its difficulties, and their alternative solutions. These can then be related to the choice among particular types, or options, for the reform of the areal distribution of powers. In explicating these connections, this chapter suspends the chronological presentation, which will be resumed in Chapter 6.

THE ROUTINIZATION OF CHARISMA

In 1962, the Gaullist party, the UNR, comprised a group of Assembly deputies with no local roots. Municipal and departmental councils remained firmly in the hands of the other parties. Even in the largest of France's thirty-eight thousand communes it would have been difficult to find evidence of a local UNR organization. Gaullism was a movement, a set of leaders with a mass following. Its appeals were more personal, emotional, and ideological than material or "interest"-oriented.[1]

These characteristics derived in part from newness; there had not been time to build the other kind of organization. It also stemmed from de Gaulle's desire to maintain the UNR as a "movement," one which would not be *un parti comme les autres*. That de Gaulle did not like political parties is well known. He saw them as inherently particularistic, seeking to gratify partial interests rather than general ones. Also, parties were for him limiting, or constraining; being the head of a party provided an organizational base, but it also imposed constraints. The interests of the members and the voters had to be looked after in a very immediate way. De Gaulle rejected the model of Konrad Adenauer and Alcide de Gasperi. He did not wish to derive his power from being head of a large organization, spiritual or secular.

When he came back to office in 1958, de Gaulle refused to

---

1. J.Q. Wilson and Peter Clark, "Toward an Incentive Theory of Organizations," *Administrative Science Quarterly* 6 (September 1961): 129–166; and J.Q. Wilson, *Political Organizations* (New York: Basic Books, 1974).

mobilize the vast resources now at his disposal in order to build a party machine. This would not have been so hard to do. The opportunities for patronage were immense. An organization could have been constructed from the ground up—a party which would cater to the needs of countless individuals and groups for special treatment or help from the state.

Instead, de Gaulle preferred autonomy from party constraints. The constitution had been designed to make this possible. The executive had formidable power, provided that the two heads worked in concert. And the referendum gave the president an instrument of immense leverage. Even these tools were not enough, however. De Gaulle supplemented the constitution with unique personal resources. His past gave him great authority in the present. The man of the *appel du 18 juin*, the leader of the government in exile, a conservative who hated Vichy, a reformer who was not a radical, the man who imposed France on the Allies—these endowments helped generate the kind of following and power no formal set of institutions can alone confer. The *auctoritas* of the institution was supplemented by the *authority* of the person.[2]

To govern as he wished, de Gaulle required the ability to demonstrate, repeatedly if necessary, that he enjoyed mass backing. Even the constitution could not eliminate that need. To keep the prime minister subordinate to the president required the cooperation of the National Assembly. Thus the system did not free de Gaulle of the need to win elections. It gave him instruments by which he could pressure the politicians, even the ones nominally in his camp, to remain loyal, or at least passively accepting, but these instruments still had to be used, skillfully, to mobilize popular support.

2. The phrase *auctoritas* is borrowed from Bertrand de Jouvenel, *The Pure Theory of Politics* (New Haven: Yale University Press, 1963); for an application of the distinction between *auctoritas* and authority see Peter Gourevitch, "Political Skill: The Case of Pierre Mendès-France," *Public Policy* 14 (1966). See also Stanley Hoffmann, "Heroic Leadership in Modern France," in *Decline or Renewal?: France since the 1930s*, ed. Stanley Hoffmann (New York: Viking Press, 1974), pp. 63–110.

In the long run, however, these techniques, while viable for de Gaulle, could not work for his successors. Routinization replaces charisma, or at least the creation of charisma must be routinized. The direct election of the president would help the new occupant of that office, but it would not suffice. No individual could hope to have the prestige of the founder. To the leverage provided by the constitution would have to be added that of organization and interests. The movement would sooner or later have to become a more conventional party, woven into the fabric of French life at every level. It would have to create not only a national staff, but local headquarters as well. It needed card-carrying adherents, militants, professionals, and as large a network of local office holders as possible. It needed to become an instrument for the servicing of the concrete interests of social actors, a mechanism for the distribution of patronage, the granting of favors, the fulfilling of ambitions. It had, in short, to become something like *un parti comme les autres*.

Just what such a party would be like was, though, an open question. However inevitable a gradual settling down from movement to party may have been, the precise *direction* that evolution would go was not so foreordained or obvious. The Gaullists were, after all, quite internally diverse. Many different sorts of people joined in 1958. There was variety in motive, interest, and outlook. Each wanted to take Gaullism to a somewhat different place. After 1962, these elements fought with each other to shape Gaullism's future.

COMBINATIONS WITHIN GAULLISM

We may identify three principal groupings within the Gaullist movement, which can be labeled the Loyalists-Nationalists, the Modernizers, and the Conservatives. The Loyalists-Nationalists were those attached primarily to the person of de Gaulle and to his emphasis on French grandeur. They had rallied to him in the past (in 1940 and 1947), and by now to the reasons for having done so was added a powerful cathexis to the individual himself, to his ideals, vision, and legend. The Loyalists would go wherever de Gaulle led them. In his absence, the question of being true would loom large; for them the question, "What course of action would de Gaulle want us to take?" would be very important. Generally, the Loyalists were strong nationalists in foreign policy. On social matters they would support whatever reforms seemed necessary to permit French activism. Michel Debré is the most outstanding member of this camp; others include Roger Frey, Alexandre Sanguinetti, Christian Fouchet, and Pierre Messmer.

The Conservatives saw in Gaullism protection against radicalism and rapid change. They feared the left and socialism. They also feared the harsh winds of international market forces. They looked to Gaullists to shield them against both: to stop the progress of the left, and to take the sting out of change. The state would help obviate the necessity to modernize, or if that was impossible, absorb much of the cost of doing so. The Conservatives were willing to make common cause with any groups willing to support such a program, whatever the partisan attachment. The Conservatives generally liked the nationalist foreign policy, but it was not essential to them. Some of them admired de Gaulle deeply; others resented him for the attack on Vichy and for having "let" Algeria go. If the resentment turned to hate, they joined other parties of the right, or went into exile (Georges Bidault, Jacques Soustelle). Examples of the traditionalists include many of those who supported Antoine Pinay in 1952, and who jumped to Giscard in 1974.

Finally, the Modernizers comprised those interested primarily in the transformation of French society. They wanted industrial development, rapid growth, up-to-date technology, larger factories, bigger companies, better trained managers, education designed for modern economic needs, better and more housing for growing cities, improved transportation—in short, progressive management of a modern society. Their vision was technocratic. These things were desirable in themselves. If they helped sustain a nationalist foreign policy, so much the better. Some Modernizers may have been attached to de Gaulle's person, but that was not the essence of their involvement with the movement. Many were too young to feel quite so deeply the

meaning of 18 June 1940, and had been more influenced by
the premiership of Mendès-France in 1954. They followed de
Gaulle because he seemed interested in change, and capable of
generating the political support it required. They would follow
any moderate political grouping to do the same. A typical
member of this group is Olivier Guichard; Chaban-Delmas
became its leader in the late 60s.

To some degree these three *courants* derive from different
moments of the *ralliement* to the general's banner: The old
barons of Gaullism joined as part of the opposition to Vichy in
1940; the Conservatives came over in 1958; the Modernizers
and *jeunes loups* rose after 1962. Some individuals belonged to
more than one camp: Chaban-Delmas and Debré were both
Loyalists and Modernizers.

These three elements could combine in different ways. Each
combination implied somewhat different mixes of interests,
ideological appeals, and substantive programmatic relations
with other political parties. Each consequently implied quite
different fates for alternative programs for the reform of local
government and administration.

An alliance between Modernizers and Conservatives against
the Loyalists would be difficult because the first two had such
different domestic goals. The Loyalists, however, could join
with the Modernizers in support of social transformation to the
extent that foreign policy and de Gaulle required it. Or they
could slam on the brakes in alliance with the Conservatives
should that seem appropriate. The Modernizers and the Conservatives had no particular animosity to other parties and
political formations; they could work with these when necesary,
differing only in which ones; the Modernizers gravitated toward
the center parties and the Socialists, while the Conservatives
were pulled more by the Republican Independents and other
conservative groupings. To the Loyalists, however, working with
the existing parties was far harder. Their hatred and suspicion
of them went much deeper. Keeping apart was a more central
aspect of their identity and connection with the person and
goals of Charles de Gaulle.

ALTERNATIVE STRATEGIES FOR THE FUTURE

These combinations would support, then, alternative futures for Gaullism after 1962. They were not simply different strategies for attaining the same goal—survival of the regime and the movement in some form or another, though that was common to all. Rather what was at stake were competing visions, alternative destinies for the Gaullist legacy, France, and its relation to the world.

We may identify four competing combinations of these elements, or four competing strategies. Each entailed different combinations of interests, ideological appeal, substantive programs, and relationship to other political parties; each implied somewhat differing stances toward the matter of reform of local government and administration.

The four strategies arise by positioning a set of choices between two dimensions. The first dimension deals with *program:* how much change, how much reform, how much modernization of French society, economic structure, education, labor relations, what balance between modernization and preservation? The second dimension deals with *leadership:* who governs? Which set of leaders carry out these policies? What relationship do the Gaullists have to the existing parties? Do they compete with them, or cooperate? Do they replace the traditional elites with a new *équipe* working through a new organization, or do they merge with and coopt the existing formations?

This is, of course, a considerable simplification of the alternatives. There are numerous elements within each dimension—many policies, many combinations of party and leaders. The principal distortion comes from not elevating foreign policy to the level of a third dimension, since this has been a major issue which splits all categories. Here, it is domestic issues which are stressed. The foreign policy implications and complications will be treated more fully in Chapter 11. The combinations of these dimensions are represented in Table 2.

TABLE 2
Competing Strategies for Survival

| | | PROGRAM | |
		Preservation	*Modernization*
LEADERSHIP	*Replacement*	Strategy 1	Strategy 2
AND PARTY			
RELATIONS	*Reconciliation*	Strategy 3	Strategy 4

STRATEGY 1: CONSERVATIVE POLICY UNDER NEW LEADER-SHIP: This strategy would seek to make Gaullism the principal bulwark against radical change in French society. The mystique, the nationalism, the dynamism, the aura of reform—these would provide a legitimacy to the *parti de l'ordre* which Conservatives themselves could not, under their own banner, provide. This policy would be put across by a new set of leaders. Indeed, that would be part of its efficacy. It would have stronger appeal across a broader part of the electorate than would the old, *usé* politicians of the regular parties. In the nature of the appeal, though not in the authoritarianism, an analogy might be made to Mussolini prior to about 1926, or to Franco of the 1960s.

STRATEGY 2: MODERNIZATION UNDER NEW LEADERSHIP: This orientation saw in Gaullism a means of modernizing French society to bring it up to the level of its neighbors and competitors, to assure a high standard of living for its citizens, and to sustain an important role in international affairs. Nationalism and activism were valued for themselves. The party would appeal to all groups in French society, across class, religious, ideological, party, regional, and other lines. A program of reform would restructure industry and the economy, improve agricultural efficiency, develop modern infrastructure (highways, rail, canals, planes, ports), expand and modernize education, construct housing for the swelling urban population, and so on. The state would spearhead social transformation without being radical—the goal would not be socialism, but a modernized, up-to-date, mixed capitalist economy. This great effort would be led by the new *équipe* brought forward by de Gaulle, not by the old familiar politicians and parties. Strategy 2, then, would seek continuity with de Gaulle's own orientation. The difference lay largely in how the appeal was organized. De Gaulle made rulership rather personal; there were, of course, Gaullist organizations but they depended directly upon his personal authority. Strategy 2 would try to institutionalize that authority into a regular political party. An historical analogy might be made to Bismarck, who constructed a complex coalition of interests which was both very transformative (unification, a constitution with a parliament and universal suffrage, industrialization) and very conservative (preservation of the Junkers, the autonomy of the executive, the insulation of the army).[3]

STRATEGY 3: CONSERVATION AND RECONCILIATION: The programmatic goals of strategy 3 are similar to its homologue, strategy 1: defense of *les droits acquis*, tradition, property, order against pressure from the left. The difference lies in the relationship between Gaullism and other political formations devoted to similar goals. Strategy 3 places conservation as the highest goal, and cares relatively little about who does it. The other parties of the right and some on the center have similar goals. Hence, they should be enlisted in the battle. The Gaullist movement should, therefore, not seek to attack and displace these formations, but merge with them. The leaderships would be fused, in the model of the British Conservative party or the German Christian Democratic Union-Christian Social Union; or they would cooperate, in a stable, multiparty alliance. During the Fourth Republic, Pinay tried this.

3. On the uses of foreign policy in domestic politics, and on the "Caesarist" model, see Hans-Uhlrich Wehler, "Bismarck's Imperialism," *Past and Present* 48 (1972). On the impact of the international system upon domestic politics more generally, see Peter Gourevitch, "The Second Image Reversed: The International Sources of Domestic Politics," *International Organization* (Autumn 1978).

STRATEGY 4: MODERATION AND RECONCILIATION: Here the programmatic homologue is strategy 2: moderate reform and modernization of French economics, society, structures. The difference is that strategy 4 does not seek to impose the Gaullist elite upon the political coalition which supports these policies. Like strategy 3, it is willing to work out cooperative relationships with the other parties committed to similar goals. Again, this could mean sharing leadership in a broad single party, or sharing via a multiparty coalition. In either case, integration and mutual cooperation would be tried, rather than frontal attack upon the existing formations of the center and the right. Both strategies 2 and 4 seek to dominate politics from the center, to resist polarization of the system, to deny the relevance of left versus right, to appeal across categories to all sectors of the population. Strategies 1 and 3 seek to mobilize all social groups, but via polarization, against the left. An example of a strategy 4 leader might be Aldo Moro in Italy.

IMPLICATIONS FOR REFORM

Each strategy has its own contradictions and tensions:

Strategy 1: Can it maintain the appeal across classes, which it needs to stay in power, while being conservative in policy? Will nationalism suffice to obscure this contradiction?

Strategy 2: Can reform and institutionalization be reconciled? Is it possible to root the Gaullist movement in a soil of interests and commitments, without losing the autonomy from particularistic concerns needed for a broad reform program?

Strategy 3: Can Gaullism be wed to the traditional right without losing its identity? What remains of Gaullism?

Strategy 4: Again, is it possible to root the movement without losing the capacity for reform?

Strategies 1 and 2 share the problem of trying to attain certain goals (preservation and reform, respectively) without drawing in the help of potential allies who share the same goals but have different partisan attachments.

From an organizational point of view, strategies 3 and 4 have a great advantage: they try to work with groups interested in their substantive policy goals. In that sense, they attempt to work with interests, rather than trying to dominate them, or impose themselves upon them.

Strategies 3 and 4 are, therefore, probably the "natural" course. The decline of a movement is part of a life cycle of political formations: from fervor, élan, charisma to routine, interest, and material incentives.[4] Sooner or later, the movement elites are likely to compromise with the other social forces and other leaders. For a time, the movement elites may actually occupy the reigns of power, but after a time they are likely to fade away and make room for the others. Thus over the long run, the distinction among the strategies is likely to blur.

In the short run, however (that is, a decade or two—a political lifetime), the difference can produce very sharp political battles. When the Gaullists follow strategies 1 or 2, their relations with the other formations of the center and right are obviously very bad. If they follow strategies 1 or 3, French politics will be sharply polarized; every election will appear to present the possibility of a sharp discontinuity. If they follow strategy 2 or 4, political life may appear calmer, but there is always the risk of drift and immobilism endemic to any Third Force approach in French politics.

What implications do the different strategies have for reform of the areal distribution of powers in France? Strategy 2 led to the greatest receptivity to such reform, strategy 3 to the greatest hostility toward it. (It remains to be seen whether this is inherent or conjunctural.) Strategy 1 is generally hostile to major reforms, but the antagonism to other parties may push it toward some kinds of change. Strategy 4 is potentially receptive to such reforms since it includes some of the elements in French politics who have traditionally been the most interested in the regions, and in strengthening local society (the center). As we shall see, however, so far when strategy 4 coalitions have been in power, the more conservative elements have vetoed such

---

4. Wilson and Clark, "Toward an Incentive Theory of Organizations."

moves. The realization of the coalition's reformist potential probably requires an alliance with the left, as in Italy (see Chapter 9).

STRATEGIES AND POLICY

The connections between these political strategies and policy toward local government over the past decade and a half are summarized below.

1962-1965. Strategy 2. Confrontation and reform provides support for Decrees of 1964 and conflicts during the municipal elections of 1965. Policy of administrative deconcentration, regionalization, and corporate representation supported by Debré and early Pompidou.

1965-1968. Slow shift from strategy 2 to strategy 3. Growing strength of conservative sentiment, interest in institutionalization of UNR, cooptation and reconciliation of traditional elites, while policy publicly remains that of strategy 2.

1968-1969. Sharp confrontation between strategies 2 and 3. *Les événements* provoke crisis for de Gaulle and Gaullism. Pompidou pushes for strategy 3, de Gaulle for strategy 2, which leads to the Referendum of 1969. Victory of strategy 3.

1970-1974. Strategy 3 in power. Pompidou becomes cautious, especially concerning local government. Shifts emphasis to communes and departments, *les villes moyennes* (middling France). *Loi Marcellin* and *loi Frey* attempt to gratify demands for reform in most cautious way. Major challenge to this from Chaban-Delmas who wants to continue strategy 2, without yet moving to strategy 4. Chaban-Delmas defeated first by Pompidou, then by Giscard.

1974-1978. Increased discord among Gaullists. Giscard tries to govern with a strategy 4 alliance, but winds up being strategy 3. Gaullists conflict among strategy 4 proponents (Chaban-Delmas, Peyrefitte, Guichard) and the "Loyalists" who wish to retain hegemony of the Gaullist *équipe* but waver between a reformist and a conservative policy stance (strategies 1 and 2).

TABLE 3
Political Leaders and Strategies

	PRESERVATION	MODERNIZATION
REPLACEMENT	Strategy 1 late Chirac (after 1976)	Strategy 2 Debré, early Pompidou, Chaban-Delmas of 1970
RECONCILIATION	Strategy 3 early Chirac (pre-1976) Pompidou after 1968, Giscard pre-1978	Strategy 4 Chaban-Delmas of 1978, Peyrefitte, Guichard Giscard after 1978

The positions of the various political leaders in relation to the strategies are summarized in Table 3.

In a very well-known book on pre-Revolutionary France, Franklin Ford analyzes the *Marriage of Robe and Sword.*[5] The new nobility, of the Robe, possessed considerable powers through its control of bureaucratic offices, but had inferior prestige and privilege. The *noblesse d'épée*, conversely, had plenty of privilege and status, but little formal power. Intermarriage between the two forged a combination more powerful than either alone. The nobility was now in a position to resist the monarchy quite effectively, and of course the noble reaction helped bring about the events of 1789.

This story has analogies with the situation in France after 1962. The Gaullist party, the UNR, controlled the government at the top. It monopolized the Council of Ministers, and its deputies formed the largest bloc in the National Assembly. At the local level, however, the UNR was quite weak. Municipal and departmental councils remained firmly in the hands of the

5. Franklin Ford, *Robe and Sword* (Cambridge, Mass.: Harvard University Press, 1953).

traditional parties. Gaullism was a movement, a set of leaders with a mass following; the regular parties had a dense infrastructure.

Gaullism and the other parties needed one another. The Gaullists could use a local base. The center and right parties could use mass appeal at the national level. Each had reason to be wary of the other as well. The Gaullists wanted to remain in control. The others wanted in. Several outcomes were possible. And the story is not over. In the next three chapters, we shall unravel it up to 1978.

CHAPTER 6

GAULLISM AFTER ALGERIA, 1962–1969

When the *Accords d'Evian* loosened the constraints on partisan conflict in France, the immediate challenge to Gaullist rule came primarily from the parties of the center and right. De Gaulle had never counted on the regular support of the left in the National Assembly to sustain his cabinets, but he did need the votes of the MRP and the Independents. In the evolution of the UNR, therefore, its relationship with those formations would necessarily be extremely important. The question was whether the UNR would choose a strategy of attack or a strategy of cooperation.

Flush with the success of having dispensed with France's most intractable problem, it is not surprising that the dominant coalition inside the party was inclined toward confrontation. Free of Algeria, de Gaulle and Gaullists wanted to complete their mission: restore France to a central role in world affairs, remake the economy, and solidify the new political system. Each goal required the others. A strong foreign policy depended on an economy capable of paying for new weapons systems, supporting autonomous economic policies (a strong franc, independence of the dollar), and sustaining French influence within the Common Market. Policies favorable to economic modernization and growth required public support; the electorate had to share the vision and receive enough of the material dividends to accept the strains of adaptation and change.

Within the UNR, these goals drew the support of the Nationalist-Loyalists and the Modernizers. In the context of strife with the other parties, together they were drawn toward strategy 2 rather than strategy 4, that is, change plus partisan confrontation, rather than change and reconciliation. Both groups thought their substantive program could be carried out only by the new leadership *équipe*. The politicians of the other parties were too compromised by their particular commitments, thought the Gaullists, to do what was necessary. Besides, why share power with them, which is what reconciliation implied, when it might be possible to get away with shoving them aside? The Conservatives inside the UNR were thus put into the background. They disliked both the substantive program involved in strategy 2, its commitment to change, and its political logic, confrontation with the other parties combined with an effort to retain the support of important elements of the left electorate.

Strategy 2 in these years sustained a favorable disposition toward reform of the areal distribution of powers. To the incrementalism of previous years, it added two ingredients: a political incentive to go farther, and the possibility of mobilizing political support to do so. The political incentive stemmed from the differing degrees of implantation of the Gaullists and their rivals in the existing structures of local government. Since the former were weak and the latter were strong at the local level, the Gaullists had no particular motive in preserving local structures, and ample interest in shaking them up. The introduction of new institutions would loosen present relationships. During the transition, the Gaullists could attempt to bring forward new leaders committed to them rather than to their rivals.

The Gaullist analysis of society led, moreover, to the presumption that plenty of potential pro-Gaullist leaders did in fact exist. Hostility to Gaullism, it was thought, came from *la classe politique*, the politicians, journalists, and lobbyists who comprised an artificial elite which perpetuated sterile, ideological cleavages in order to sustain itself in power. The natural leaders of society were the heads of *les forces vives*, the businessmen, engineers, scientists, doctors, workers, farmers, family specialists, and so on, who dealt with practical problems of daily life. The central political problem of France was that the institutions of local government still lay in the hands of *la classe politique*, not *les forces vives*. Having eliminated the notables from control of the executive in the center, the Gaullists now wanted to drive them out of the periphery as well. New modes of representation would enable these new elites to come forward. Their *apolitisme* would be, the Gaullists assumed, the equivalent of support for Gaullist rule. Such was the reasoning which provided the political rationale behind a set of moves culminating in the Decrees of 1964.

MOVES TOWARD REFORM

Change of the administrative structures had always been regarded as risky, but the end of the Algerian crisis facilitated a greater openness to risk-taking. So long as the conflict lasted, the Government was unwilling to tolerate the confusion in the lines of command which any major reform of administrative structures would inevitably create. Now, a bit of short-run chaos would not bring down the state and might bring some significant long-term gains.

The groundwork for reform had already been laid. A core of civil servants and interest-group leaders had developed the arguments and the recommendations for more extensive rationalization of the administrative structures. A decree of 7 January 1959 created a regional prefect and some harmonization of ministerial districts. More change required only the political interest in pushing aside the numerous sources of resistance inside and outside the bureaucracy. Even while the Algerian crisis was at its height, Michel Debré, whom no one could possibly accuse of wanting to weaken the majesty and authority of the state, himself took charge of the reform agenda. His authority allowed the working groups preparing proposals to go farther toward regionalization than would otherwise have been the case.

After Debré's departure in 1962, the Pompidou government
was able to take advantage of the new political situation post-
Evian to keep momentum going forward.[1]

A major innovation was the creation in 1963 of the DATAR
(*Délégation à l'Aménagement du Territoire et à l'Action Régionale*). The DATAR was to be for the regions what the *Com-
missariat au Plan* had been for national planning—a guiding
spirit, a prod, a center of knowledge and initiative, a source of
energy. It had little formal power, and only very limited finances.[2] Its influence would come from the quality of its personnel, their political contacts, and its location in the system. In
its early days, the DATAR attacted a group of young, bright,
energetic *énarques*, full of new ideas and ambitious about doing new things. This personnel was well-connected; it had all
the predictable links to the *Grands Corps*, and it reached into
the top of the Gaullist leadership as well. Its first head was
Olivier Guichard, who had good credentials among Loyalists
and Modernizers alike. Finally, the DATAR was attached to the
office of the prime minister, so that it was well-placed to put its
finger into everything. Over the next decade or so, the DATAR
would flood France with a vast quantity of impressive studies,
plans, and proposals emphasizing the regional dimension of the
country's problems. Its creation in 1963 foreshadowed the more
conspicuous and controversial Decrees of 1964.

The *Decrees of 1964*

The *Decrees of 1964*, which have been examined in admirable
detail by Catherine Grémion, had two "wings."[3] The one having to do with regions attracted the most attention; the other
aspect dealt with departments, and while less spectacular, re-
veals much about the motivation behind the whole package.

1. Aside from being remarkably detailed and thorough, Catherine Grémion's work on the Decrees of 1964 constitutes one of the first studies of decision-making in France. Catherine Grémion, *Profession: décideurs—Pouvoir
des hauts fonctionnaries et réforme de l'Etat* (Paris: Gauthier-Villars, 1979).
2. Ibid., chs. 5 and 6 on the DATAR.
3. Ibid., passim.

The regionalization measures rationalized the incremental steps of the previous fifteen years, and extended them. The twenty-one *régions de programme* took shape as institutions. Each region would now have an executive, the *préfet de région*, supported by a staff, the *mission régionale*. A committee known as the CAR (*Conférence Administrative Régionale*), composed of the departmental prefects and the departmental treasurers, would get the very important job of apportioning credits delegated from Paris among the departments in the region. The national budget and the national plan would be regionalized more thoroughly with stronger input from regional planning bodies themselves. A representative assembly would be established, known as the CODER *(Commission de Développement Economique Régionale)*. Half its members would be designated by functional groups, one-quarter by the departmental councils who could choose either mayors or departmental councilors, and the remaining quarter by the prime minister.[4] The mayor of the regional capital and the president of the *Comités d'Expansion Régionale* would sit in the CODER by right.

The departmental decrees sought to clarify the chain of command between Paris and the countryside. The confusion wrought by the proliferation of external field services would be eliminated by restoring the primacy of the prefect in the department. The prefect would be recognized as the principal representative of the government to whom all other representatives of the state (therefore, members of other ministries and corps) would be subordinate.

These changes amounted to a kind of streamlined Jacobinism. They modernized rule from the center via administrative deconcentration. The new institutions remained wholly dependent on the government in Paris. The identity of the executive,

4. Elisabeth Dupoirier and Gerard Grunberg, "Vote municipal et vote legislatif: Evolution de 1965 à 1971 dans les villes de plus de 30,000 habitants," *Revue française de Science Politique* 22 (April 1972). See the other articles on the March 1971 elections in that issue.

the source of the funds, the actual scope of powers, the administrative personnel, and at least one-quarter of the regional assembly members were named by the government, which did not have to consult Parliament in making its choices. The CODER had purely consultative functions. It had no power over the *mission régionale*, the regional prefect, or the CAR. Its influence could be that of persuasion, of a good dossier, but it had no formal power. In terms of the categories developed in Chapter 3, the Decrees of 1964 combined elements of option A (those dealing with the departments) and elements of option B (those dealing with the regions).

Reaction to the *Decrees of 1964*

While the Decrees of 1964 were hardly revolutionary, they did involve a major rationalization of the previous measures and did provoke considerable opposition both inside and outside the governing majority. Among the politicians of the UNR, many feared the new measures would weaken the authority of the state. They worried most about two aspects of the package: the regions and corporate representation. These Jacobins of the right were suspicious of regions, which smacked too much of the old regime, of particularism, of loyalties to entities other than the nation-state. Being small, departments were not dangerous. Even if affective attachments developed for the department, the cathexis would be broken up among many units, no one of which had enough followers to threaten the center. Smallness was also a protection against political enemies; a department, even if captured by the opposition, lacked the resources to be much of a base for launching an attack on Paris. Regions, however, being so much larger, would be more visible, more legitimate, and hence more dangerous. They could provoke useful weapons in the hands of an enemy. Corporate representation was disliked on similar grounds: it gave too much weight to particularistic interests; it violated the sanctity of the state; and it threatened to undermine the capacity of the state to represent and implement the national interest. The Jacobin conservatives were more sympathetic to the departmental decrees. They accepted the argument that order had to be restored to the state's management of its affairs, and that this was the way to do so.

The criticisms by the politicians of the left and center parties were in some respects similar, in others not. They too were especially critical of the regionalism clauses and corporate representation. They defended republican legitimacy which they equated with departments and universal suffrage based on geographical districts. Corporatism was for them fatally compromised by its association with fascism. The new institutions were seen as profoundly undemocratic because they vested power in bureaucrats beyond the reach of any elected representatives.

All the non-Gaullist parties charged the government with political opportunism in promoting these reforms. They accused it of trying to transfer power from institutions in which the oppositions were strong to institutions whose personnel the government could control. Here, as in later discussions, opinions about the substance of the reform (levels of government, procedures, modes of representation) were strongly colored by the context in which the proposals were put forward. Because the initiative came from the Gaullists, in a setting of considerable tension between the UNR and other parties, politicians who, in another conjuncture might be more favorable to certain elements of change, were here quite critical. Because the issues were complicated, multidimensional, and confusing, it was not hard for all sides to be contradictory and inconsistent.

Finally, the way in which the reforms came about was itself an object of controversy. Everything was done by decree. None of it was ever put before the National Assembly even for its advice, to say nothing of its consent. The decrees were discussed on the floor of the Palais Bourbon, but only through questions, not because of any *projet de loi*. This procedure drew accusations of an attack upon republican legitimacy.

Whatever the opinions of the opposition, the government could of course impose the reforms so long as it wished to do so. The interesting thing is that it did in fact desire them. That was the case, it is being argued here, because the Loyalists and

Modernizers wanted to strengthen the Gaullist movement by giving it a local base. Shaking up the system, devising new institutions and new types of representation, helped do that. These were not the only motives behind the reforms. They provided the political rationale for them. Institutional change was not such an obvious, self-evident necessity that it could impose itself without a political rationale. When the rationale dried up, so did the process of change.

IMPLEMENTATION AND THE
MUNICIPAL ELECTIONS OF 1965

The next steps in the application of strategy 2 were the implementation of the Decrees of 1964 and the municipal elections of 1965. In each case, the Gaullist leaders saw an opportunity to bring forward local elites loyal to them. As the CODER were set up, the "natural elites" would have a platform from which to express themselves, providing an alternative voice to that of the local politicians. What nature did not do, the appointive powers of the prime minister would supplement. While the CODER were a sapping operation, undermining the enemy's ramparts, the municipal elections would be a frontal assault. The Gaullists would storm local mayoralities, running candidates not only against the left, but against the center and right as well, hoping to drive them out.

In both cases, the Gaullists failed. They did not achieve the hoped for breakthrough in the municipal elections. Where they ran candidates in coalition with the center and right parties, the Gaullists performed respectably. Where they ran candidates in direct confrontation with those parties, the Gaullists were beaten. Thus it proved impossible to take the local bastions of their political neighbors by storm. If, to switch metaphors, they wanted to sink local roots, some other way would have to be found.[5]

5. Pierre Grémion and Jean-Pierre Worms, *La Mis en place des institutions régionales* (Paris: Copédith, 1965); idem, *Les Institutions régionales et la societé locale* (Paris: Copédith, 1968).

The results of the CODER scheme also turned out to be meager. The hope that the natural elites would be pro-Gaullist proved illusory. The representatives chosen to sit in the CODER were very much like the people who already dominated French local life; indeed they were very much the same individuals. Pierre Grémion and Jean-Pierre Worms, examining the *mise en place* of the regional institutions, have demonstrated how these were "neutralized" by the politicians, interest-group leaders and civil servants who dominated the old system. They simply absorbed the regional structures, integrating them into the existing network of relationships. Instead of being a vehicle for a new elite, the CODER gave the old ones yet another platform.

New Alliances for the Gaullists

As the impact of these reverses sank in, some Gaullists began to look around for an alternative way of stabilizing the movement and the regime. Some decided that confrontation was foolish. The politicians of the center and right parties were potential allies, not enemies. They should be drawn into the Gaullist orbit, not attacked frontally. A broad alliance should be constructed, dominated by the Gaullists to be sure, but in an accommodating way. If a certain moderation of reformist zeal was the price to be paid for such accommodation, so be it. The UNR would have to become a party like others, with an organization, a local base, offering services, distributing patronage. In short, strategy 3—reconciliation in party relations, caution in policy program.

After 1965, Pompidou, then prime minister, moved slowly in this direction. He supported Robert Poujade, secretary of the UNR, in the construction of a modern party machine, replete with research staffs, opinion pollers, and professional managers. Contacts were made with other centrist and conservative elites, and with interest group leaders.

Strategy 3 entailed a *renversement des alliances*. The Loyalists would abandon the Modernizers and link up with the Conservatives. The new alignment inside the party would be strengthened by its ability to make alliances *outside* the party. In the

mid–sixties, the major alternative was strategy 4: improved relations with other formations, combined with continued commitment to reforms. This would stress alliance with the progressive center, not incorporation of the right. It is only clear in
retrospect that Pompidou was headed in the direction of strategy 3, not 4. At the time, economic modernization, renovation
of the army, an active and acerbic foreign policy, criticism of
traditional elites all continued. De Gaulle still dominated
politics. From 1965 to 1968, several directions were being tried
out simultaneously. The alliance committed to strategy 2 was
still in place; yet experiments with other directions were also
underway. This confusion and ambiguity might have continued
for quite a while. In the spring of 1968, the strikes of May and
June forced a choice, and helped tip the scales toward strategy 3.

DE GAULLE VERSUS POMPIDOU (1968–1969)

The events of May and June 1968 affected the reform of local
government in contradictory ways. At first they seemed to help
the cause of change. The explosion gave vent to a growing
disenchantment with the state, on the left as well as the right,
and it induced de Gaulle to propose further reform of center-local linkages via the Referendum of 1969. At the same
time, *les événements* also produced a reaction, which led to the
defeat of the referendum, de Gaulle's departure, and the emergence of Pompidou's political orientation, less open to reform.
In the end, 1968 proved to be another opportunity for change
in this domain which slipped away unused.

De Gaulle's interest in reform of local government did not
begin with *les événements*. He had of course accepted the
Decrees of 1964 and shared Debré's conviction that preserving
the strength of the state required reforming it. After the instal-
lation of the regions from 1964 to 1968, some of the civil servants most interested in this sort of innovation were already developing proposals for going farther in various ways: elevating
the regions to the formal status of a local government, giving

them more powers, having an elected assembly, giving more power to departments and communes, increasing administrative deconcentration.

Again such proposals aroused considerable opposition inside and outside the administration, and again could not go forward to overcome these "topocratic" lobbies without political support.[6] De Gaulle, along with the Modernizers and some of the Loyalists, appears to have become convinced by the late sixties that the long-run interests of the state as well as Gaullism required going ahead.

In March 1968, de Gaulle spoke at Lyon, delivering a speech frequently cited to prove that he had already come to some of these conclusions *before* the pressure of the May events began to weigh on him.

> General trends are carrying our country toward a new equilibrium. The centuries-long effort at centralization, which had long been necessary in order to realize and maintain France's unity, despite the diversity among the provinces which had successively been attached to her, is no longer imperative. On the contrary, it is regional activity which appears to be the basis of economic power in the future.[7]

Several weeks later, Guichard, head of the DATAR, spoke at Nantes about the importance of developing institutions which were new with respect both to the size of the territory (regions) and to the type of representation (mixture of territorial and functional elites).

The Challenge to Gaullism

A variety of schemes could have met the general requirements of these broad proclamations. Different projects were under consideration in the administrative "pipeline." It is not clear which of them would have been put forward, nor following

6. The word "topocratic" comes from Samuel Beer, "Federalism, Nationalism, and Democracy in America," *American Political Science Review* 72 (March 1978): 9–21.

7. Charles de Gaulle, "Discours de Lyon," *Le Monde*, 26 March 1968.

what timetable, had the explosion of May not intervened. What happened was that *les événements* altered quite dramatically the political context and meaning of the issue. Prior to May, de Gaulle moved toward reform as a way of improving the efficiency of the state machine and as a way of strengthening those forces in French society favorable to the Gaullist vision of the future. After May, de Gaulle used reform of the areal distribution of powers as a way of solving challenges to his *personal* authority. He did this twice. The first time came at the end of May, the second with the Referendum of 1969, the following April. The magnitude of the crisis of 1968 was not initially appreciated by either de Gaulle or most of the government. De Gaulle actually went off on a state visit to Roumania, and Pompidou on a trip to Afghanistan. As the strikes spread after 14 May, leaders began to appreciate that something special was happening.

The authority of the government was being challenged at a very basic level. Something had to be done, but what?

De Gaulle's initial response was simultaneously to belittle the whole affair and to say that he was the appropriate person to make things better. In his speech of 24 May, he proposed a referendum on *la participation*. The French would be invited to reaffirm their belief in democracy by endorsing the need for improved mechanisms of participation whose precise nature were not made clear. In so doing, the electorate would of course also be reaffirming its support for de Gaulle, over the heads of the party leaders who were presumably responsible for the mess. In short, de Gaulle proposed an old solution to an old problem—to obtain autonomy from *la classe politique,* he would go directly to the people.

The speech was a political disaster for de Gaulle, one of the gravest misjudgments he ever made. Everyone, from the mass public to the Gaullists in office, found him completely out of touch. Things had gone much too far for a vaguely worded referendum whose real meaning was "leave everything to me." Suddenly, de Gaulle seemed old, weak, unsure, unmasterful, not, somehow, his usual self. Suddenly, the very core of the system seemed hollow. Authority had disintegrated. The result was panic on the side of government supporters and intensification of pressures from the opposition. Talk began circulating about the formation of a new, left government and there was even speculation as to who would have which ministry.

Pompidou understood somewhat more quickly how serious the situation was. He argued that something more drastic had to be done. He persuaded de Gaulle to adopt a different tactic: less talk of conciliation, reform, problem solving; more outright assertion of authority, the firm hand at the top, the will to govern, the élan to fight back. Pompidou saw that the referendum de Gaulle had proposed on 24 May would no longer have any effect. The only way to combat the impact of strikes and street demonstrations was with the greater legitimacy of a different type of popular consultation. He persuaded de Gaulle to dissolve the National Assembly, thereby forcing the left to worry about elections. Big counterdemonstrations were organized on the Champs–Elysées, and gasoline suddenly became available for the beautiful weekend weather. Government negotiators sat down to deal with the strikers and business representatives. Pompidou relied on the efforts of the unions and the PCF to confine the workers' protests to traditional labor market issues, rather than to broader political ones.

The ploy worked. The Gaullists won a smashing victory in the elections of June, the first time indeed in French history that any single party got an absolute majority of seats in the National Assembly. This success did not come without costs, however. Because of this victory, and the events which led to it, the Gaullist movement would change character, and its leader would be squeezed out of office.[8]

Changes in Gaullism

The two months of May and June 1968 brought about two extremely important alterations in Gaullism. First, it gravely undermined the ability of Gaullism to present itself as a grand,

---

8. Raymond Aron, *La Révolution introuvable* (Paris: Fayard, 1968); Daniel Singer, *Prelude to Revolution: France in May 1968* (New York: Hill and Wang, 1970).

national movement, above the political left-right spectrum, appealing to all groups and classes, offering a *troisième voie*. The government had come down foursquare on the side of capital, aggressively so. All the moral suasion incarnated by de Gaulle and Gaullism was used not to sustain a new foreign policy and social transformation, but to mobilize mass resistance against the left, to defend the system.

Pompidou's strategy produced impressive short-run results —the legislative victory of June 1968, and his own massive victory in the presidential elections in the spring of the following year. The long-run cost was polarization and the loss of important support for Gaullism on the left. In the sixties the social profile of the Gaullist electorate resembled that of society as a whole. It drew on cadres, patrons, workers, the retired, the young, the rural, the urban, the poor, and the rich, not equally, perhaps, but enough to claim to represent a broad spectrum of French society. Gaullism could plausibly assert that it was neither left nor right, that it appealed to the nation. A key element in that appeal was the support given by voters who previously had voted on the left. The UNR was not quite a catch-all party in the sense of a purely pragmatic seeker of votes but, having a broad and diverse base of support, it did have some of the potential for becoming one.[9] With support from the other parties of the center and right, the Gaullists were able repeatedly to turn back challenges from the left.

For this to continue, the Gaullists had to retain the ability to siphon off some portion of the left electorate. This became increasingly difficult in the late sixties. In the elections of 1967, the left recovered its earlier vote levels (about forty–seven percent). The events of 1968 temporarily stopped the shift leftward by frightening the electorate back toward de Gaulle. After 1968, the trend resumed, but faster. The Gaullist profile changed. As left voters slipped away, a corresponding shift, of lesser proportions, took voters from left to right: small property

9. Suzanne Berger, *The French Political System* (New York: Random House, 1973); Guy Michelat and Michel Simon, "Religion, Class, and Politics," *Comparative Politics* 10 (October 1977): 159–186.

owners, the retired, farmers, businessmen—people whom
republican traditions and anticlericalism had put on the
left—now became increasingly frightened of that position, and
switched sides. Whereas the Gaullists could once claim to represent the future (the young, well–educated, economically
dynamic), they now attracted the past (the old, the retired, the
workers in traditional occupations).[10]

The impact of these shifts would be to change Gaullism. As
it filled up with particular social categories having concrete programmatic needs tied to the defense of certain interests, it lost
its character as a movement, above ideology, above interests. It
became instead a moderate-to-conservative party *comme les
autres*. As we shall see, this evolution limited both the willingness and the capacity of the party to support various social
reforms.

This shift was perhaps inevitable. Sooner or later, élan
diminishes. The zeal of a movement ossifies into a structure of
interests. The UNR had become a governing organization.
Naturally it gravitated into a relationship with dominant social
forces, not with the unions and the radical left. Nonetheless,
this could have happened sooner or later, faster or slower, with
more or less internal opposition and fragmentation. Without
the events of May 1968, the ambiguity of several different directions could have gone on for a while. Instead, a choice was
forced, and it was strategy 3 (preservation and reconciliation)
which won out.

This happened in part because of deliberate decisions made
by Pompidou. His emergence into the spotlight was a dramatically new and important feature in the configuration of French
politics. Hitherto, there had never been a "successor." The
only alternatives to de Gaulle seemed to have been the army,
civil war, or the immobilism of the previous republics. Much of

10. For a recent analysis of the changing social composition of the electorate, see Panayote Dimitras, "Social Classes and Voting Behavior in France:
The Political Economy of Class Voting in the Fifth Republic" (Paper delivered
at conference, Two Decades of Gaullism, mimeographed (Brockport, N.Y.,
9–11 June 1978).

de Gaulle's leverage had always derived from this situation; he who is indispensable has power.

Les événements changed this in three ways. First, de Gaulle no longer seemed so infallible. Second, the reformism of his policy stance became repugnant to the intensified conservatism of much of the electorate. Third, there was now, indeed, a plausible successor, Georges Pompidou.

Pompidou came forward not only because of his years as prime minister, but because of his handling of the May and June events. When de Gaulle faltered, it was Pompidou who got the credit for figuring out what to do and for organizing the smashing victory in the legislative election of June. Pompidou behaved the way people had expected de Gaulle to behave: firm, cool, authoritative, aggressive.

The upshot of these new developments—in the electorate's ability to locate Gaullism politically, and the declining sense of de Gaulle's indispensability—made for an instability in the political situation, only partly obscured by the size of the governing majority. De Gaulle himself was weakened. The majority had become more conservative. De Gaulle had not. The majority was willing to insist that its leader subject himself to its wishes. De Gaulle was not. In the months after June 1968, both the substance of the government's domestic policies and the character of de Gaulle's ruling style would increasingly come under attack.

De Gaulle's Provocative Referendum

De Gaulle had two choices. First, he could accept the new situation by becoming more accommodating in both policy and style. Indeed, part of his problem was that he could not easily do one without the other. Trimming his sails in policy would be interpreted as yielding to pressure, which would diminish his autonomy. Alternatively, de Gaulle could refuse the situation and fight back, trying to recover both his autonomy and support for his policies. To do that, he needed some way of demonstrating convincingly that he still had personal standing with the population. He had to challenge the politicians in the National Assembly, and beat them.

Enter regionalism. The instrument de Gaulle chose for the reassertion of his authority was the reform of France's structures of local government, administration, and representation, all of which were to become parts of the Referendum of 1969. As we shall see, de Gaulle's political needs account for certain characteristics of the referendum project which are otherwise hard to explain—aspects of the project which he knew were unpopular, even among his own followers, but which he inserted nonetheless into the text, contributing to his defeat.

Why this set of issues as the subject for the referendum? Largely because the alternatives were even more controversial and politically tricky. De Gaulle's interpretation of how to combat the effects of May and June was to have more reform, orderly reform, not a *chienlit* but reform nonetheless. The broad theme behind such reform was to be *la participation*. Three areas were involved: the factory, the universities, and local governments. The first two were loaded with political booby traps, land mines of sensitivity, interest, and ideology which could blow up at any moment. Businessmen would be extremely unhappy about any serious push for autogestion in the factories, or even milder schemes such as profit sharing. The electorate, the schoolteachers, and the students were an explosive combination concerning the universities. Something had to be done about each of these, but they were better talked about in the National Assembly, in ministries, in contacts with the interest group leaders than in the open and unstable forum of a national referendum. Both were made subjects of *projets de loi*. Both laws were passed by enormous margins in the fall of 1968.

These margins were not indicators of unanimity and consensus, but, on the contrary, of subjects so touchy that the deputies preferred to dilute responsibility by voting them *en bloc*, thus getting them out of the way.[11] Local government, while having

11. Otto Kirchheimer, ''The Transformation of the Western European

controversial elements, was less explosive. It had a progressive cast to it, but not the quasi-revolutionary aura of worker and student involvement in management.

Work began on the projected referendum in the late summer and early fall of 1968. The government undertook a vast survey of elite opinion on the subject. It sent out questionnaires to every municipal and departmental council, to the CODER, and to every conceivable interest group asking a very long series of questions about the organization of local government and administration in France, both as it presently functioned and as it should function.[12] The answers showed how extraordinarily complex and confusing the whole matter was. As Chapter 3 noted, there were so many dimensions involved (the type of executive, limits of the regions, relations between regions and departments, powers of the assembly, finances, and so on) that it was hard to pull out any clear messages. For the government, the survey provided useful publicity. All the people who had to fill out the questionnaire had to think and talk about what they thought. At the same time, the government could demonstrate its good faith in seeking to consult society and involve it in decision-making.

The job of writing the actual text was given to Jean-Marcel Jeanneney as *Ministre d'Etat pour l'Administration et la Réforme Régionale*. Jeanneney consulted widely, inside the government and out. In late December, just before the Christmas recess, Jeanneney laid the matter before the National Assembly. The deputies were invited to talk, to advise, but not decide. The text was never made a question of law, so there was no legislative committee study or report. During the debate, there

Party System," in *Political Parties and Political Development*, ed. Joseph LaPalombara and Myron Weiner (Princeton: Princeton University Press, 1966), pp. 184–192.

12. These questionnaires generated an extraordinary quantity of information about French opinions of the distribution of authority. The author looked at the reports themselves, thanks to the Ministry of Administrative Reform which had them filling a remote room of their building. The author also consulted analyses of these reports prepared by the SOFREAS.

was not even a tentative text. The deputies thus did not know what they should attack or defend. This was to become one of the controversial aspects of the whole proposal—that it had never been adequately laid before the representatives of the people, that it was written by a closed circle of technocrats.

In the debate, the many conflicting opinions emerged quite clearly. Indeed, the absence of a precise text worked like a psychological projective test: everything people thought, felt, and feared came out. The desire to loosen the bonds of Parisian control was real, but not unlimited. Decentralization was popular, but also troublesome, and not popular enough to carry with it any and all related but different issues. Left and right alike worried about too great a weakening of the state. Though they worried about somewhat different dangers (the Marxists' concern was with the coherence of planning, the ability to manage a publicly owned economy; the Gaullists worried more about disorder, fragmentation, and the Communists), most deputies shared some understandings about the *nature* of the common good, as opposed to its *content*, which hindered the acceptance of extensive decentralization. That is, they stressed the primacy of *la nation* over its parts, the superiority of general interests over particular ones, the need for an institutional structure capable of identifying the public good and then implementing it. Even the most enthusiastic partisans of decentralization acknowledged that it implied more fragmentation of policy formation, the possibility of divergence of policy among different regions of the country, conflict with the central government, and the possibility that partial interests would have their way. No one developed an argument that reconciled the tension between collective and particular interests as applied to local government, that is, an argument able to demonstrate that the common good can emerge from the pursuit of a series of local, hence, inherently partial, interests.[13]

The debate also revealed considerable reservations about other aspects of what might go into the referendum; corporate

13. For further elaboration on this point see Chapter 1.

representation still smacked of fascism to a large number of deputies, both right as well as left. Departments and communes still enjoyed considerable legitimacy. Politicians were worried about their power bases. Left and right feared the other would be the main political beneficiaries of a revised system of local government. The left and the center insisted that, in any new assembly, the territorial representatives should be directly elected. The debate provided ample warning of political danger. That the left would criticize was overdetermined. But the project was also under fire from the majority.

The government's text called for the elevation of regions to the status of *collectivité territoriale*, equal legally to communes and departments. The executive would be the regional prefect. Powers were fairly broad in subject matter—housing, urbanism, transport, and so on—though the meaning of these clauses would depend on further legislation and policies set in Paris. The civil servants would be part of the national system. Finances would depend on what money Paris chose to give, either in taxing powers or in grants.

Representation in the regional assembly would be shared between territorial and functional leaders. One college of the regional assembly would be territorial, though chosen at the second degree by towns and departmental governments. The other college would be functional, and the government would have considerable leeway as to which groups in what proportions would actually be chosen. The mix of powers between the two colleges was complex: both would vote on all matters but, in case of conflict between them, the territorial representatives would prevail.[14]

In the language of Chapter 3, this was an extended version of option B. It went beyond pure administrative deconcentration in giving some role to an elected assembly, but the real activity of the new institutions would remain almost entirely dependent on Paris. It stressed regions rather than departments and cities

14. On the referendum, see Jean-Luc Bodiguel et al., *La Réforme régionale et le Referendum du 27 avril 1969* (Paris: Editions Cujas, 1970).

as the object of activity. And it was far more functionalist than many would have liked.

Reasons for de Gaulle's Defeat

In each dimension, the regional clauses drew criticism: the left objected to the powers of the functional elites and their mode of designation; they objected to the nature of the executive, and to the feebleness of the money and powers granted, all the while defending the departments and communes. On the center and the right there was complaint also about the functionalism, about the undermining of departments and cities, about the vagueness of the powers. And there was complaint that it went too far.

The text failed to mobilize the enthusiasm of ardent reformers, who thought it all too feeble (such as Mendès-France). At the same time it worried the Jacobins, who thought it went too far (Sanguinetti). Nonetheless, the creation of a new level of government, the regions, was itself sufficiently popular that, by itself, it might well have carried. Instead, the government chose to add to the creation of regions a set of measures (functional representation and reform of the Senate) which, while logically connectable, could have been omitted. These other measures were far less popular among the mass public, and vastly less popular among the political elites.

Functional representation was unpopular on all sides. It ran too deeply against the presumption that group interests were partial and particular, that only territorial interests could elicit the common good. For the left, it also appeared to be an explicit attack upon the only mechanisms of representation in which they were strong: local governments.

The Senate had no particular standing among the French public, but was an old institution—there had always been an upper house, of varying powers. The title "senator" carried some modest prestige. For the left the Senate was suspect because it favored rural and conservative France; senators are chosen indirectly by the municipal and departmental councilors. The Gaullists disliked the Senate because the mode of

designation greatly favored the traditional centrist and conservative elements which had resisted the Gaullist party and
program all along.

Resistance to abolishing the Senate came of course from precisely the elements well represented in it. The politicians themselves seem to have been particularly disturbed at this blow to
their authority, and the conservatives saw this as yet another
adventurist scheme on de Gaulle's part. Resistance was made all
the more intense because of the connection between abolition
of the Senate and corporate representation. Elevating the
Economic and Social Council to the position of second
chamber, even one with very limited powers, aroused all the
hostilities which the functionalist clauses at the regional level
also provoked.

Thus, to each popular dimension of reform was added a
rather unpopular piece. Those who might have overcome other
misgivings to support regionalism were repelled by the precise
project proposed. Those whose antagonism to the Senate would
have been clear found themselves wondering whether the existing machinery was not preferable to the corporatism of the new
proposals.

In the end, the actual content of the referendum text probably proved less important in determining its fate than did
judgments about the future of de Gaulle himself. Inevitably, as
in all referenda, the issue and its political ramifications were in-
tertwined. By April, the election had turned into a referendum
on whether to keep de Gaulle in office. He himself had made
quite clear he would resign if the project lost, which, of course,
it did. Was this defeat necessary? Could de Gaulle have produced a more acceptable text? Need he have engaged his personal future in it? It is argued here that the first questions must
be answered in the negative, the third in the positive. To explain why, it is necessary to put those choices in a broader political context.

The left, even that sizable segment which had proregional
sympathies, urged a negative vote. Having been frozen out for
so many years, the left wanted a chance at power. A defeat for

de Gaulle would be the first step to that end. It would at least
unblock French politics, and weaken the center and right. From
looking at François Mitterand's poll in the presidential race of
1965 (forty-five percent), and the left's poll in the legislative
elections of 1967 (forty-seven percent), we may infer that even
if the whole left electorate voted *en bloc* against the referendum, it still would have passed. To produce the defeat required, therefore, an important defection from the previous
Gaullist majority of about six percent to seven percent of the
total electorate in order to reach the losing margin of fifty-three
percent to forty-seven percent against.[15]

Who were these defectors? Two kinds of people: first, conservatives who had become more fearful of de Gaulle's reformism
than of his departure. Such people disliked de Gaulle's response to 1968. They wanted less rather than more change.
They wanted protection from modernization, not more of it.
Pompidou offered the possibility of beating the left without
conceding too much reform. The second source of opposition
came from local office holders; mayors, town and departmental
councilors, even those who belonged to the majority and might
normally have defended their side against the left, spoke out
very sharply against the referendum, the abolition of the Senate
in particular, and mobilized some of the electorate in defense of
traditional republican institutions. The number of voters dis-
placed by such arguments was doubtless small, but it did not
take many to push the solid bloc of negative left votes over the
margin.[16]

To some degree, therefore, the content of the referendum
did matter. De Gaulle lost in part because of what the text said.
Much of the opposition was eminently predictable, and predicted at the time. Why, then, did de Gaulle allow it to be
written that way? Why not write a text which maximized the

15. Ibid.
16. Ibid. and *Le Monde*, 28 April 1969. A SOFREAS poll on the Referendum shows that feelings concerning its regional aspects were quite different
from feelings concerning reform of the Senate:

changes of passage? A more palatable text might be one which called for: regions with directly elected assemblies, a divided executive on the departmental model, a modest budget, and a purely advisory, functionalist council. This would have caused some anxiety among the Gaullist Jacobins and the conservatives of the majority, but arguably less than the attack on the Senate and the corporatism of the actual referendum text. And the centrists and left elements sympathetic to regionalism and decentralization might actually have voted for a clearer chance to get them.

Or de Gaulle might have offered a vague statement of principles, focusing on the regions, leaving it up to Parliament to fill in the details. The controversial elements could thereby have been left obscure. This course was urged by Raymond Marcellin, minister of the interior, who was in close touch with local notables, and sensed very keenly the mix of conservative hostility and institutional jealousy which motivated them; Marcellin also happened to be somewhat antiregionalist anyway. This was also urged by the DATAR group around Olivier Guichard, which was ardently proregionalist, and feared seeing its pet project sunk by the burden of other preoccupations.[17]

Yet another tactic might have been to avoid making the ref-

Question: Dans l'ensemble, êtes vous plutôt favorable ou plutôt opposé:
—à la réforme régionale
—à la réforme du Senat

	enquête des 14–18 mars	enquête des 29–31 mars	enquête des 11–12 mars
Réforme régionale			
—plutôt favorable	54%	55%	52%
—plutôt opposés	20%	21%	22%
—sans opinion	26%	24%	26%
Réforme du Sénat			
—plutôt favorable	26%	28%	30%
—plutôt opposés	33%	30%	31%
—sans opinion	41%	42%	39%

SOFREAS, ''La Réforme régionale et le Referendum,'' Table 2, mimeographed (poll carried out 11 and 12 April 1969).

17. See Paul Camous, ''La Genèse du projet gouvernmental,'' in Bodiguel

erendum a test of de Gaulle's future, to prevent the *engagement personnel*. The merits of the case could have been divorced from the political dimension had de Gaulle refused to make clear that he would depart if beaten. This is apparently what Jeanneney, the minister in charge of writing the project, urged. He wanted a detailed text on all the issues, including the Senate and corporate representation, but nonpoliticization of the vote. "This was our chance," said one high civil servant in an interview. "We have to make the public swallow as much as possible for we will not soon get another opportunity."[18]

De Gaulle did none of these things. He allowed Jeanneney to write a detailed text, dealing with all the issues, including the Senate, including functionalism, leaving nothing in the shadows. He personally approved the whole thing. At the same time, he engaged himself in a clear, unambiguous way. He would resign if beaten. Why? It has been suggested that this was "presidential exit by suicide."[19] De Gaulle knew he would have to go sooner or later. He was considered by some to be obsessed with the form of his departure from public life. It had to be dramatic; it had to fit the shape of his whole life. He was thought, moreover, to be moody, and annoyed with the French people because of *les événements* and the grumbling that went on afterward. Thus, pride and arrogance led him to follow deliberately a risky course which led to defeat, where a prudent line might have prevented it.

This interpretation is possible, but it is also superfluous and

---

et al., *La Réforme régionale*. My interpretation of the politics of the Referendum is based on: books such as the Bodeguel volume; interviews with ministers, civil servants, deputies, party leaders, mayors, the leaders of voluntary associations and interest groups, and academic researchers; materials from a variety of organizations such as the *Mouvement National pour la Décentralisation et la Réforme Régionale*, the *Assemblée des Présidents des Conseils généraux*, *L'Association des Maires de France*, and the various party-related associations of local government politicians; the documents gathered by the government as part of the consultation in the late summer and early fall of 1968; and the debates on Jeanneney's presentation to the National Assembly, 11–14 December 1968, and to the Senate as well.

18. Interview with a member of the Jeanneney cabinet, Paris, 1972.

19. J.E.S. Hayward, "Presidential Suicide by Referendum," *Parliamentary Affairs* 22 (Autumn 1969): 289–319.

unnecessary. There were powerful, compelling, *political* reasons underlying de Gaulle's conduct. We do not need the hypothesis of mental unbalance, suicidal impulses, and other disorders. Occam's Razor suggests we try to do without it, since it is the most cumbersome and least demonstrable of the interpretations.

De Gaulle needed not just any victory, but a particular kind of victory. *Les événements* had undermined his authority. He had to reassert it. The challenge to his position came not only from the left, which was predictable and manageable. More seriously, it came from his own camp, from those voters and deputies whose support had been part of Gaullist majorities from the beginning. From July 1958 onward they grumbled increasingly about their leader. They pressed in on de Gaulle, wanting him to cut back his activity, to be more responsive to them and their needs. If de Gaulle gave in, he would become the conventional leader of a majority, having to tack and trim with the winds. This, of course, de Gaulle had never wanted to do, and did not wish to do now. He wanted to recover his freedom of action, his autonomy from *la classe politique*. He wanted to prevent the regime from sinking to the level of pluralistic pushing and shoving by private interests, where he would have to negotiate every move, and even lose a number of times. De Gaulle wanted to govern autonomously. To do so, he had to challenge the grumblers *in his camp*, among the center and right electorate, inside the UDR (formerly the UNR) itself, and beat them.

To do that, a provocative referendum was necessary, not an ameliorative one. It had to contain elements visibly distasteful to his erstwhile and ostensible supporters. The passage of such a text would constitute not only an affirmation of de Gaulle but a rejection of politicians by the mass electorate. When, in the winter of 1969, the referendum was quite obviously headed for trouble, de Gaulle could not trim his sails by reefing in the text, since appearing to run before the storm blown up by the *notables* would undermine the meaning of any victory. De Gaulle was trapped. The worse the project fared in the polls, the more he had to personalize. If he amended the text, the victory would become ambiguous; he would not have reasserted in a direct way his capacity not only to remain in office, but to govern as he wished. If he stuck with the text, he risked defeat. Also, he believed in it.

The Struggle among the Gaullists

From June 1968 onward, one can see signs of a continuing struggle between de Gaulle and his own camp. In the summer, he replaced Pompidou with Couve de Murville. Did he feel menaced by Pompidou's increased prestige? Did he and Pompidou disagree on strategy? Did he seek to shift blame for the events onto someone else? Did he see Pompidou as a plausible successor, for whom a period of silent exile would be beneficial? A bit of all of these things, perhaps, but we cannot be sure. From a distance, the political dimension bulks large. De Gaulle sensed instantly that Pompidou was a rival, stronger among some of the Gaullists than he himself.

In the fall of 1968, the gap widened. Deputies in the governing coalition took few pains to conceal their dislike of de Gaulle's policies; they objected to the education law's framing by Edgar Faure, and to the bill on the rights of unions in factories. Though almost all the deputies voted for these measures, the conservatives found them too radical, too conciliatory, too adventurous. In November, the repercussions of the wage settlements of May and June showed up in a monetary crisis; conservative property owners expressed grave distrust of the government by sending capital out.

Throughout this period, Pompidou maintained a silence whose effects were deafening. There was open discussion that he would replace de Gaulle. In January 1969, Pompidou turned the screw just a bit tighter; he said to a group of French journalists in Rome:

> It is not, I believe, a mystery for anyone that I will be a candidate for President of the Republic. But I am not in a hurry.[20]

20. *Le Monde*, 18 January 1969.

Immediately there was speculation that Pompidou was trying to force de Gaulle out. In a radio interview a few days later, Pompidou qualified his earlier remarks:

> I am not presently making any electoral campaign. Thank heaven, General de Gaulle is well installed.[21]

On 23 January, de Gaulle felt compelled to declare to the Council of Ministers:

> In the accomplishment of the national task which befalls me, I was reelected December 19, 1965, President of the Republic by the French people for seven years. I have the duty and the intention of finishing this mandate to the end.[22]

Despite the denials, the idea remained: if de Gaulle should go, Pompidou was ready and willing to take over.

As the situation worsened, many loyal Gaullists urged that, in case of defeat, de Gaulle should not resign. After all, as *La Nation* put it in an article of 27 February 1969:

> This referendum, in reality, is very different from the preceding one. It is the first time that a referendum does not involve any of the grand, fundamental orientations of Gaullism. One cannot claim that decentralization and the transfer to the provinces of a certain number of decisions traditionally taken in the capital has ever figured in the "Gaullist" system of thought.[23]

In its bulletin of 1 March 1969, the *Association Nationale pour le Soutien de l'Action du Général de Gaulle* said exactly the same thing. The referendum was not a vote of confidence in the president because "less than a year ago the French people once again gave him a massive vote of confidence."[24] Only that vote was a legislative vote, not a direct personal one.

Other Gaullists gave out contrary signals. Robert Poujade said in January that this type of election "was inevitably a vote

21. Ibid., 19,20 January 1969.
22. Ibid., 24 January 1969.
23. Ibid., 28 February 1969.
24. Ibid., 6 March 1969.

of confidence." Jeanneney put it more ambiguously, "It is a political question, but it is not one of the fundamental policies of the regime."[25]

Much hung on the resolution of the ambiguity. If, as *La Nation* suggested, the reforms were so unimportant, why go through the trouble of a nationwide election? If the proposals mattered so little to the regime, why should anyone vote for them? Moreover, whatever de Gaulle said in advance, Poujade's observation would prove true; a defeat would inevitably be interpreted as a defeat. If, on the other hand, the referendum really dealt with significant issues, it must be a piece of the *orientations fondamentales*, if not of Gaullism, at least of de Gaulle and his government in the spring of 1969. In that case, the referendum *was* a vote of confidence, and the government would have to mobilize an all-out effort to win. But then it would become a plebiscite on de Gaulle, not the issues. Those sympathetic to the reforms but hostile to Gaullism would then be forced to vote no, and de Gaulle might lose.

In early March, de Gaulle took the plunge. The referendum would not be delayed. It would not be rewritten, amended, pared down, simplified, lightened, fudged. The whole package of reforms would be presented, and to it he would tie his continuation in office.

The organizations on the left had already recommended a "non." The center and non-Gaullist right had been inching in that direction, and by the first week in April did so openly. Only the Republican Independents seemed to remain with the UDR, and even Giscard let drop his famous "Oui, mais," and the "Je refuse mon oui." On 11 April de Gaulle definitively announced that he would resign if he lost. As everyone knows, the gamble failed, the referendum lost, and de Gaulle left.

CONCLUSION

The argument here has been that the process which led to 27 April 1969 had begun in the mid-sixties, and was considerably

25. Ibid., 8 March 1969.

intensified by *les événements*. For years de Gaulle had managed
to reconcile contradictory pressures: he got conservatives to accept more reform than they wanted, and he got the progressive
center and left to settle for less, by forcing both to realize that
they had little alternative, and by offering other gratifications—stability, international grandeur, defiance of the super-
powers, economic growth. This was an extremely difficult political line to sustain. Inevitably the conservatives would demand a
halt, the progressives would demand more, and the techniques
for bridging the gap would be strained to the breaking point. It
might have worked for some years more, but we believe it
would have broken sooner or later. And *les événements* did
break it. The Gaullist synthesis snapped. The left defected
when it saw Gaullism coming down so firmly on the side of order. The conservatives defected when they saw de Gaulle trying
so hard to resurrect the compromise through reformism. Many
politicians defected when they saw that de Gaulle continued to
attack them in particular. To paraphrase Marx's comment on
Louis-Napoléon, we may say that part of the extra-parliamen-
tary bourgeoisie turned against its own representative. In 1851,
it supported the executive against Parliament, whereas this time
it supported its parliamentary representatives against the
incumbent president.[26]

For reform of the areal distribution of powers in France, the
defeat was, of course, a major setback. An opportunity had
been lost. In the late sixties, there was widespread support for
some kind of reform, even the creation of a wholly new level of
government. Interest in regionalism was at its high-water mark.
There had been a veritable explosion of awareness about it from
many different sources: autogestion and participation, submerged cultures, planning, rationality, urbanization, industrialization. Regions seemed new, modern, progressive, innova-
tive, democratic, sensible. These were not necessarily enduring
sentiments, and might not last forever. Nonetheless, there was
a reservoir of enthusiasm to be tapped. Support for change was

26. Karl Marx, *The Eighteenth Brumaire of Louis-Napoléon* (New York:
International Publishers, 1973).

real but not unlimited; something could have been got through, but not everything.

The failure of the referendum blocked that energy, and eventually dissipated it. After April 1969 the situation was terribly confused. No one could be sure what the outcome meant for the substance of the issues. Was it purely a verdict on de Gaulle? Or did it also mean that, whatever people said in the polls, they were in fact attached to the existing system? Was it functional representation they disliked? The Senate reform? The whole issue area seemed uncertain and dangerous. It was not clear anymore how anyone could make political capital out of it, if at all. More important, the defeat marked a shift in the balance of political forces in France. Despite the continuity of Gaullism in the Palais Bourbon and the Elysée Palace, the changeover signalled a considerable weakening of the forces seeking reform in French society.

CHAPTER 7

GOVERNING WITHOUT
DE GAULLE, 1969–1978

The change in person, from de Gaulle to Pompidou, in April and May 1969, was itself, of course, very important for French politics. No one could do what de Gaulle had done, nor rule as he had ruled. With the change in personality, there came also a structural shift. Pompidou owed his career to de Gaulle, who lifted him from obscurity to the office of prime minister and, implicitly, to the position of *le Dauphin*. Nonetheless, despite the appearance of great continuity, Pompidou reorganized the elements which comprised the Gaullist movement. A new alignment emerged: the Nationalist-Loyalists and the Conservatives against the Modernizers. With the new alignment came a shift in policies.

The policy and political orientation of the government went from strategy 2 toward strategy 3, from modernization and partisan conflict to conservatism and conciliation. Where de Gaulle held the neighboring party formations at arm's length, Pompidou, lacking de Gaulle's personal clout, moved to integrate them. His first cabinet took in the Giscardians and the most cautious of the centrists. This enlarged the government's base of support in a way which reinforced its conservatism. Gradually, the Modernizers were forced to choose: accept the new orientation, or leave.

Pompidou moved carefully so as not to offend the Nationalist-Loyalists, who were the critical swing group. He could not appear conspicuously to be abandoning de Gaulle's positions; yet at the same time, he had to gratify the pressure for a slower pace. In June 1969, Edgar Faure was eased out as minister of education: his *loi d'orientation* had been intensely disliked by the conservative voters. At the same time, he named as his prime minister Jacques Chaban-Delmas, who had strong credentials in two camps—Loyalist and Modernizer. Chaban-Delmas wanted to continue de Gaulle's line of reformist, broadly centrist, vaguely nonpartisan appeal. In a widely publicized speech to the National Assembly in September 1969, he criticized the "société bloquée," calling for a variety of reforms, among them more regionalization. (The speech was heavily influenced by Michel Crozier.) Chaban-Delmas was to be disappointed. Pompidou went the other way. Eventually he dismissed Chaban-Delmas, partly to reaffirm the superiority of the presidency, partly because the two had divergent understandings of policy and politics.[1]

This shift had important implications for the fate of local government reform. Everyone knew that the Referendum of 1969 had not really expressed French opinion about regionalization and decentralization. Pompidou could easily have interpreted the referendum results as a personal defeat for de Gaulle, or for corporate representation, or as a victory for the Senate. Regionalization could have been pulled out of the April 1969 package and brought forward on its own. Instead, Pompidou took a much more cautious line. He chose to interpret the referendum failure as indicating resistance to any form of experimentation, especially that which touched the privileged place of departments and communes in French political life.

THE CAMPAIGNS OF SERVAN-SCHREIBER

At first it looked as if the regionalization project would be shelved permanently. In his public discourse, Pompidou emphasized towns and rural areas. He made well-publicized visits

---

1. Chaban-Delmas' departure also had something to do with a controversy over the low level of taxes he was paying. What he had done was perfectly legal, however, and the constant innuendo in the press was more a symptom of his political isolation than a cause.

to *villes moyennes*, and the countryside, and increased contacts with traditional social groupings.[2] Some programs of aid to towns were announced, but little was done until political pressure appeared. It came in the form of a challenge from the center, led by Jean-Jacques Servan-Schreiber.

Servan-Schreiber had taken over the ruins of the Radical party or, more precisely, part of the ruins, since that group, already small, split. One part moved left, becoming the *Radicaux de Gauche*, aligning with the Socialists and Communists as signatories to the Common Program. The other part stayed in the center, a component of the shrinking and fragmented forces neither linked to the left nor absorbed into the majority; it was this part which Servan-Schreiber captured. In his leadership campaign, he took up the cause of local government reform generally and, in particular, the cause of regions. Indeed Servan-Schreiber became the only politician, and the Radicals the only party, to make regionalization and local government reform the centerpiece of a political program. The proposals were indeed far-reaching: directly elected regional assemblies; downgrading the prefect from chief executive of the region to the government's representative in the region; replacing the prefect in the former capacity by an elected official; more funds; more powers. The Socialists and Communists were to come quite soon to similar official positions, but these demands were not as prominent in the campaigns and priorities of the Common Program as they were for Servan-Schreiber's Radicals.

For a time this program of reform appeared to have some appeal. In the late spring of 1970, Servan-Schreiber took the issue into a by-election to represent Nancy in the National Assembly. This district was a propitious place for him and his arguments. The Lorraine was in crisis, with aging industries and factories and rising unemployment. Increasingly, residents of the area saw that their problems were regional in character. Paris seemed insensitive, blocking projects that would tie the region to the

2. Suzanne Berger, "D'une boutique à l'autre: Changes in the Organization of the Traditional Middle Classes from the Fourth to Fifth Republics," *Comparative Politics* 10 (October 1977): 121–137.

booming markets of Germany and the Benelux; it seemed also to favor the rival city of Metz.

Servan-Schreiber's victory was dramatic. He defeated a Gaullist by a wide margin. The result gave some momentum to the reformist critics of Pompidou, who wanted the government to take a more centrist, less cautious stance. In September, Servan-Schreiber tried to keep up the pressure with another spectacular act: he ran against Chaban-Delmas in another by-election in Bordeaux. A Radical victory there would very badly embarrass the majority, and of course propel the victor into the public spotlight with dramatically enhanced leverage over events. Servan-Schreiber miscalculated badly. Bordeaux remained completely loyal to its long-time mayor and Servan-Schreiber was crushed.

The Government Response

Nonetheless, the campaigns of Servan-Schreiber had some effect on the political situation and hence on policy-making. He had reasserted the local government question at a time when Pompidou was letting it slide. He had shown that reform continued to have some support, that the Referendum of 1969 did not have to be interpreted as a complete rejection of regionalization. Servan-Schreiber was applying pressure to which Pompidou felt compelled to respond. Three measures came out of the government over the next two years: a new set of decrees extending administrative deconcentration, a law on the consolidation of town governments, and a new bill on the regions. Pompidou would allow reform but only cautious ones; these measures added up to a measure of deconcentration, but very little participatory decentralization or corporatism.

The regulations promulgated in November 1970 became known as the *décrets anti-remontées*. Their goal was to discourage the constant tendency to refer local matters to Paris for judgment. State expenditure would henceforth be classed according to the unit of government most affected: nation, region, department, and commune. Those affecting the last three would be remanded down to the state's agents at the regional level and below. The budget would classify expenditures according to levels; the funds for the lowest three levels would similarly be handed down to the regional administrations. There, the funds would be divided up among departments by the CAR *(Conférence administrative régionale)*, which comprised the prefects and treasurers of each department. None of this could be appealed back to Paris.[3]

The law on consolidation of towns was an effort to deal with the problem posed by the existence of thirty-eight thousand communes in France, more than in any other country in Europe, and a number virtually unchanged since the Revolution. Many of these are so tiny as to be unable to organize a wide range of services. Rural life is effectively handled by various branches of the *Grands Corps*. Governments have long discussed consolidating these rural communes, as most of the other European governments have done. This is stoutly resisted by the *élus locaux*, who wish to retain their titles as mayors and town councilors. The measure brought in by Pompidou and Raymond Marcellin, minister of the interior, called for fusion of communes, but voluntary fusion—no communes would be forced out of existence. Rather, they would be encouraged to link up by a variety of inducements. Clearly Pompidou had no desire to provoke the backlash from local officials from which de Gaulle had suffered in trying to eliminate the Senate. The *loi Marcellin* was passed in 1971, and has produced very few *regroupements*.

A NEW BILL—LOI FREY

To preside over the drafting of a new bill on regions, Pompidou appointed Roger Frey, an old-time Gaullist with both Loyalist and Modernizer credentials. Frey and Pompidou sought to avoid almost everything that had alienated the center-right electorate in 1968–1969. Instead of a referendum, the new pro-

3. Jean-Jacques and Michèle Dayries, *La Régionalisation*, Ser. *Que sais-je*, no. 1719 (Paris: Presses Universitaires de France, 1978).

ject would be a bill, presented to and passed by Parliament, hence by the existing *classe politique*. Consultation would be long, extensive, detailed, and open. Frey spent many months meeting with every conceivable sort of local notable, from mayors, to town and departmental councilors, to the various associations of local government officials. The content of the project itself allayed the fears of the defenders of departments and communes, and the opponents of corporatism. The regions would be given a juridical status clearly inferior to that of other local governments; whereas de Gaulle's referendum proposed classifying regions as *collectivités territoriales* along with towns and departments, the *loi Frey* made them *établissements publics*, along with the Paris Metro authority or intercommunal units for coordinating sewerage disposal. The Senate would remain untouched. The regional representatives of socio-professional groups would meet as a distinctly different and clearly inferior body. Legislative power would be vested exclusively in an organization of territorial representatives, which would be elected indirectly. The regional assembly would be chosen at the second degree, that is, by municipal and departmental councils. The budget would be limited to the revenues derived from the fees on drivers' licenses, plus additional taxes not to exceed a total of twenty-five francs per inhabitant. Powers were vague, and depended really on what the government chose subsequently to delegate. The executive would be a prefect. And all deputies in the National Assembly would sit by right in the regional assmebly—clearly there was no thought of bringing forth a "new" elite, but rather to reassure the existing one.[4]

The government's text did draw criticism. Some Giscardians and centrists attacked the inclusion of deputies in the regional assemblies as favoring the Gaullists, who were overrepresented at the national level in relation to their local base. Some centrists thought the bill was too cautious in the powers and finances it gave regions. The left attacked the number of regions,

4. The analysis of the *loi Frey* is derived from interviews conducted by the author during the period it was written and passed, fall, 1971 to summer, 1972. See also Dayries and Dayries, *La Régionalisation*.

the role of the prefect, the slender powers and finances and, most vehemently, the indirect selection of the representatives and the nonresponsible executive. They argued that the government's version of reform was designed less to open up government to the citizens and local concerns than to streamline control from Paris. The left's positions are analyzed further in the next chapter.[5]

The final version of the *loi Frey* did not reach the floor of both Chambers until June 1972, over a year and a half after Frey was charged with the assignment. The bill was supposed to go through earlier, but then got delayed when Pompidou called the April referendum on Britain's entry into the Common Market. Implementation of the new law was delayed another year and a half until after the legislative elections of March 1973. These delays are characteristic of the whole pattern of local government reform in the postwar years; something else was always getting in the way, taking precedence, tossing the issue of reform this way and that. Delay has always been a symptom, not a cause.

Six months after yet another delay to turn back the left in the *législatives* of 1973, the regional institutions called for in the *loi Frey* were finally set up. In sharp contrast to Italy, where the establishment of regions in the early seventies was an event of major political importance, the equivalent process in France attracted little attention—the difference is due largely to the mode of selection of the regional councilors: direct in Italy, requiring a separate election; indirect in France, hence parcelized and fragmented. (See Chapter 9 on Italian regions.) As with the CODER, the new bodies are dominated by people already prominent in French political life: among the first presidents of the regional councils were Faure, Guichard, Michel D'Ornano,

---

5. The *loi Frey* is Loi no. *72-619 du 5 juillet portant création et organisation des régions* (*Journal Officiel*, 9 July 1972). The text plus summary of the discussion may be found in *Notes et Etudes Documentaires*, no. 4064, *La Réforme régionale, Loi du 5 juillet 1972* (Paris: La Documentation Française, 19 February 1974). The bill was debated in the National Assembly, 26–28 April 1972, and in the Senate, 31 May–2 June 1972.

Pierre Mauroy, Alain Savary, René Pleven, Gaston Defferre, André Chandernagor, Chaban-Delmas, and Servan Schreiber. Three-quarters of the regional assemblies were controlled by center-right alliances. Five have been taken over by the signatories of the Common Program, in each case with a Socialist president getting Communist support: the Nord, Limousin, Midi-Pyrennées, Languedoc-Rousillon, and Provence-Côte d'Azur. The large left gains at the municipal elections of 1977 have also given it control of the Auvergne.[6]

Implementing the New Law

Implementation of the *loi Frey* was entrusted by Pompidou to Alain Peyrefitte, a Modernizer with strong Nationalist-Loyalist credentials. Peyrefitte wanted to interpret his mission broadly, to work out a whole program for reshaping the structure of French local government from top to bottom. Pompidou demurred. Peyrefitte describes his discussions with Pompidou in *Le Mal français*, a widely discussed critique of the French style of authority and governance.[7] Pompidou's comments are revelatory:

> The (re)organization of local governments . . . ? I don't see it. And neither did the General, who was so lucid in other domains and so blind in this one. Or rather, I see very well what *we must not do*—regional power and other irresponsible schemes. But what *must we do?* The commune, the canton, the arrondissement, the department such as they exist now are sclerosis-ridden structures, outdated institutions. We must find alternatives. I don't know which. You want to fight against the cancer of the Parisian bureaucracy, but you must prevent it from metastasizing in the regional metropoles.[8]

Pompidou had rejected an experiment proposed in 1970 to create two *régions-tests* (Champagne-Ardennes and Rhones-Alpes) with an executive responsible to directly elected assemblies. If all went well, the scheme would be applied to other regions.

6. See Dayries and Dayries, *La Régionalisation*.
7. Alain Peyrefitte, *Le Mal français* (Paris: Plon, 1976).
8. Ibid., p. 451.

It's a dangerous undertaking! The restoration of our national
unity and of the state is still too recent to risk it. As soon as we
were to embark on this experiment of the two regions, all the
others would immediately want to take advantage of it without
waiting. Bretons, Corsicans, and Alsatians would step right in.
They would be insulted because the experiment had not started
with them. A few hundred autonomists can get hot under the
collar and sweep their regions into violence. This would be a
frightening risk for France! Why venture it?

. . . What we must encourage are the little and middle-sized
towns where the quality of life is good. Thus, we must try to
favor the departments, not the regions.[9]

I can't do everything at once. My first and main aim is to industrialize, and to do this, I don't need regionalization. Let us
industrialize within the framework of the structures which grew
out of our history and geography. Thereafter we shall see. Let's
take it one day at a time.[10]

Let us consider . . . Italy's regionalization. As long as this
country was satisfied with having a central government, the
Communists, though pretty strong, could not touch it. Because
at that level, a party that wants *everything or nothing* gets
nothing. But if we subdivide the question, we subdivide the
answer as well. That is how several Italian regions have elected
or will elect Communist executives. You can be sure of one
thing: once the Communist party gets power in one region, it
will not let go of it any more. And once people get used to the
Communists in small doses, they will try them wholesale. In the
regions that are not yet Communist, there is a holy mess, since
no one knows who is giving the orders, Rome or the region.
And the Communists, of course, take advantage of any mess.
When the central government has the upper hand, its orders are
more or less carried out; but as soon as it hands its power over to
the local governments, everything goes haywire.

The aftereffects of the Third and Fourth Republics are still
with us. The risk of relapses still persists. Don't you sense that
France has a tremendous need to consolidate itself? Don't you
see that de Gaulle's attempt to foster regionalization and participation was premature and ill-prepared? The country knew

9. Ibid., p. 451.
10. Ibid., p. 453.

what it was doing when it refused to go along! Five, ten years
from now it will be another story. *Ci va piano.* . . . I won't be
like those people who, wanting to be on the left, imagine that,
by provoking a mess, they contribute to progress. Pope John
XXIII is the prototype of those apprentice-sorcerers. He opened
the valves of a torrent and the torrent flooded everything. As far
as I am concerned, the last thing I want to do is to leave a topsy-
turvy France to my successor.[11]

Peyrefitte put together an informal group of civil servants
and intellectuals in order to study the problem and make
recommendations. He outlined to Pompidou a set of reforms:
regrouping of tiny communes; revamping the apportionment of
seats in departmental councils so that they would represent
towns and inhabitants; holding all local elections on the same
day; eliminating staggered terms for departmental councilors;
reshaping the region into a syndicate of departments, with a regional council comprised of representatives of the departmental
councils, having no deputies or mayors sitting by right; an executive rotating among the heads of the departments (which
would prevent it from becoming too important and would give
voice to the smaller departments in each region); and the reduction of the bureaucracy's *tutelle* over local government.[12]

Pompidou rejected the whole thing. Indeed, one of his ad-
visors remarked to Peyrefitte that now that the *loi Frey* had
been applied and the regions set up, it would be *plus normal*
for supervision of the regions to revert to the Ministry of the Interior, as was already the case for departments and communes.
Since Peyrefitte's mission had been accomplished, he would
now be *sous-occupé.*

> We must not tamper with the territorial structures for a long
> time. *Vous vous êtes assez amusé comme cela.* . . .[13]

11. Ibid., p. 455.
12. Alain Peyrefitte et al., *Décentraliser les résponsabilites* (Paris: La
Documentation Française, 1976). The volume presents reports from the working group that surrounded Peyrefitte during his ministry, as well as his own
comments; the other authors include Michel Crozier, Jean-Claude Thoenig,
Octave Géliner, and Elie Sultan.
13. Peyrefitte, *Le Mal français,* p. 459.

The next day, the prime minister, Pierre Messmer, reshuffled the Cabinet. Peyrefitte's ministry was abolished, and he was switched to Cultural Affairs and the Environment. At the next Cabinet meeting, Pompidou told him:

> You know, your reforms, they will be for my second term. Don't be sad. Continue thinking about these problems. It's a gigantic undertaking, a long-range matter. It can't be launched at the end of a term.[14]

Not long afterward, Pompidou was dead.

In applying the *loi Frey*, Peyrefitte obeyed instructions and kept to a narrow interpretation of the law. He annulled a discussion in the regional council of the Limousin which proposed creating a regional bureaucracy. In touring the country he found sentiment for going farther with the regions, and sentiment against it; among the latter, he cites several cases of mayors objecting to being put under the thumb of the largest city in the region (Nice and Marseilles, Evreux and Rouen, Biarritz and Bordeaux). Jacques Médecin, mayor of Nice, commented, "I will not let myself be annexed by the Phoenicians."[15]

Peyrefitte captures quite well the various elements of Pompidou's position: a sense of the fragility of French unity and of France's political system; fear of the Communists; an innate caution and conservatism; other priorities, in particular, industrialization; a political strategy of reconciliation, harmony, building a stable alliance for the future. Perhaps even more than de Gaulle, Pompidou seems to have worried actively about what would happen after him. Unlike de Gaulle, he seems to have thought he could do something about it. He could leave a structure in place which could function even without an exceptional person.

Pompidou sought to stabilize Gaullism by marrying the Gaullist leadership to the centrist and conservative base—a modern version of the fusion between Robe and Sword. This

14. Ibid., p. 460.   15. Ibid., p. 454.

was no easy operation. The marriage contract facilitated the original version. The present attempt requires considerable juggling, compromise, and reconciliation of interests. The Loyalists take offense at excessive concessions to Gaullism's traditional enemies among the old-line parties. The Modernizers resent the shift away from reform. The non-Gaullists resent the continued dominance of the general's heirs in leadership positions.

In such conditions, there could be little reward and much risk in pushing such reform of local government. The new allies would interpret these reforms as an attack on them, as had been the case under de Gaulle. The Gaullist Loyalists were at any rate inclined to Jacobinism and didn't believe in such reform anyway. And everyone on the center and the right feared the left, in particular the Communists. Though the distribution of the vote meant the center-right would control most local governments and most of the regions, Communist access to even a small bit of power was unacceptable. The majority would rather no one had much control over local life than to allow the Communists control over *some* areas. Political polarization between left and right thus worked along with the dynamics of interparty relations among the center and right formations to inhibit reform of local structures.

AN EXAMPLE: THE CASE OF THE NORD

The implications of Pompidou's preference for conciliation and caution may be illustrated with a brief look at a particular region, the Nord. Comprising only two departments, the Pas de Calais and the Nord, this region is one of the oldest industrial areas of France. The industries which propelled its development belong to the early stages of the industrialization—textiles and coal. Both have experienced severe difficulties in the past three decades: stiff foreign competition, old equipment, inefficient practice, and overabundance of firms. Shortly after the war, several residents of the area founded a study group, the *Commission d'Etudes Régionales, Economiques, et Sociales* (CERES), whose purpose was to persuade both the local population and the government in Paris that northeastern France was headed for very difficult times requiring treatment in regional terms, rather than from purely national, departmental, municipal, or even individual-firm perspectives. The founders of the CERES came largely from progressive Catholicism; they included a leader of the Catholic trade union, the *Confédération Française des Travailleurs Chrétiens* (CFTC); a moderate Catholic deputy from an old textile family; and a prominent dean of the university.

For the first fifteen years or so of its existence, the CERES was unpopular among the elites of the Nord and Pas de Calais, both left and right. The dislike stemmed both from its composition, and its arguments. To the Communists and Socialists, the founders were too Catholic; to the parties of the center and right, the cross-class implications of trade-union presence was troublesome. At the same time, the regionalist analysis clashed with established opinion. The major business leaders were suspicious and skeptical of the regionalist argument. They had well-established links with the central government, via party and bureaucracy, all based upon the contacts of individual firms or upon towns and departments. The regionalist arguments smacked both of undue collectivism and challenge to existing relationships. Economic distress also helped depress wages. For most of the decade of the fifties, the CERES found itself fairly alone, its arguments and its political strategies rejected.

In the early sixties, the hostility to a regionalist analysis found new fuel in the government's actions. Non-Gaullist formations of the center and right were strong in the Nord. Gaullist policy on regions was seen as an attack. At the same time, however, the proportions of the economic crisis in the Nord became unmistakable to everyone. It became obvious that the problems transcended individual firms and individual localities and that some kind of collective effort had to be undertaken. Predictably, the local CODER was taken over by the existing elites who now also took over the arguments originally developed by the CERES, which they had hitherto scorned. The inventors themselves were frozen out, being persona non grata to the Gaullists, to the traditional elites, and to the left.

As the reconciliation line began to take shape after 1965 within the Gaullist camp, the antagonism began to soften. The region had already been chosen to be the cite of new steel and port installations (Dunkirk-Calais). Government spending and subsidies helped provide the base for the political integration of the local elites and the national leadership group. After Pompidou's accession to the presidency in 1969, this became evident. Certain important Gaullist ministers were parachuted into the region; they were accepted by the local conservative and center elites as their candidates for the National Assembly. Thus we see that, in contrast to de Gaulle's line, the Pompidou strategy permitted at least a partial integration of the traditional center-right with the Gaullists. The adaptation of regional policies, from assault weapons upon conservative strongholds, as in the early sixties, into ramparts of the governing majority, was now complete.[16]

GAULLISM AFTER POMPIDOU: GISCARD AND CHIRAC

The presence of a new man in the Elysée appeared to augur somewhat better for the reform of local government. Giscard had criticized earlier projects as too timid. When Jeanneney was preparing the referendum text in the fall of 1968, Giscard had urged that the regional executive not be an appointee of the central government. Just before the referendum he stated:

> A dynamic solution would entail the election of regional councilors by universal suffrage. And a sound decentralization supposes, at least eventually, an elected regional executive.[17]

In expanding the governing coalition toward the center after taking office, Giscard was adding to the majority political forces known to be among the most sympathetic to further reform: the Radicals of Servan–Schreiber and the centrists of Jean Lecanuet. Both had criticized the *loi Frey* as too timid; both had

16. This analysis of the Nord is based largely on interviews carried out there in 1971–1972 and 1976.
17. Dayries and Dayries, *La Régionalisation*, p. 112.

called for further change, including an elected assembly which would choose for itself the regional executive.[18]

Instead, policy in this area has remained much the same. The political logic which constrained Pompidou continues to limit Giscard as well. Like his predecessors, Giscard faces a choice of political strategies. Indeed, his predicament is, if anything, more difficult and complex. In domestic policy, he can be reformist or conservative: either he can try to build a strong center by avoiding polarization and pushing for moderate change, or he can try to erect a conservative hegemony on the right by attacking the Communists on the left. In party relations, Giscard would hardly be expected to defend the organizational interests of the Gaullist survivors, but he has had an analogous choice to make there as well: either attack the Gaullist bloc, trying to break them up; or conciliation, compromise, papering things over, working quietly to narrow the distance without an open break.

The strategies sketched out in Chapter 5 were framed with the Gaullists in mind. They can easily be adjusted to show the comparable choices for Giscard. Strategy 1 would mean driving out the Gaullists plus conservative policies. Strategy 2 would mean driving them out and modernizing policies. Strategy 3 would mean conciliatory posture toward the Gaullists and conservative policies. Strategy 4 would mean conciliation and modernization.

Each strategy has major difficulties. Giscard cannot govern without the Gaullists; to rely on them less means relying on the center more, which pulls away from clearly conservative policies—the liabilities of strategy 1. Strategy 2 might appeal to some of the Gaullists in policy terms, but not in organizational ones, and the policy goals would offend the Giscardian right. Strategies 3 and 4 make for better relations with the indispensable Gaullists, but require management of the antagonisms and jealousies built up over many years toward them on the part of the centrists and conservatives. And the coalition is

18. Ibid., p. 113.

very heterogeneous so that the constant pull between reform and caution, between moderation and polarization is very great.

Strategies 1 and 3 would be polarizing: the enemy would be the left. Strategies 2 and 4 would be moderating: they would seek to deny the relevance of left and right to build up the center. The choice was between models, Pompidou's or de Gaulle's. Pompidou's model was to run against the left. The majority presents itself as the force of order, stability, and liberty, the only defense against adventurism, chaos, bankruptcy, and possibly even against an escalating process of instability leading either to totalitarianism or a military coup. De Gaulle's model was to define the issues in a way that placed the president above partisan factionalism, ideology, and petty interests; nationalism and foreign policy became crucial in doing this. A less exalted version of the model was that tried during the Fourth Republic by the parties in Third Force coalitions: to be spokesman for moderate, reasonable reform, defending the Republic against the extremes of both left and right.

Choices have now to be made under conditions which are, if anything, even more difficult than those faced by Pompidou and de Gaulle. The presidential majority has become more heterogeneous while the whole has shrunk. Economic growth, urbanization, industrialization, aging of the electorate, renewed vigor of the left, changes inside the left parties—these forces appear to be reducing the categories of electors who vote for the majority parties, to the benefit of the left parties. Giscard's margin of less than fifty-one percent has loomed large in everyone's thoughts since 1974. Somehow, Giscard must not only keep the majority together and dominate it, but expand it as well, to provide a safer and surer margin. Giscard is not, moreover, entirely free to pick his own way either. He is constrained by the behavior of others (Chirac and the Gaullists, the centrists, the left), and by international forces beyond the reach of all of these people.

Since coming to office, Giscard has oscillated among strategies. At first, it appeared he would embrace wholeheartedly

strategy 3—reformism and conciliation with most of the Gaullists, though not all. He expanded the government toward
the center by bringing in such people as Lecanuet, Servan-
Schreiber, Simone Weil, Françoise Giroud. A Gaullist was
made prime minister, but not just any Gaullist. Debré, Guichard, and Chaban-Delmas were all left out. Chirac was chosen
because he was too young to be an old-time Nationalist-Loyalist, and because he could appeal to the Conservative Gaullist
deputies. Indeed, at the time, Chirac was suspected of being
Giscard's Trojan horse inside the Gaullist camp. There was
speculation that he might help Giscard break up the UDR. This
would then make it possible to reassemble the pieces of the center and right parties in a new alliance, freezing out, as the anti-
Gaullists had long wanted, the men of the *appel du 18 juin*,
the Loyalists. In policy terms, this would entail *décrispisation*,
or a toning down of political rhetoric, plus a certain degree of
reformism, at least in discourse, if not in reality.

In fact, things worked out quite differently. Chirac proved
more resilient than expected and more complex. He held the
UDR together, became its leader, and made himself the driving
force behind a stridently anti-Communist, conservative appeal
shrouded in Gaullist language and forms. Servan-Schreiber left
the cabinet, and Poniatowski, minister of the interior, kept up a
steady fire of attack on the left. Some reforms went through to
keep alive a centrist image, notably Mme. Weil's bill on abor-
tions, but mostly the reforms were very tepid and widely understood as such—the tax plan of 1976 is a good example. Giscard
seemed to be following the conservative line of his predecessor
in the Elysée Palace, under the tutelage of Pompidou's own
protegé, Chirac.

In the summer of 1976, Giscard appears to have shifted his
stance somewhat. The cantonal elections of March showed that
his political allies were slipping, while the UDR held its ground
and the Socialists gained substantially. Chirac proposed antici-
pated legislative elections for the fall of 1976 (instead of March
1978) to be fought as a war against the collectivist left. Giscard
refused. He judged that he would be the major loser from

polarization, and if he acceded to Chirac's demand, he would gradually lose authority to his own prime minister. Instead, he chose to use the time remaining before the elections to rebuild his reformist, moderate credentials, in order to woo votes from the center-left by moving in its direction. The replacing of Chirac by the more apolitical Raymond Barre symbolized the new orientation. In the end, of course, Giscard was vindicated by the results of the 1978 elections.

Giscardian policy toward reform of local government structures mirrors these political shifts. In his first cabinet, Peyrefitte was dropped and not replaced. There was no talk whatever of altering the *loi Frey*, or making another attempt at a *fusion des communes*. Giscard thus appeared to embody perfectly the axiom that politicians are sympathetic toward decentralization while in the opposition, against it when in power.

Forces Favoring Change

At the same time, though, other forces were pushing in favor of change. As the regions were set up in however limited a way, they acquired some life of their own. The *cumul des mandats* allowed some of France's most prominent political figures to add yet another position to their list, that of president of the regional council. Given the size of the regions, these posts are the most visible office a French politician can now occupy outside the government in Paris. In prestige, if not real power, it is rivalled only by the deputy-mayor. In the hands of the opposition, the regional presidency can be especially useful. In the Nord, for example, the *Bureau Executif* has become a large operation, making use of dozens of people formally employed in other posts. The regional government publishes a magazine, distributes brochures, sponsors meetings, invites all sorts of visitors, both French and foreign. This is all minor in relation to the government in Paris, but it does help make the regional president, the important Socialist politician, Pierre Mauroy, more widely known than he would be if he were only mayor of Lille.[19]

19. Interviews in Lille, May 1976.

The new regional structures themselves became the source of pressure on behalf of further change. In November 1974, the presidents of the Regional Economic and Social Councils met with the prime minister to ask for more vigorous devolution in the context of the 1972 law. In the spring of 1975, the presidents of the regional assemblies met with Giscard to press the same case. The left parties continued to assert their platform on this matter: direct election of the assemblies, a politically accountable executive, more funds, less *tutelle*. The situation resembled that under Pompidou a year or two after coming into office: the "honeymoon" dissolves, various forces begin challenging the authority of the president, urging him to go this way or that. A malaise develops. What does he want, this man? Is he capable of governing? Will he support more reform or less, and which kind? Eventually some action must be taken, a line asserted, some change of one kind or another announced. At the comparable juncture, Pompidou put an end to agitation for extending the regional reform, appointed Roger Frey to write a narrow law, and forced Chaban-Delmas out. Now Giscard parted ways with Chirac, made a tough speech on decentralization, and set up a commission to bring in a report which would recommend nothing fundamentally new. Despite the clash, Giscard's policy stance on local government is not different from Chirac's. Both are extremely cautious and defend the "state."

Given the political constraints on Giscard, and his inclination for caution, his response to pressure from the "topocrats" would in any event have been limited. Events during the summer of 1975 made sure of it. Between July and September, numerous disturbances occurred in the winegrowing area around Perpignan. The complaints attached to these outbursts were largely economic, but their location gave them an "ethnic tinge and raised the specter for some of Occitan nationalism. In August, several Corsican nationalists kidnapped some officials and barricaded themselves in a cave near the town of Alesia. Some police were killed flushing them out. The incident blazed in the national press and was treated as an example of the forces lurking beneath the surface ready to disrupt national unity.[20]

These events helped push Giscard to assert a position on the whole problem of devolution in a major speech at Dijon, November 1975:

> The region was not created, nor asked by public opinion, to duplicate the work of communes or departments, or to become another barrier between public power and the citizen. It is nòt part of the region's role to administer or rule, nor to substitute its interventions for the decision-making power of existing local governments, which, on the contrary, should be developed and reinforced. The region's role is to provide a structure appropriate to the coordination of our economic development. This is an essential role which no other institution can provide: not the commune, too involved with itself; not the department, too limited with respect to the significant zones of production and trade; nor, except for major decisions, the state, which is too far away and too Parisian.

As for the other levels of government:

> [The commune] is the site of local democracy, the organ of decentralized, elected power, the institution through which Frenchmen and Frenchwomen can take charge of their daily lives, provided they are given the responsibilities and the means to carry them out . . . . [The] department is, par excellence, the seat of the coordinated management of space, and must be affirmed and used as such.[21]

Giscard went on to applaud the law of 1972 on the regions and to make clear that he envisaged no reform of it over the next few years. These parts of the speech, which attracted the most attention, were interpreted widely as a very aggressive *coup de frein* for the regions in particular and areal reform in general. This is true in that Giscard clearly wished to put an end to the

20. *Le Monde*, *Le Point*, *L'Espress*, summer and fall, 1975.
21. "Discours de Dijon," 24 November 1975, author's translation of text published in *Le Monde*.

mild *frondeur* grumbling he had been hearing from the regionalist groups. In other parts of the speech, though, he attempted
to give some satisfaction to reformers, and to hold the way open
for further change. First he announced that measures were being drawn up to transfer, in the context of the *loi Frey*, decision-making power on about two billion francs from the prefect of the region to the regional assembly, which would then
carve these funds into departmental packets. Other measures
assigned certain tasks concerning unemployment and school
construction to the departmental prefects. Inside the administration, civil servants dubbed these measures (promulgated by
decree in January and February 1976) *déconcentralisation*—a
fusion of decentralization to the regions and deconcentration to
the departments; they saw them as contradictory and confused.

A Policy of Prudence and Caution

Finally, having apparently defined in this speech the appropriate role of the various levels of government, Giscard created a
commission to study the question further. If the legislative elections of 1978 were the long-range concern, the municipals of
1977 were the immediate problem. The job was given to
Guichard, an interesting choice. Guichard was one of the
Gaullists left out in the formation of the first Giscard government. To entrust him now with a politically sensitive albeit
minor task—anything involving local governments was understood to be sensitive—marked clearly an effort to reintegrate
formally the Gaullists into the government, and an effort to
isolate Chirac. Guichard was a Modernizer as well as a Nationalist-Loyalist. Indeed, as the first head of the DATAR, he had
been a prime mover in the Gaullist regionalization efforts. The
commission Guichard headed was composed entirely of elected
officials from the majority; the only Socialist resigned when he
realized his solitude. With them worked about a dozen high
civil servants from the appropriate ministries—Interior, Equipment, Agriculture, and the DATAR. The report was not trivial
in content, but was certainly cautious. It recommended that all
existing local governments be kept in their present form, hence

no coercive fusion of communes, no abolition or consolidation of departments, no democratization of regions or change in their formal status. Communes should be encouraged to undertake collective action; urban conglomerations should be given representation in departmental councils; departments should receive greater responsibility for such matters as education, health, and civil order, and should have wider powers of taxation; regions should be freed of the legal limit on taxation, presently twenty-five francs per inhabitant, and should obtain new competences in culture, transport, tourism, and regional development. The state should lighten its *tutelle*, and create a "National Conference of Local Institutions"; as the "permanent organ of coordination between the state and local governments," it would be the "overseer of decentralization." The report called for the preparation of a law containing these items for the next session of the National Assembly, and another phase of reform beginning in 1985.[22]

Nothing was done with the report till after the legislative elections of 1978. Then, with stability restored to the political scene, the government began cautious consideration of which items it would actually propose. In the summer of 1978, discussions were held in Parliament. In December of that year, the Council of Ministers approved the bill which was to be taken up in the spring of 1979. The government's legislation proposes: the lightening of *tutelle* on communes; the transfer of certain costs from the communes to the state, and of certain credits

22. Interviews conducted during May 1976. *Le Moniteur du Batiment et des Travaux Publiques* remains an indispensable source of information and opinion on the French administration. See in particular the following articles: On the decrees of January and February 1976, see the issue of 28 February 1976, pp. 43 and 163; François Lefebvre, "La Déconcentration des compétences ministerielles en matière d'équipment collectifs," 21 November 1970; articles of 2 January 1971; 16 January 1971; 31 July 1971; 1 January 1972; 5 February 1972; 29 July 1972; 20 January 1973; 14 April 1973: Jacques Lefevre and Christian Charlet, "Régionalisation du budget et le budget régional," 26 January 1974; idem, "L'Evolution de la régionalisation à travers la planification: La Régionalisation du budget de l'état et le budget régional," 15 February 1975; 12 and 19 April 1975; Victor Convert, "Les Communes françaises à l'aube du VIIᶜ Plan," 14 February 1976.

from the states to communes and departments; provision for full-time mayors, receiving a remuneration; greater control by mayors over their civil servants; voluntary intercommunal cooperation; and certain procedures rendering the functioning of towns and departments more public, such as the publication of agendas, and the possibility of communal referenda.[23] None of this appears to arouse very strong feelings, pro or con. In this domain, like his predecessor, Giscard continues to manifest prudence and caution. This is especially interesting in contrast to the government's behavior in the economic sphere; once the left's defeat diminished immediate political pressures, market forces were unleashed on French industry, leading to extensive closing of plants and firing of workers. Political capital and energy are thus invested in economic modernization, not institutional reform. Indeed, Giscard, again like Pompidou, clearly feels that the former requires the absence of the latter; the government needs administrative stability and centralized control to preside over social transformation. More reform in the field of center-local linkages requires, then, some important change in political conditions. Among these could be an opening to the left, or a left government. How might that change policy?

23. Commission de Développement des Résponsabilites Locales (La Commission Guichard), *Vivre ensemble* (Paris: La Documentation Française, 1976).

CHAPTER 8

THE LEFT AND
THE REFORM OF LOCAL
GOVERNMENT, 1945–1978

So far, the story has been told from the perspective of the relations among the parties of the center and the right. These do not, of course, develop in isolation. Among the major problems facing the groups who now comprise *la Majorité* is how to cope with the left parties—that is, how to prevent them from coming to power and how to prevent them from imposing certain policies, even while still out of office. With respect to local government, the majority has so far thought that the maintenance of centralization serves its interests.

The problems of the left are the converse: how to come to power, how to influence events while still out of power, how to keep power if ever it is won, how to achieve left goals? The answers to these questions have implications for the areal distribution of power. Within the left, conflicting traditions can be identified pointing to different answers and, therefore, different prescriptions for center-periphery relations. The Jacobin tradition stresses the highly centralized, strong state. What we may call the Proudhonian tradition questions the centralized state, and seeks instead citizen participation through a variety of decentralized institutions.

The balance of strength between these two traditions has oscillated back and forth over long periods of time. When the left has governed, the Jacobin tradition has predominated. When the left has been in opposition, the Proudhonian views have gained ground. Recent developments continue this pattern. A

series of sharp political setbacks in recent decades has shaken
the Jacobinism of the left parties, in particular the Socialists and
Radicals, and to some degree even the Communists. To recover
their fortunes, the left parties have sought new ideas with which
to mobilize new people. The success of this appeal has forced
further change; new elements moving into the parties have
pressed for even more change in traditional positions and programs. Large segments of the left now call for democratization
of all aspects of French life: autogestion in the factory, debate
in the party, and decentralization in the state. In the early
1970s both the Communists and the Socialists adopted plat-
forms calling for democratization of regional governments and
other forms of decentralization, and these goals were written into the Common Program, signed in 1972. Today, the major
source of pressure in France for reform of local government
structures comes from the left. At the same time, it is far from
clear what would happen were the left actually to form a government. The Jacobin current remains strong, and the magnitude of problems any left government would face might well
discourage tampering with all the levers of power provided by
the existing administrative apparatus. This chapter explores the
evolution of the conflicting positions on the left toward reform
of the areal distribution of powers in France, in quest of an
interpretation of the magnitude and durability of the recent
shift in the relative influence of each policy position.

THE JACOBIN TRADITION ON THE LEFT

The distrust of local government as somehow inherently reactionary and unprogressive goes back to the Old Regime. It was
the monarchy which pushed for uniformity, rationalization,
and equality of treatment before the law. In resisting such reforms, the nobility defended local government against the central bureaucracy. Decentralization and local liberties thus took
on quite a different coloration than they did in Britain and the
United States.[1]

1. Stanley Hoffmann, "The Areal Division of Powers in the Writings of
French Political Thinkers," in *Area and Power*, ed. Arthur Maass (Glencoe:
Free Press, 1959).

These associations were accentuated by the experiences of the Revolution. Under the pressure of invasion from without and resistance from within, the Girondin position of trying to reconcile an effective executive with limited, decentralized government collapsed. In mobilizing the nation to defend the Revolution, Jacobinism was born, fusing together democratic values and highly centralized rule from Paris. Progressive tasks in the Jacobin view require a strong state capable of controlling the very powerful forces inside French society opposed to social change. Napoleon confused the democratic left; he continued the work of the Revolution, but as a dictator. Can authoritarian methods be used for progressive purposes, or is this a contradiction in terms? That debate has smoldered constantly on the left, at times flaring up into genuine conflagrations. The left came out of the revolutionary period strongly Jacobin, but with countercurrents warning that a strong state could also destroy revolutionary goals.

With the Restoration, the left entered a long period of opposition, stretching from 1815 to 1870. Frozen out of governing, the left had the space and the incentive to develop a critique of the existing model. We may identify two strands in that critique, which remain quite distinct down to the present day. One strand stresses the need for democratic participation via local bodies which have benefited from an extensive devolution of power from Paris. The other strand stresses the need for democratic modes of representation, that is, the election of all officials directly by universal suffrage. The first of these is more intensely antistatist and anticentrist. In the nineteenth century, this idea developed in the writings of Proudhon, who considered the state not the protector of liberty, but a major menace to it. For him, a decentralized corporatism was the remedy; the inherent arbitrariness of the state could be curtailed if the domain of politics itself was reduced. People would be organized as producers, not citizens. These producing communities would be the targets of devolution, not local government which was inherently part of the domain of the state. It was upon this line of thought that the very strong currents of anarcho–syndicalism were to be built, eclipsed in the twentieth century by a particular version of Marxian scientific socialism, and reemerging in the late sixties as autogestion.

The other school of left thinking accepted the need for a state, and sought to analyze the role of local government in it. Its complaint about the nineteenth-century system was that democratic methods of selecting representatives had not been applied at the local level. Town and departmental councils remained in the hands of a narrow elite, either named by the central government, or by an extremely reduced electorate. Just as the suffrage should be expanded for national elections, so too it should be expanded at the local level. If liberty meant choosing those who govern you, then town governments as well as the national government should be based on universal suffrage. Ideals thus fused with interest. Having little hope of being able to use the central government for its own purposes, the left sought to expand the local domain in which it might play some role. Direct election of representatives, itself a democratic ideal, would serve to do this. Note that, by itself, democracy in representation does not necessarily require any large transfer of power to the local level—the democratically chosen representatives may have little to do. The stress on this type of democracy did not therefore require as fundamental a critique of the state as did the Proudhonian ideals, and as a consequence it could be assimilated into the Jacobin tradition.

This is precisely what happened after 1871. With the founding of the Republic, the problem for the left became one of defending itself, rather than preparing either for opposition or conquest of power. Once again, the principal danger was seen to come from conservative elites, the curé and the landlord. To break their grip over the peasants, the state would inculcate republican virtues via the schoolteacher, backed by the prefect. Local governments would be democratized, but not greatly strengthened, since they could still fall into the hands of the Republic's enemies.[2] Thus the exigencies of political survival

2. On the Third Republic, see David Thompson, *Democracy in France since 1870*, 5th ed. (New York: Oxford University Press, 1969); and Gordon Wright, *France in Modern Times* (Chicago: Rand McNally, 1960).

helped revive a certain appreciation of the state's powers amongst the republican victors of the 1870s. This impulse was reinforced by economic goals as well. The small producers and professionals who supported the Republic against one version or another of the monarchy wanted state assistance in building an economic infrastructure (the Freycinet Plan) and for tariff protection (the Méline Tariff).[3] A really weak apparatus would not be able to do either one, particularly the former.

As the republican left rediscovered Jacobinism, there emerged among the Socialists an increasing emphasis upon state power. With the industrialization of France and the spread of Marxism, the Proudhonian, anarcho-syndicalist traditions began to lose influence. Instead of producers' cooperatives, Socialists came to demand public ownership and planning, which would immensely enhance the role of the state. After the Russian Revolution, Leninism provided the model for a highly centralized party organization, which was developed to its full authoritarian potential by Stalin and imposed on the French Communist party. While the Socialists (the old SFIO—*Section Française de l'Internationale Ouvrière*) never went to the Stalinist extreme, its model of authority in the party was also quite centralized.

By 1945, both Marxist parties had developed an understanding of the meaning of socialism, of the political difficulties in reaching it, and of internal party structures which reinforced each other to produce a thoroughly statist, centrist, and hierarchical outlook on the organization of authority. Socialists and Communists alike focused on the conquest of the state apparatus, not on dismantling it. They did not want to transform the machine; they thought that it was being used for the wrong purposes, a condition which could be remedied by turning its

3. See Sanford Elwitt, *The Making of the Third Republic: Class and Politics in France, 1868-1884* (Baton Rouge: Louisiana State University Press, 1975); Peter Gourevitch, "International Trade, Domestic Coalitions, and Liberty: Comparative Responses to the Crisis of 1873–1896," *Journal of Interdisciplinary History* 8 (Autumn 1977): 281–313; James Kurth, "The Political Consequences of the Product Cycle: Industrial History and Political Outcomes," *International Organization* 33 (Winter 1979): 1–34.

levers over to them. Like all political forces in France, the Marxist parties were shaken up by the catastrophe of 1940. In the immediate postwar years, however, their criticism of republican
structures focused on incomplete democratization; they wanted
an end to the overrepresentation of rural districts on departmental councils, local referenda on key issues, and a locally
chosen departmental executive. Little attention was paid to
redrawing the administrative map or to transferring powers
from one level to another.[4]

The new political alignments after 1947 wrecked even these
aspects of the left's interest in reforms. As part of Third Force
cabinets, the SFIO refused to share power with the Communists
at any level, national or local, and feared the Gaullists as well.
Feeling pressure from both directions, the Socialists stuck to the
state machine as it existed. Division on the left inhibited support for decentralization still further, since winning local elections required a kind of interparty cooperation which was not
forthcoming.

The circumstances under which the Fifth Republic came into
being were hardly conducive to spurring interest in administrative reform; the left as well as the Gaullists thought that the
machinery at de Gaulle's disposal helped save the country from
the army and the extreme right. Down to the early sixties, then,
the Jacobin current remained hegemonic among the parties of
the left. Other ideas existed, but had yet to make much headway in any of the major parties.

THE REVIVAL OF AN ANTISTATIST LEFT

We may identify two stages in the emergence of critical positions by the left parties concerning the areal distribution of
powers in France. The first stage is primarily intellectual. From
the end of World War II to the late sixties, traditional under-

---

4. Gordon Wright, *The Reshaping of French Democracy* (Boston: Beacon
Press, 1948); Yves Mény, *Centralisation et décentralisation dans le débat
politique français, 1945–1969* (Paris: Librairie Générale de Droit et de Jurisprudence, 1974).

standings of socialism were increasingly contested, and new analyses put forward. These new currents of thought had only a very limited influence on the major formations, the SFIO, the PCF, and the Radicals, who stuck to their Jacobin positions. Frozen out of the regular parties, the critics went into other political groupings—clubs, civic action associations, study groups. The second stage involved the absorption of these new currents by the regular party organizations. This came after 1968–1969; the events of May and June sharply accentuated the general contestation of all organized forces in French life, including the parties of the left. The debacle of the presidential election of 1969 forced the SFIO in particular, and the left in general, to open its doors to new recruits, the bearers of new ideas, and to adopt new political strategies.

The intellectual critique of the Jacobin model had itself several sources. Perhaps the most important was the disillusionment with the Soviet model of socialism. Many leftists had already been shaken by reports of the great purge trials of the thirties; more were shocked by the Prague coup of 1948 and its aftermath. The great trauma came with Krushchev's speech of 1956 to the Twentieth Party Congress and the repression of Hungary later the same year. People left the PCF, and the SFIO became more resolutely anti-Communist.

Less conspicuous, but nonetheless important, was a certain disappointment with Western socialist experiments. Extensive nationalization had occurred after the War, but these industries didn't seem to be very different from private ones; the policies pursued in both nationalized and private industries were about the same, and workers had similar experiences in both types of industry. Some attributed this to the continued subordination of the state as a whole to capitalism, denying therefore the relevance of the nationalization experiences to date as a test of socialism. Others began to wonder whether there was more to socialism than public ownership and planning. The latter began to develop alternative analyses to the traditional Marxist views, arguments which turned increasingly toward the question of the organization of authority itself.

Whereas the traditional definition of socialism stressed collec-
tivized ownership of the means of production per se, the new
view stresses the role of the worker in the management of the
factory. The realization of human potential, full citizenship in
advanced industrial society, requires that the worker have a say
in the management of the place of his employment.

While the major focus among the *autogestionnaires* has been
on the factory, the argument has important implications as well
for other constellations of authority, the state and the party.
The inadequacy of nationalization derives not only from the
persistence of hierarchical relations in the nationalized enterprise, and from the continued influence of private capital over
state policies, but also from the inadequacy of quinquennial or
septennial elections as a link between the popular will and governmental policy. Elected governments can still be authoritarian
ones. Further nationalization will not itself make the state more
democratic. So long as a small group of people in Paris command a vast apparatus comprised of an elite *Grands Corps*,
mass participation in governing will be impossible. The state
must itself be democratized. The reasoning which leads to
autogestion implies extensive decentralization of the state.

The emphasis on participation and democratic decision-
making also has implications for the organization of the
political parties themselves. While the SFIO organization remained less authoritarian than the PCF, the grip of the central
bureau under Guy Mollet was nonetheless quite great. To the
new activists of the fifties and sixties, this form of leadership
was unacceptable. Party positions should emerge out of genuine
consultation of *la base*. Rather than be an exclusive band of
militants held together by purity of doctrine and fidelity to the
leader, the party should open itself to new forces in French
society, and encourage the widest possible discussion. (Some of
the same criticisms were levelled at the PCF from within, but
these arguments surfaced somewhat later than they had appeared among the Socialists.)

While anti-Stalinism and the autogestion current have been

the primary forces behind the critique of the traditional republican, Jacobin model of the state, there have been other influences as well. Left authors have shared in the rediscovery of regional imbalances and the submersion of nationalities in the building of France. Robert Lafont, Michel Philliponeau, Michel Rocard, Yves Durrieu, and others helped awaken consciousness on the left of the existence of a certain internal colonialism, whereby the peripheral regions are to the dynamic regions in France as colonies are to the mother country.[5] The system operates so as to transfer resources to the center, thereby aggravating, rather than correcting, territorial inequalities. The hegemony of the center is cultural as well as economic. To make the France of the Hexagon, the culture of the peripheral regions had been destroyed. Whereas the building of a centralized structure had always been considered a great accomplishment by both left and right in France, now doubts were being raised. Perhaps cultural uniformity was not such a virtue. Respect for the masses means respecting their culture, even if these differ. What made the new critics different from traditional leftists was the former's insistence that, while capitalism was crucial, it was not everything. Eliminating capitalism would not by itself transform the position of the poor regions unless socialist governments allowed a greater degree of diversity and autonomy. Socialism could be overly centralized as well.

Another contribution to left criticism of the Jacobin model came from an unusual source—the Catholics. As the MRP crumbled under the blows of its Fourth Republic failures in colonial policy, and the capturing of its political base by Gaullism after 1958, French Catholics scattered in many directions. One current moved leftward, entering the socialist stream for the first time. Progressive Catholics sought to put aside the school issue in order to make possible an alliance of all forces in French society committed to significant change. While many Catholics

5. Michel Philipponeau, *La Gauche et les régions* (Paris: Calmann-Lévy, 1967); Yves Durrieu, *Régionaliser la France* (Paris: Mercure de France, 1969).

turned to the Marxist analysis of society, they also brought to the left certain modes of thought which helped nourish the growing interest in participation, diversity, and decentralization. The Catholic view of society has always been more corporatist than the secular republican one; it respects intermediate associations, both public and private. Its criticism of capitalism applies also to the French version of democracy; the individual is atomized by market forces in the economy and politics. Unions, associations, local governments, regions—these all help root the individual in a series of meaningful relationships in which the development of personality and the exercise of freedom can occur.

Yet another source of new thinking about the areal distribution of power in France came from the Academy. Social scientists working in a diversity of fields helped introduce new categories of analysis which loosened the hold of traditional orthodoxies, be they Marxist, liberal, or conservative. Geographers such as Jean-Francois Gravier and economists such as François Perroux created the framework for regional planning. Sociologists such as Michel Crozier worked via social psychology to formulate a critique of all manner of French institutions. Political scientists such as Maurice Duverger put French parties into a comparative perspective, thereby helping to introduce alternative models to the often closed world of French discourse. Another political scientist, Georges Quermonne, published one of the early studies of regional institutions in 1962. Marxism became more diverse, at times more empirical, at times more abstract, but increasingly interested in giving theoretical underpinnings to different models of socialism.[6] These intellectual influences were varied, and by no means confined to the left. The same ideas were often taken up by contrasting political forces. What this academic ferment did was to contribute a certain type of backing to the questioning of traditional models of public authority.

6. Yves Mény, *Centralisation et décentralisation*, provides an excellent guide to the evolution of views about these issues.

A final influence upon left analysts of center-periphery relations was that of the process of rapid social change itself. As France urbanized and industrialized, certain concrete problems emerged—housing, sewage, transport, water, industrial renovation, technological obsolescence, new school curricula, and so on. The issues posed by these problems could not be easily assimilated into traditional categories of left versus right. The ideological meaning of the classic issues concerning schools, the constitution, and nationalization was clear. The political meaning of these newer issues was not. It was not at all clear to politicians, militants, or electors on the left what a progressive treatment of a sewerage treatment problem or a traffic system would mean, and how it would differ from a "nonprogressive" treatment. Political activists mobilized by such issues felt frustrated with the left parties. By sticking to their traditional orthodoxies, charged the activists, these parties failed to grapple with the practical problems of daily life in cities and towns. Nor were the parties of the center and right much better. New types of analysis, new types of political organization, new relations between Paris and the countryside—these were the demands of the new civic activists, demands quite congruent with those of the other critics of the traditional left orientations.[7]

THE ORGANIZATIONAL CRISIS

To a considerable degree, this ideological efflorescence took place outside the major party formations of the left. While the collapse of the Fourth Republic was certainly a disturbing event to the Communists, Socialists, and Radicals, all of them adapted to new political realities without any major revision of party personnel, organization, or ideology. The Communists and the Socialists especially remained much as they had been since the late forties: highly centralized in party organization, firmly committed to a highly statist conception of socialism

7. Suzanne Berger et al., "The Problem of Reform in France: The Political Ideas of Local Elites," *Political Science Quarterly* 84 (September 1969).

(albeit different ones of course), and staffed by a tightly knit band of veterans of a long history of combat. Neither party showed any strong interest in opening itself to the new currents in French politics. As for the Radicals, their party organization was far too fragmented to offer much of a framework to anyone.

Finding little interest among the regular political parties, the new activists turned to other outlets: clubs and civic associations. Hundreds of clubs were formed in the sixties, in the provinces as well as in Paris. The label "club" covers a very wide assortment of organizations. Some were ginger groups, or think-tanks, seeking to influence the parties and events by ideas; an example is the Club Jean Moulin. Others were the political vehicles of particular individuals, temporarily left out of any regular party; for example, Alain Savary's *Socialisme et Démocratie*. Still others sought to provide a meeting ground for persons of varying partisan backgrounds (such as Catholics and Socialists), for example, the *Groupe de Recherches Ouvriers-Paysans* to which belonged André Jeanson and Albert Detraz, officials of the *Confédération Française Démocratique du Travail*. Some clubs tried to work within the political parties: the *Centre d'Etudes de Recherches et d'Education Socialiste* was formed in 1966 as a club inside the SFIO whose honorary first president was Guy Mollet; this was the same organization which a decade later, under the leadership of Jean-Pierre Chévenèment, has become the major dissident left faction within the PSF.[8]

While fragmentation gave each club the autonomy to work out its own viewpoints, it also undermined their political leverage. From the beginning there were efforts to draw them together, to develop structures of cooperation that would focus and magnify the raised voices, rather than dissipate their energy in so much discordant cacaphony. Presidential and legislative elections provided the practical incentives for such efforts. In

8. Frank Wilson, *The French Democratic Left: 1963-1969: Toward a Modern Party System* (Stanford: Stanford University Press, 1971); Harvey Simmons, *The French Socialists in Search of a Role, 1956-1967* (Ithaca: Cornell University Press, 1970).

1964, two national conferences were held, the *Assises de la Démocratie* and the *Convention Préparatoire des Institutions Republicaines*, the former tending to attract the more intellectual clubs, the latter the more politically oriented ones. The following year, many of the clubs joined the FGDS (the *Fédération de la Gauche Démocrate et Socialiste*) to help fight the presidential election of 1965.

The major obstacles to such cooperation between parties and clubs were organizational rivalries and programmatic divergences. Indeed there are strong parallels here with the situation among the center and right parties analyzed in the previous chapters: who would lead, and toward what goals? The parties wanted to absorb the energy of the clubs, but without yielding leadership, nor altering their ideological commitments. To the clubs, this was of course unacceptable. They had come into existence precisely to contest the existing opposition to Gaullism, to force the center and left to change. To win over the clubs, the parties would have to make more extensive concessions then they appeared willing to do in the mid-sixties.

Another outlet for political energies in this period, besides the clubs, were civic action groups. Formed in cities and towns all over the country, these associations attracted people who were both: (*a*) discontented with the way their municipalities were being run, and (*b*) repelled by the way the political parties were handling local problems. Instead, they proposed to mobilize citizens on a nonpartisan basis for the purpose of examining the concrete problems facing their communities and proposing what they thought would be nonideological, pragmatic solutions. The most well-known of these associations were the *Groupes d'Action Municipale*, or the GAM, among which the one which attracted the most attention was the GAM of Grenoble. The GAM there began with a controversy over water pressure. Grenoble was growing very rapidly; indeed its department, the Isère, was one of only two departments in all of France to which more people moved from Paris than left it to go to Paris. Many of these new arrivals were highly educated cadres, coming to work in high technology industries, such as the nuclear research center and the hydroelectric equipment factories for which Grenoble had long been famous. This great influx of people and industry apparently overtaxed the city's water system; water stopped moving beyond the lower floors of apartment buildings. Complaints by individuals got no results. These newcomers were not the sort to accept such treatment. They formed a study group which analyzed the problem, then went to city hall and fought for their solution. The experience got them to form the GAM. One of its leaders put their approach as follows:

> . . . in eight out of ten cases our choices are really logically decided. In municipal problems often there is only one solution. There are not ten different ways to pick up garbage. There is no need for a left and a right on that issue.[9]

For the GAM, the objective nature of contemporary issues obliges men of all political opinions to work together. The method of modern politics is essentially a technocratic one, in which the ideologies inherited from the past have no relevance.

In France and other European countries, this has traditionally been an argument made by the right, particularly as a complaint against parliamentary politics. Partisan conflict through elections was seen as sterile, as encouraging false divisions among the electorate in the interest of the political class. As a result, concrete problems were neglected or distorted. The cure would be turning power over to natural elites, as de Gaulle argued on behalf of corporate representation. A striking development in the postwar period has been the partial disassociation of these views from their conservative corporatist connections and their subsequent spread into the left. Complaints about wornout categories of analysis or of inappropriate ideologies no longer mark someone as an antipolitical elitist, seeking an authoritarian alternative to a constitutional system.

The GAM militants were indeed by no means antiparliamentary. On the contrary, their demand was for more citizen participation, for the democratization of government in

9. Berger et al., "The Problem of Reform in France," p. 447.

general, local government in particular. They wanted less interference from Paris, more power for local governments, and a reshaping of local structures to allow more opportunity for participation. The GAM helped create community associations within each neighborhood, *les unions de quartier*, where residents could debate problems and solutions, and subject public officials to some kind of ongoing accountability.

For the GAM and the other civic associations, the reforms needed were of a piece. Improving the quality of decision-making by public bodies required at the same time bypassing the parties, putting aside ideological categories of little relevance to actual problems, and decentralizing the state quite drastically. Each acquired its full potential only if done in conjunction with the others.

In comparison with the Club Movement, the GAMs initially sought to keep their distance from electoral politics at the national level. The struggle for power in Paris was, for them, tainted because it corrupted the parties and diverted attention away from local matters. To win municipal elections, of course, the GAM had to form alliances with the regular party formations. They did so *faute de mieux*, and quite pragmatically; that is, they would ally with whichever parties offered the greatest chance of adopting new methods and ideas. In some places, this meant alliance with the right, in others with the left. In Grenoble, for example, it happened that the municipality in office at the time of the water incident was a center-right one, so there the GAM went left. In the early days, then, the GAM avoided politicization. Eventually, that became impossible for them and the clubs.

Together, the clubs and the GAM were important sources of pressure for change of the organization of public authority in France. The clubs contributed to a torrent of writing on regions, city government, urban planning, management of open spaces, *l'aménagement du térritoire*, public administration, and so on. They spewed out all sorts of ideas for reshaping the politico-administrative map of France, from a few grand regions *à l'échelle européenne*, to strengthening the existing twenty-one regions, to eliminating prefectoral *tutelle* on departments, to creating a formal system of neighborhood and metropolitan governments. The GAM contributed a certain grassroots activism, a mass of educated, involved citizens restless with the existing left, repelled by the parties of the center and right as well, receptive to new ideas and techniques.

The effervescence of the clubs and GAM did affect the parties, especially the Socialists and the Radicals, less so the Communists. A growing minority of these first two formations became interested in the new arguments. Michel Phillipponeau, an activist of long standing inside the CELIB and other Breton organizations, helped promote a consciousness of regions and decentralization among the Conventionnels and Radicals through his many writings and activities. Michel Rocard, then leader of the PSU, held a *Rencontre Socialiste* at Grenoble which was to become famous among the left parties as one of the major turning points toward more proregionalist and anti-Jacobin positions. Rocard's *Rapport* to the meeting called for quite sweeping changes: redrawing the map on the basis of functions, having as units the *quartier* and the village, the urban agglomeration, and the region; eliminating the *tutelle* and the regional prefect; democratization of suffrage at all levels; ample financing.[10] In 1962, Pierre Mendès-France published his *La République moderne*, which proposed ten large regions and some institutionalized place for corporate representation.[11] Other publications which attracted some notice in this period include Robert Lafont's *La Révolution régionaliste*, one of the stronger statements on behalf of the "oppressed" peripheries and ethnic minorities; the Club Jean Moulin's *Les Citoyens au pouvoir: 12 régions, 2000 communes;* and Michel Philipponneau's, *La Gauche et les régions.*[12]

10. Mény, *Centralisation et décentralisation*, pp. 475–502.

11. Pierre Mendès-France, *A Modern French Republic*, trans. of *La République moderne* (London: Weidenfeld and Nicolson, 1963).

12. Robert Lafont, *La Révolution régionaliste* (Paris: Gallimard, 1967); idem, *Décoloniser la France* (Paris: Gallimard, 1971); Club Jean Moulin, *Les Citoyens au pouvoir: 12 régions, 2000 communes* (Paris: Le Seuil, 1970); Philipponneau, *La Gauche et les régions.*

In the academic milieu as well, this was a period of intense interest in regionalism and decentralization. Michel Crozier and his associates carried out in-depth studies of the regional structures set up by the Decrees of 1964. Their work showed how meager were the results of the actual reform, and by implication, how much more needed to be done. Crozier himself worked through the Club Jean Moulin, while some of his associates' connections were with the PSU and the more politicized clubs of the left. The DATAR contracted with the *Institute d'Etudes Politiques* of Grenoble to publish an annual yearbook on regional matters, which included everything from bibliography, to summaries of official actions, to analytic essays. Grenoble became one of the places where the younger researchers tried to work out some sort of a synthesis between critical Marxism and the newer applied social-science methods and ideas about urbanism, planning, community-oriented architecture, and the like.

The sixties, in sum, or more precisely the years between the end of the Algerian War and *les événements,* were an era of great intellectual ferment concerning reform of the links between Paris and the countryside. Democratizing and modernizing the state was one of the major themes among the Club Movement and the civic associations, through which passed some of the most energetic political activism of the period. These ideas and the organizations which advocated them had influence on the existing party formations, but that influence remained limited. Those parties, the Communists, SFIO, and Radicals knew they faced major problems—a loss of militants, a decline of enthusiasm, an unstable electorate. They thought, nonetheless, that they could continue as before. They would try to coopt the new movements, but on the parties' terms, not on the terms of the clubs and the GAMs. The clubs and the GAMs, conversely, to varying degrees wanted to force change in the party system, but again, on their terms. As with the comparable situation among the Gaullists, this confused state of affairs could have gone on for quite a while. Instead, a sudden crisis forced the hand of all concerned: *les événements* of 1968 and the debacle for the left of the presidential election of 1969.

THE CRISIS AND ITS AFTERMATH

Les événements started a process which eventually drove the GAM-Club Movement and the parties into some sort of fusion. It did this by politicizing the former quite acutely, and by shaking the confidence and organizational solidity of the latter. Even before May 1968, some activists among the GAM wondered if their antipartisan stance was realistic. If the obstacles to local reform were located in Paris, was it really possible to pretend that political control over the government was not important? If certain programs of importance to citizens were frustrated by the activities of financiers, speculators, corporations, and foreign capital, could one really continue with an analysis wholly local in its outlook, ignoring the social and economic contest in which the problems of towns actually existed? The events of May shattered many illusions and drove many activists into regular party politics.

The clubs had already moved partially in that direction before 1968. Mitterand drew many of them into the regular party struggles by running against de Gaulle in 1965. Another attempt was made at club and party cooperation through the *Fédération de la Gauche Démocratique et Socialiste* of the 1967 legislative elections. The turmoil of May and June produced wild lurches in contrasting directions: at first the left drew together, tantalized by the prospect of actually replacing the Gaullist government. Then the sudden reversal of fortunes in the legislative elections of June led to acrimonious dissension. Each party and group blamed the other for a variety of sins, from adventurism to cowardice. The deterioration among the left formations continued in the following months such that, whereas all had united around Mitterand in 1965, each ran its own candidate against Pompidou in 1969. (The cooperation to bring down de Gaulle in the Referendum of 1969 had been purely negative, as it required no agreement on what would take his place.) The results of the first round are well known:

Jacques Duclos rallied the core PCF electorate to get about twenty percent; Gaston Defferre polled a humiliating six percent for the Socialists; Rocard and Alain Krivine each got a trivial handful of votes; many voters swung to Alain Poher, leaving the left with no candidate in the *ballotage*.

It was this debacle for the left parties which induced them to make major changes which are still being worked out in French political life. After the euphoria of 1968, the presidential election of 1969 was like a blow to the stomach. All the political formations on the left were forced to see that the continuation of past policies confined them to isolation and irrelevance and would leave the future entirely to the center and right. Some effort at greater cooperation was therefore imperative.

For the Communists, the shock of 1968–1969 provided opportunities. Within the framework of an overall weakening of the left, the relative strength of the PCF increased. Most of the electorate which had defected to Gaullism in the sixties came back; Duclos' twenty percent showed that the ghetto was at least not shrinking and that the Communists retained their very impressive organizational strength at a moment when the Socialists and Radicals shattered completely. Hence a coalition of left forces would doubtless put the PCF in a hegemonic position. The construction of an alliance would occur among rather unequal partners. Cooperation would allow the PCF to break out of its isolation in very favorable conditions, with it as the dominant force.

At the same time the PCF's behavior in 1968 made it more attractive as a partner to its potential allies. While the PCF's restraint during *les événements* was a bitter disappointment to some, it was also quite reassuring to many others. It gave credence to the PCF's claims of having accepted the rules of the game, that it was trustworthy. The PCF's criticism of the Soviet intervention in Czecheslovakia had similar effects. While not as strong as many would have liked, the party's remarks helped allay fears that it was still *téléguidé* by Moscow. Over the next years, the PCF moved toward the stance which came to be known as Eurocommunism, seeking to share power within parliamentary systems on terms which varied according to national political conditions.

While the content of the PCF's positions changed, the organizational continuity was great. The events of 1968–1969 provoked a change in strategy by the leadership; it affected the militants, it caused departures and new arrivals, but it did not wreck the apparatus. The party leader was changed, but by decision of the same central committee, ruling as it always had.

For the Socialists, the process of change was profoundly different. The SFIO was shaken to pieces. The party of Guy Mollet lay in ruins. The organization decomposed into a set of fiefdoms, based upon strength derived from positions in local government and the trade union movement. Rebuilding there meant more than a new strategy. It meant recreating a new structure which in turn required throwing open the doors to as many new recruits, groups, individuals, clubs, and associations as possible.

The *Parti Socialiste Française* was thus born out of the fusion of the old SFIO with the clubs and politicized civic associations who had been unable to force their way in beforehand. The price the old SFIO leadership had to pay was to make place for new leaders and for new ideas.

It is in this way that the parties of the left came to adopt new positions on the matter of reforming the areal distribution of powers in France. The people who flooded into the PSF were the very ones who had in the sixties led the way in contesting the traditional understanding of the connection between socialism and the organization of the state.

The case of Grenoble may again serve to illustrate this process. In 1970–1971, the Socialists organized a series of meetings in different parts of France to debate in open forum the various substantive issues which would make up the party platform. Negotiations with the PCF over a contract of union were approaching. The PSF wanted to establish its positions, and to do so in a manner which would contrast sharply with the PCF's process, thereby helping build membership. The meeting to discuss local government was held near Lyon in the fall of 1971. To it were invited not only PSF members, but other "interested" persons. Among those who attended were the members of the Grenoble GAM, including Mayor Hubert Dubedout, who was pointedly introduced during the proceedings. The PSF adopted many of the arguments which the clubs and the GAM had been putting forward: local government was the *cellule* of citizen participation in the state; to allow it to play such a role,, decentralization was an imperative; regional government should be democratized and strengthened. Not long afterward, Dubedout formally abandoned his GAM's *apolitisme*, agreeing to run for the National Assembly as a Socialist. In 1973, he won.

Similar experiences were repeated all over France. The non-Communist left came back to life, but not as a "sanitized" de-Marxified catch-all party; 1971 was not to the PSF what *Bad Godesberg* had been to the Social Democratic party of Germany in 1959. The PSF developed its own brand of socialist militancy in which participatory themes were prominent. Its understanding of socialism was the democratization of all aspects of industrial society; the economic sphere (autogestion and socialization of key industries) certainly held ideological primacy, but to many in the PSF economic democracy could have no meaning if other power structures were not simultaneously democratized—the party and the state. The analysis of the economic sphere led, therefore, to a critique of the Jacobin model in the realm of state organization.

The Communists arrived at similar positions on local government reform but via a somewhat different route. Regional problems, argues the PCF, derive from capitalism. The only way to solve them is to abolish capitalism, which for the PCF means nationalization. Nothing in that understanding of economic democracy impels decentralized local government; on the contrary, it implies a strong, centralized, state apparatus.

The PCF's attitude toward local government derives instead from its efforts to take up the mantle of republican legitimacy and from its strategic interest in forming alliances with other parties and social groups. Republican traditions dictate that power stems from popular sovereignty. All formal units of government must be based on universal suffrage, local as well as national. Existing units of local government may be criticized for failing to meet that standard (malapportioned departmental councils, a nonresponsible departmental executive), and new units should meet it as well. Before regions existed, the PCF was not among the leaders in calling for their creation. On the contrary, like the SFIO, they resisted this innovation precisely on the grounds of defending republican tradition. Once the fact had been accomplished, the application of republican tradition came to mean democratizing what had been created. The PCF's position became, essentially, that so long as capitalism existed, regions were useless, but if regional governments were to be created anyway, they must be based on universal suffrage. The discussion of actual powers of regions, and of their relation to other local governments, tends to be vague and there is always room in the PCF projects for a substantial government *tutelle* behind the democratic facade.

The strategic source of the PCF's interest in local government concerns the evolution of its policy toward alliances with other parties and social groupings. The PCF has always attributed considerable importance to maintaining a "presence" in all intermediate organizations, from trade unions to cultural associations, to government advisory boards to local institutions. Activity in such organizations helped sustain the image of the party as "tribune" of the people, working ceaselessly to defend the workers' interests in all possible locales.[13] When the party decided to seek an alliance with the other forces on the left, these intermediate organizations took on a new dimension. They provided arenas for the working out of more cooperative relationships. While the new partners could not be induced to join the party formally, they could be drawn within the sphere

13. Georges Lavau, "Le Parti communiste dans le système politique français," in Frederic Bon et al., *Le Communisme en France* (Paris: Armand Colin, 1970), pp. 7–81.

of party influence through the framework of other organizations or institutions.

The decision by the PCF, following the events of 1968–1969, to seek a union of the left led it, therefore, toward developing a new platform on local government. The ideological rationale was provided by republicanism; the pragmatic rationale by the desire to attain hegemony on the left via cooperation. In preparation for its negotiations with the Socialists, the PCF produced its own statement of program, in which it called for democratized regional government along lines fairly similar to the PSF's new positions.[14] The big difference is perhaps in doctrine: whereas the PSF fuses republican traditions with its views of industrial democracy, these remain for the PCF somewhat distinct.

That difference, somewhat ironically, has proved indispensable in allowing the two formations to reach a common stance on local government reform and stick to it. The major conflicts among the signatories have been over industrial democracy: how many industries to nationalize, which ones, the role of the market, the nature and primacy of autogestion, and so on. Were the Communists to derive their local government reform positions very tightly from the economic ones, the conflict in one domain would spill over to the other. Instead, each domain can be kept insulated from the other. Indeed, the existence of conflict over economics has made agreement on local government, if anything, more important. It allows the parties to show they agree on something at least. (The same mechanism operated in Italy; the Italian Communist party (PCI), the Socialists, and the Christian Democrats (DC) supported regionalization as proof that they could make the opening to the left work—see Chapter 9.)

14. Parti Socialiste Française, *Changer la vie* (Paris: Flammarion, 1972); Parti Communiste Française, *Programme pour un gouvernement démocratique d'union populaire* (Paris: Editions Sociales, 1971); and *Programme commun de gouvernement du parti communiste et du parti socialiste* (Paris: Editions Sociales, 1972).

The document signed in 1972 calls for: direct election of regional councilors; a purely consultative socio-professional body; an executive elected by the regional assembly; replacing the prefect by a *commissaire du gouvernement*; a regional administration controlled by the elected officials; regional financing and regional powers not very clearly specified; a redrawing of the map to create ten to twelve large regions, instead of the present twelve; and elevating regions to the status of *collectivités territoriales*.[15]

At the same time, departments and communes are to be retained, and the Common Program says little about the distribution of powers, functions, and funds among the different levels. Is there room in France for four levels of government (communes, departments, regions, plus the state) in addition to metropolitan agglomerations, intercommunal and interdepartmental syndicats, and a whole host of *établissements publics?* What relationship should there be among them? The left parties, indeed any of the parties, are unwilling to come out for abolition of one of the existing levels. For the left, the issue can be sidestepped by focusing on the question of representation. All structures can be democratized formally, and none have any power. Would the left carry out this program were it to win a national election? Speculation on that question will be saved for Chapter 11.

---

15. Jean-Jacques and Michèle Dayries, *La régionalisation* Series *Que sais-je*, no. 1719 (Paris: Presses Universitaires de France, 1978), p. 116; Yves Mény, *Partis politiques et décentralisation*; mimeographed (Rennes University, 1978). Howard Machin, "All Jacobins Now?: The Growing Hostility to Local Government Reform," mimeographed (Hull University, 1978).

PART THREE

COMPARISONS AND CONCLUSIONS

CHAPTER 9

ALTERNATIVE OUTCOMES
The Creation of Regional Government in Italy

France was not the only European country which confronted reform of the areal distribution of power as a political problem in the postwar years. In other places as well, the units of administration and local government were old and in various ways inappropriate for contemporary purposes. Nowhere was reform easy, but it does appear to have gone much farther in other countries than in France. Sweden and Britain have drastically reduced the number of local governments. Italy has set up regional governments which resemble those demanded by the left in France. Why this difference? Why has reform in France been more limited than elsewhere?

This chapter explores that question through a loose application of the "most similar case" method.[1] Italy is the country which most resembles France in certain ways relevant to the problem at hand. First, the existing organization of the state was similar, having been based on the French model—three levels: communes, departments (called *provincie*), and the national government, whose *tutelle* over the other two is quite extensive. Second, the nature of the reform debated in Italy was quite similar—the introduction into this schema of a new, larger level, the region. And, third, the character of the party system through which such reform had to go is roughly comparable: fragmented and polarized, with a strong Communist

1. Henry Teune and Adam Przeworski, *The Logic of Cmparative Inquiry* (New York: Wiley-Interscience, 1970); Arend Lijphart, "Comparative Politics and the Comparative Method," *American Political Science Review* 65 (September 1971): 682–693; J.S. Mill, *The Philosophy of Scientific Method* (New York: Hafner, 1960), bk. 3, ch. 8.

party in a divided left and a divided center and right as well. What critical difference allowed a similar country to produce a more extensive reform? Can we find factors congruent with those used to explain the French outcome?[2]

As in France, Italian historical experience suggests that the opposition tends to be more sympathetic to decentralization than do the forces in power. The Italian monarchy adopted the French model to solve a comparable political problem: how to impose effective rule from the center over widespread opposition of various kinds, particularly from the Church and local particularisms. The Fascists certainly never felt secure enough to decentralize. In the postwar period, fear of the Communists has been considerable and for a long time blocked change as well. Nonetheless, in the 1970s, regional structures were set up. What was it about the Italian situation that induced governing politicians to overcome their structurally induced reluctance to permit some decentralization?

To some degree, the difference reflects the uniqueness of the problem in each country. In Italy, regional disparities in wealth and development are much greater. A much later national unification left much stronger regional identities and communal traditions. No single city dominates all aspects of Italian life the way Paris does in France. These factors all plausibly encourage greater decentralization in the one country than in the other.

What these variables do not explain in any direct way, however, are the politics of decentralization and regional reform. In exploring the French case, considerable emphasis was put on political factors, that is, on the factors which shape politicians' evaluations of the costs and benefits of reform to their parties and their personal careers. In the interests of parallelism, we should look for factors which encouraged Italian politicians to see more opportunity in change than did the French. These may be found in the following areas: (1) the dynamics of

2. Much of the material in this chapter is adapted from the author's "Reforming the Napoleonic State: The Creation of Regional Governments in France and Italy," in *Territorial Politics in Industrial Nations*, ed. Sidney Tarrow, Peter Katzenstein, and Luigi Graziano (New York: Praeger, 1978), pp. 28–63.

alliance combinations among the parties; (2) party strength at the national and local levels; (3) the geographic distribution of electoral support; (4) the efficacy of existing institutions; (5) ideological presuppositions concerning the proper areal distribution of power; and (6) the content and context of specific reform proposals.

As in France, regional reform in Italy has been a highly dependent issue. Its fate was always a byproduct of other, more decisive quarrels and cleavage issues. Even when regionalism found itself in the center ring, the spotlight was someplace else. The periodization of the debate over regional reform bears the influence of these other issues, especially the Cold War and domestic economic crises. The four phases which follow are similar to those used for France:

1944-1948: Constitution-making and Opportunity. A period of flux at the Liberation brought to an abrupt end by the Cold War. The new Italian constitution calls for the establishment of regional governments.

1948-1960: The Cold War and Immobilism. Polarization, expulsion of the left, leading to immobilism; regional clauses not implemented.

1960-1969: The Thaw and Fluidity. Gradual reduction of tensions. Partial reintegration of the Communists, and the opening to the left. Passage of legislation implementing the constitutional clauses on the regions.

1969 to the present: The Hot Autumn, Higher Tensions, and Ambiguity. Sharpening of domestic antagonisms. Recrudescence of hostility to regions by governing coalition, stronger support by the left. Regions set up, but constrained by Rome.

In each period, local government policy was a function of broader political developments.

PHASE 1:CONSTITUTION-MAKING
AND OPPORTUNITY (1944–1948)

The Italian euphoria after the war was if anything greater than the French. The Liberation marked not only the expulsion of the occupying armies, but the destruction of the Fascist

Regime. A large slice of recent history was in disgrace, and the coalition interested in change was broad. The writing of a constitution provided an opportunity for forces long shut out of power to remake the institutional structure of their country. Within each of the major parties which dominated the immediate postwar years could be found conflicting traditions concerning the proper areal distribution of power.

Though thirty years of continuous rule since the late forties make one forget the fact, the Christian Democrats at the time had never been a governing party. They had therefore little of the identification with the instruments of rulership which could be found among the French Socialists, Radicals, and Independents. The Christian Democrats had suffered from centralization under both the monarchy and Mussolini. Party members tended therefore to think in terms of the *motivazione garantista,* according to which strong local government is seen as a valuable bulwark against whatever depredations may emerge from Rome. Progressive segments of the party also valued mass participation in politics for itself. Conservative elements, on the other hand, feared from the beginning that decentralization would cede too much power to the Communists. Over the next thirty years, the policy of the Christian Democrats (DC) toward decentralization shifted back and forth with the changing fortunes of the different factions within it.[3]

The parties of the left in Italy were also divided in attitudes toward the organization of the state. At the Liberation, they

3. On the politics surrounding the creation of regional institutions in Italy, see the extremely informative series of articles, full of valuable footnote references, by Franco Bassanini, *Relazioni sociali,* nos. 1–4 (1970). Other useful materials include *Proceedings,* Acpol Congress, "Le Regioni de fronte alla crisis del sistema politico italiano" (Rome, Acpol, 25–27 November 1969); C. Palozzoli, *Les Régions italiennes* (Paris: Librairie Générale de Droit et de Jurisprudence, 1966); Ettore Rotelli, *L'Avvenuto della regione in Italia* (Milan: Giuffre, 1967); Andrea Villani, *Il Potere locale* (Milan: F. Angeli, 1969). See the bibliography cited in Sidney Tarrow, "Local Constraints on Regional Reform: A Comparison of Italy and France," *Comparative Politics* 7 (October 1974): 1–37; also Norman Kogan, "Impact of New Italian Regional Governments on the Structure of Power within the Parties," *Comparative Politics* 7:3 (April 1975): 383–406.

were emerging from twenty years of underground organization, planning, and social reconstruction, all of which required strong central authority. Hoping to share power at the national level, they opposed any weakening of the state. Regions appeared to be nonessential for the realization of major programmatic goals, and threatened to put important arenas of power out of reach just at the moment when the left appeared closest to sharing in it. As in France, the Italian left stressed direct election of representatives, not decentralization of powers, as the key element in the democratization of local life.

At the same time, the Marxist tradition in Italy contained elements more sympathetic to decentralization than French Marxism. As with the Christian Democrats, alienation from the central government spawned an appreciation of the value of local institutions in supporting the party organization. The Socialists had a tradition of *isole rosse* stretching back to the days of the monarchy—left strongholds in the midst of a hostile bourgeois state and society—a tradition revalidated by the Fascist period. Unlike their French counterparts, the Italian left had no tradition of ever having governed or even shared power. That experience in France during the Third Republic helped revive the left's identification with the Jacobin state. In Italy, this had never happened. Whereas the French left stressed action in the political sphere, Italian theorists argued the importance of action in civil society, in which the local level might be particularly important.[4]

Both the Marxist and the Christian Democratic parties, then, contained within themselves conflicting attitudes toward decentralization. In both groupings, power considerations helped tip the balance first one way, then another. In the immediate

4. On Italian Marxism see Donald Blackmer, *Unity in Diversity: Italian Communism and the Communist World* (Cambridge and London: MIT Press, 1968); Donald Blackmer and Sidney Tarrow, eds., *Communism in Italy and France* (Princeton: Princeton University Press, 1975); John Cammett, *Antonio Gramsci and the Origins of Italian Communism* (Stanford: Stanford University Press, 1967); and Sidney Tarrow, *Peasant Communism in Southern Italy* (New Haven and London: Yale University Press, 1967).

postwar period, the Christian Democrats were proregional and the Marxists antiregional. With the onset of the Cold War, the two sides switched positions. The Communists and Nenni Socialists rediscovered the utility of local government as shelters in a storm. The DC rediscovered the utility of the centralized state as an instrument of control. In the short interval before this *renversement des positions* was fully completed, the Constitution was adopted. During those months, the DC was still committed to decentralization and the creation of regional governments, and the Marxist parties were becoming more sympathetic to it. Title 5 of the Italian Constitution calling for the creation of regional government thus had the backing of both sides.

Compared to any of the proposals put forward by French governments over the past thirty years, Title 5 gives regions more competence, legitimacy, and funding, though it falls far short of federalism. Regions have a juridical status equal to communes and provinces.[5] Their organization follows a parliamentary model: powers are vested in a unicameral regional council, which selects from among its members a regional executive council (the *giunta regionale*) and a president of that executive council.[6] Regions may propose laws to the national Parliament and may initiate national referenda. Title 5 prevents the very common French practice of *cumul des mandats* ("multiple elective offices") in that regional councilors may not sit in Parliament.[7] The list of competences formally mentioned seems broad—the regional aspects of urbanism, tourism, transportation, agriculture—and Parliament can delegate more.[8] Regional councilors will be territorial, not functional, though the precise number and mode of designation were left to future legislation.

The government in Rome retains vast powers of control over

5. Constitution of 1946, Title 5, arts. 121, 122, from Norman Kogan, *The Government of Italy* (New York: Crowell, 1962).
6. Ibid., art. 121.
7. Ibid., art. 122.
8. Ibid., art. 117.

the regions. It can oversee regional administration through a *commissario del governo* ("government commissioner"), resident in the regional capital, and an administrative council charged with supervising the legality of regional activities.[9] The government may dissolve or dismiss regional councils for any one of a variety of reasons: violation of the national constitution, national security considerations, and paralysis of the regional government. Rome may veto legislation of the regional council, which may then repass the bill, which then is sent by the national government for adjudication either to Parliament or the constitutional court.[10] Title 5 specifies what regions shall be created: five special ones (Sicily, Sardinia, Trentino-Alto-Adige, Friuli-Venezia Giulia, and the Valle d'Aosta) and fifteen ordinary ones.

> Despite the limits and deficiencies . . . of the constitutional design [it] was sufficiently precise to make plain that the regions were conceived not just as centers of administrative decentralization for purposes of efficiency, but, on the contrary, as entities endowed with political autonomy, that is to say, . . . centers of democratic self-government, capable of elaborating, adopting, and realizing its own political line, eventually divergent from that of the central government.[11]

Any constitutional text can be subverted, as we shall see below. Nonetheless, these clauses did strengthen the supporters of regionalism in Italy by putting beyond discussion some of the issues that in France proved to be objects of controversy. These included the legal status of regions, some aspects of the organization of regional government, and the territorial and noncorporatist character of representation. Not the least important were the ample powers given the government in Rome to supervise the regional governments. Though it was precisely this last provision that has been used to weaken the regional reform, it also facilitated implementation of Title 5 by reassuring the conservatives. Because the Italian Constituent Assembly had gone

9. Ibid., arts. 124–125.
10. Ibid., arts. 126–127.
11. Bassanini, *Relazioni sociali*, p. 166.

so much farther than the French, the hurdle to be overcome in the mid-1960s was in Italy that much lower.

PHASE 2:COLD WAR AND IMMOBILISM,1948–1960

The sharp polarization of politics brought on by the Cold War blocked regional reform in Italy for almost two decades.

Title 5 of the Constitution had called for elections to the regional council within a year of ratification, and implementation of the whole regional council within three years. Decentralization implied allowing the Italian Communist party control of some units of local government. Unwilling to tolerate this, the DC blocked implementation of these constitutional clauses. First, it simply failed to bring forward the required enabling legislation dealing with regional finances and elections. Second, in 1953 the government enacted a de facto modification of Title 5 (the *legge Scelba* on regions), so that regions would be weak if some day political pressures forced their creation. Where, for example, the Constitution gave regions enough control over their own internal organization to permit some diversity and autonomy, the new law imposed considerable uniformity and central supervision over such matters as the number of vice-presidents and secretaries of the regional council, the precise dates of its meetings, and the filling of vacancies on the *giunta regionale*. It also narrowed the definition of regional competences and provided for a prefectoral *tutela* by Rome.[12] In short, it laid down detailed regulations governing the life of institutions that did not exist and whose creation it did nothing to promote.

Without the support of the governing party, regionalism could not progress. Support from other forces was either lacking or wholly isolated. Unlike its French counterpart, the Italian bureaucracy generated no reform movement from within. The Communists, on the other hand, were frozen out at the national level. By becoming the most outspoken proponents of Title 5, they helped to prevent its implementation.

12. Ibid., pp. 172–187.

PHASE 3: THE THAW AND FLUIDITY, 1960–1969

By the end of the 1950s, important shifts in international and domestic politics restored an element of movement to political life in Italy. The attack on Stalin eventually lessened the isolation of the Communists; in the short run, Hungary widened the breach between them and the left Socialists. In Italy, this helped bring about the opening to the left. (In France, these shifts were overshadowed by Algeria.)

Regionalism is perhaps the principal accomplishment of the opening to the left in the 1960s, though by no means its principal goal. The shift leftward altered the positions of proregional and antiregional forces. The progressive elements inside Christian Democracy who wanted regions were able to use the alliance with the proregional Socialists to free themselves, at least on this issue, from the negative influence of the antiregional right.

Hailed as the answer to immobilism, the new center-left coalition found itself unable in fact to enact much significant new legislation. Though forced to acquiesce in the new coalition strategy, conservatives inside the DC were able to block its progress. The government, increasingly embarrassed by this stalemate, pressured by the Socialists and progressive Catholics inside the majority and by the Communists from without, turned to regionalism for much the same reasons that de Gaulle had in 1968. As a reform, regionalism demonstrated the will to constructive action. As decentralization, it had a democratic participatory ring. Since it was limited, somewhat technical, and easily rendered vague, it was less controversial than many other issues. With the approach of the elections scheduled for 1968, the coalition partners feared that the Communists would score heavily with a campaign based on the inactivity of the great experiment in Italian politics. To forestall that attack, the government brought forward legislation allowing implementation of Title 5.

The debate over the regional election law in 1967 touched off the longest filibuster in Italian history (10 July to 31 October). Most of the opposition came from the Liberals (PLI), the

Monarchists (PMI), the Fascists (MSI), and the conservative wing of the DC. Most of the vocal support came from the Communists. Observers of the debate found it odd that those who were formally responsible for the bill—the dominant DC bloc—sat silently while those outside the government did the talking on both sides.

On numerous points, the Italian debate foreshadowed the French one of the following year. Proponents of regionalism argued that Parliament dealt with too many bills of purely local interest and that the geographic boundaries of provincial-based administration no longer corresponded to the realities of Italian demography and economic life. They also maintained that the *provincie* were too small for planning purposes, that control from the capital suffocated initiative, and so on. Opponents warned of the pettiness of local interests and of the danger of undermining the coherence of national planning and economic policy through decentralization. In addition, they worried about the Communist menace and the incompatibility of regional diversity with equality before the law.

In other important ways the two debates differed. In Italy, the value of local autonomy seemed more strongly appreciated, especially on the left. The reasons for the difference are as varied as the reasons for the divergences between the Communist parties of the two countries. Much sooner than its French homologue, the PCI sought to break out of its isolation. Among European Communist parties, it pioneered the strategy of developing contact with other social and political forces in order to neutralize hostility toward it and lay the groundwork for collaboration on substantive reforms. In that strategy, local government has an important role to play as an arena for such contacts and a place to demonstrate commitment to democratic values. The PCF has been much slower in adopting this strategy, and there is of course much debate as to whether it ever has. In the sixties, therefore, when the PCF was still attacking regional reform and other decentralization projects, the PCI had already become their strongest supporter in Italy.

Another contrast between the debates in the two countries was the absence in Italy of any serious charge that regions were tainted by corporatism, feudalism, and fascism. To some degree this was due to the difference in content. Socio-professional representation had no place in the Italian constitutional scheme and did not therefore arise as a subject in the 1967 parliamentary discussion. Also, the Fascists had been against both regions and decentralization, so there was no equivalent of the Vichy regional experiments to contend with. Finally, there was less quarrel in Italy about such details as boundaries, institutional machinery, and representation, since the Constitution and previous legislation had settled many of them.

As in France, government spokesmen, supposedly champions of reform, spent most of their time reassuring the bill's opponents that the central government retained ample authority to control the regions. In the final vote, DC leaders were unable to stop defections from party discipline; without Communist support, the legislation would not have passed the Senate.[13]

Some observers feared the government might pass this bill but then fail to bring in a regional finance law and actually hold the elections. The tensions associated with the "hot autumn" of 1969 (Italy's equivalent of May 1968) worked in opposite ways. In the short run, they continued the pressure on the government to carry out reforms. At the same time, they damaged the center-left coalition by polarizing politics and strengthening those in the DC who wanted to break off the alliance. The opponents of implementation managed to delay the elections to the regional councils, but its support held up sufficiently so that they were finally held on 7 June 1970. The results were as expected: Communist domination of three regions, DC domination of the rest.[14]

DETENTE AND AMBIGUITY (1969 TO THE PRESENT)

The immediate consequence of the May and June events of 1968 in France and the "hot autumn" of 1969 in Italy was a

---

13. *Atti Parlementari,* Cameri dei deputati, vols. 37–39 (1967).
14. Figures taken from *Rinascita,* 12 June 1970. See also Bassanini, *Relazioni sociali,* pp. 288–292.

heightening of domestic antagonisms and a rightward shift. In both countries this development was unfavorable to regional innovation.

With the implementation of Title 5 in 1970 the regions now exist; they spend money, commission studies, select executives, hire staff, and so on. As institutions, they are stronger than their French counterparts. Nonetheless, governments in Rome have limited their role by applying the regional laws in a conservative way. When the regional governments have challenged these actions in the courts, the constitutional court has consistently supported Rome. One ruling says that the listing of regional competences in the Constitution refers to what the state may transfer, not to what it is obligated to transfer; another ruling argues that these competences are not exclusively reserved to the regions; hence the state may continue to act in them. In many domains which were to be regionalized, the central government continues to make decisions and control funds.[15] When the Giannini Commission, comprised of jurists hostile to the bureaucracy and sympathetic to regions, proposed a broad transfer of power to the regions, the government pruned its suggestions to rather modest dimensions.[16]

It is far from clear how important a role regions actually play in decision-making, or whether they have or will ever become a significant locus for the allocation of funds, inititatives, and so on. The regional elections of 15 June 1975 affected Italian political life because of the sharp gain by the left (especially the Communists), not because the officials elected have much power. Regional elections in Italy appear to have become precisely what Pompidou and other French conservatives feared in their country: highly politicized contests, intimately linked to national rather than local political quarrels, affecting the relations among political forces in the national government. The

15. Bassanini, *Relazioni sociali*, pp. 288–292.
16. Sidney Tarrow, "Regionalismo incompiuto o centralismo restaurato? L'esperienza regionalista in Italia e Francia" (also in English, mimeographed). (Cornell University, Ithaca, 1978).

TABLE 4
Italian Election Results, Regional and National, 1970–1976
(in percent)

Parties	1970 Regional Elections	1970 National Elections	1975 Regional Elections	1975 Change from 1970	1975 Change from 1972	1976 National Elections	1976 Change from 1972	1976 Change from 1975
PCI	27.5	27.5	32.4	+5.3	+4.9	34.4	+6.9	+2.0
PSI	10.6	9.7	12.1	+1.5	+2.4	9.6	−0.1	−2.5
PSIUP-PDUP[a]	3.1	2.6	1.2	−1.9	−1.4	1.5	−1.1	+0.3
PRI	3.0	2.9	3.3	+0.3	+0.4	3.1	+0.2	−0.2
DC	37.6	38.7	35.5	−2.1	−3.2	38.7	0.0	+3.2
PSDI	6.9	5.2	5.6	−1.3	+0.4	3.4	−1.8	−2.2
PLI	4.6	3.9	2.5	−2.1	−1.4	1.3	−2.6	−1.2
MSI-DN[b]	6.9	8.8	6.9	0.0	−1.9	6.1	−2.7	−0.8
Miscellaneous	0.3	0.5	0.5	+0.2	+0.1	1.9	+1.4	+1.4

[a] 1970 = PSIUP; 1972 = PSIUP + PDUP; in 1973, the PSIUP split with parts going to PCI, PSI, and PDUP; 1975 and 1976 = PDUP.
[b] 1970 = MSI + PDIUM.
Source: *Rinascita*, 25 June 1976.

legislative elections of 1972 left Italian politics stalemated; all parties got about the number of seats and votes they had before. In the referendum on divorce, May 1974, the DC suffered a massive defeat. It remained unclear, however, to what extent this rejection of the DC position on that issue would carry over to other political issues. The regional elections occurred precisely at the point when this question dominated Italian political life. The answer profoundly jolted Italian political life, provoking new national elections in 1976 (see Table 4).

The PCI emerged from 15 June 1975 as the largest party in every major city of Italy (including Rome, Turin, Milan, Venice, Florence, and Naples, as well as Bologna) and the largest party in seven regions, thirty-four provinces, and twenty-six province capitals. To the three regions of the traditional Red Belt (Umbria, Tuscany, and the Emilia-Romagna), the left has now added control of Liguria, the Marches, and Piedmont. The legislative elections of June 1976 confirmed these shifts. Though some observers had thought PCI gains in 1975 were a function of the type of elections (local, not national), the PCI did even better the following year.[17]

For the future of Italian politics, and consequently for the regions, the impact of these elections is unclear. The two major parties have entered into the *accordo pragammatico* whereby the PCI negotiates policy matters with the DC without actually participating in the government. As Sidney Tarrow convincingly argues, the result appears to be a certain slackening in the PCI's enthusiasm for extending decentralization:

> In the late sixties and early seventies, the Communists had made themselves advocates of regional reform as part of a strategy that emphasized social and institutional presence, to find

17. Donald Blackmer and Sidney Tarrow, eds., *Communism in Italy and France* (Princeton: Princeton University Press, 1977); see also Peter Lange, "The French and Italian Communist Parties: Postwar Strategy and Domestic Society" (San Francisco: American Political Association, 2–6 September 1975); Sidney Tarrow, "Local Constraints on Regional Reform," in *Between Center and Periphery: Grassroots Politicians in Provincial Italy and France* (New Haven: Yale University Press, 1977).

an issue with which to whip the Socialists and Christian Democrats, and to appeal to voters in the South, where they were per-
sistently weak. By the mid-seventies, the strategy had shifted to
one of compromise at the summit with the DC, a compromise
which required *control* over the periphery—as it did over the
trade unions. Is it excessive to suspect that the PCI was concerned that *too much* regional devolution would make the
future task of national power consolidation difficult?[18]

With the DC reluctant to have further devolution, the shift in
the PCI's position helps account for the limited nature of recent
changes. An outright government of the *compromesso-
storico*, no longer needing regions as a way of proving a capacity
to act, might abandon its postwar tendency to support decentralization. Similarly, a Socialist-Communist government might
also find that the great historic tasks facing it, combined with
intense political opposition, would provide ample reason to
avoid dispersion of power.

THE POLITICAL DYNAMICS OF REGIONAL REFORM

The creation of regional governments in both Italy and France is
the story of reluctant governments driven into doing something

18. Tarrow, "Regionalismo incompiuto," p. 30. See also the extensive
work on Italian regionalism being done by Robert Putnam, Robert Leonardi,
and Raffaella Y. Nanetti, "Decentralizing Power: Initial Findings from an
Italian Case Study," mimeographed (Paper delivered to the Agnelli Italian
Studies Seminar of the Center for European Studies, Harvard University, 19
November 1977); Putnam et al., "Regional Decentralization in Italy: From
Euphoria to Realism," mimeographed (Paper delivered to the American Polit-
ical Science Association, 31 August–3 September 1978, Washington, D.C.);
Raffaela Y. Nanetti and Robert Leonardi, "Betting on the Cities: The Urban
Strategy of the Italian Communist Party," mimeographed (Paper delivered to
the American Political Science Association, Washington, D.C., September
1977, and to the Agnelli Italian Studies Seminar, November 1977); Raymond
Seidelman, "The PCI and Municipal Decentralization: The Case of
Florence," mimeographed (Paper delivered to the Agnelli Italian Studies
Seminar, November 1977); Gail Russell, "The Politics of Industrial Conver-
sion: The Case of the North of France" (Ph.D. Diss., Princeton University,
1979); Robert Berrier, "The Politics of Industrial Survival: The French Textile
Industry" (Ph.D. Diss., Massachusetts Institute of Technology, 1977).

about which they had grave misgivings. Each step forward expressed the pressure of some political problem on politicians. Usually this problem was weakness: for the Gaullists in 1964, weakness in local governments; for de Gaulle in 1969, weakness in relation to his own followers; for Pompidou, grumbling by his centrist allies, UDR modernizers, and potential competitors like Servan-Schreiber. In Italy, DC governments were forced to implement Title 5 by the logic that had propelled them into the opening to the left. In both countries, the controversy over what type of regions to create reached a highwater mark of public consciousness in the late sixties. The torrents of political agitation pushed regionalism into the main channels and pools. Before the drop in water levels, previous currents had brought the two countries to different ports. It has been my argument here that this difference can best be understood as a function of six major factors.

1. Alliance Combinations among the Parties

CENTER AND RIGHT: The different fates of Christian Democracy in Italy and France have had two important consequences for the regionalist cause. In both countries, elements of the Catholic center have been among the strongest supporters of the regions. To the strain of thought exemplified by the MRP of Robert Schumann, or the DC of Alcide De Gasperi (strongly European, anti-Marxist and anticapitalist, reformist, participatory in a corporatist way), regions permit the full play of natural social forces and help shield the citizen from both the individualistic atomism of the Jacobin model and the bureaucratic suffocation of the Soviet one. Where these ideas were strong, regionalism had powerful supporters. Conversely, anything that weakened the Catholic center weakened regionalism. Thus, the party systems were quite important. Gaullism, by wrecking the DC position in France, skewed the political center of gravity to the right, which was more antiregional, isolating the more proregional Catholic formations. In Italy, the dominant party included those formations, while a portion of the right lay outside the organization; this facilitated center-left coalitions that pivoted around the proregional center, sloughing off part of the antiregional right.

SOCIALIST-COMMUNIST RELATIONS AND STRATEGIES. As relations between the Socialist and Communist parties in the two countries have varied, so has the fate of the regions. The PCI has been considerably more interested in building links to other groups than has the French Communist pary. Regions have utility, therefore, to the PCI as an arena for the development of these alliances and for the demonstration of its abilities and probity. Closer ties between PCI and the Italian Socialist party (PSI) (again compared to the PCF and the French Socialists) have made proregionalism more rewarding by increasing the likelihood that the left could get control of some regions should they be created. In France, conversely, the PCF's greater isolation and isolationism inhibited for a long time any understanding of the political value of regional government, while poor relations with the Socialists lessened the rewards of control. The closer relations between the Socialist and Communist parties of recent years have made regional government more attractive to both parties.

2. Geographical Distribution of Voting Strength

The distribution of left voting in Italy and France differs in ways that affect the incentives to support regions. Though twenty percent of the French electorate lives around Paris, the capital district has been excluded from all regional reform projects (and did not receive its own local government structure until 1975–1976). That part of the left vote that lives in the Red Belt around Paris is therefore lost in a contest for control over French regions. In Italy, the Red Belt is itself regional. It has always been obvious that the left would control the Emilia-Romagna, Tuscany, and Umbria and would be in striking distance in some others. Indeed, it has recently come to power in Liguria, Piedmont, and the Marches, and plays an important role in Lombardy and elsewhere.

The rapprochement between the Socialist and Communist parties in France has diminished the importance of this factor in

recent years. Regional governments were set up in France during the working out of the Common Program strategy, and
together the left parties have elected five regional presidents (all
Socialists)—in Languedoc-Roussillon, Limousin, Midi-Pyrénées,
the Nord, and Provence-Côte d'Azur—and they support a left
Radical in Corsica.

3. Party Strength at National and Local Levels

New political parties probably have a stronger incentive than
older ones to support a shake-up of the areal distribution of
power. Thus the Gaullists, who after 1958 were strong nation-
ally and weak locally, hoped to outflank their rivals' local hold
through new institutions.

Conversely, well-entrenched parties have difficulty with reform of the politico-administrative system. Change threatens
not only party positions in relation to each other, but established interests within each party organization. Secure, well-
integrated, disciplined, dominant parties (like the Swedish
Social Democrats) can prevent threats to the party as a whole by
working out these conflicts within their own organization.
Looser, more poorly disciplined, and nondominant parties like
the DC find it hard to neutralize the threatening elements of
change.

4. The Efficacy of Present Institutions

However much French local elites complain of their dependence
on Paris, French centralization does give them certain benefits,
particularly that of being the privileged interlocutors between
the state apparatus and their constituents. Institutional reform
could loosen this monopoly and disrupt established relationships. Conversely, since the Italian state apparatus functions less
effectively, the benefits of established positions in relation to it
are correspondingly less. Italian politicians are therefore more
likely than their French counterparts to see a positive balance on
the account sheets of regionalism.[19]

19. This is the central argument of Tarrow, *Between Center and Periphery*.

5. Ideological Assumptions Concerning the Proper
Organization of Public Authority

The entire universe of political discourse in France appears to be more hostile to regions and decentralization than in Italy. Left and right alike have been dominated by Jacobins who equate regions with feudalism, corporatism, fascism, anarchy, and national disintegration. The French tolerance for risks in this field appears low, though the objective danger in Italy appears much higher. An event like the 1970 riots in Reggio Calabria over the location of the regional capital would certainly have killed regional reform in France for a generation. In Italy, the two major bodies of political thought—Marxism and Christian Democracy—contain strong anticentrist currents along with centrist ones. Both traditions were excluded from power during the long stretch of rule from the center (under the monarchy and fascism) and have developed greater interests than their French equivalents in the problems of local diversity.

6. The Context and Content of the Reform

The circumstances that brought forth the regions, and specific features of the proposals, gave them greater legitimacy in Italy. In Italy regions appeared to mean incorporation of the left and the extension of democratic participation through direct elections. In France, they appeared to be part of an attack on existing parties and institutions, a transfer of power away from direct to indirect suffrage.

It is not yet possible to evaluate the actual performance of the machinery created in each country. The French law is only just now being applied, and appears to have been emasculated even further—if this was possible—as the Giscard government has faced major problems. The Italian regions do function but are bogged down in juridical disputes and slowed by the more general fiscal crises of the Italian state. One can envisage two scenarios, the first narrowing the differences between the two countries, the second maintaining or accentuating them. If weak centrist governments uneasy about, or hostile toward, regionalism remain in power in Rome, they may well use the authority available to them to restrict the actions of regional institutions to the point that they begin to resemble French ones. In France, conversely, it is possible that, though participatory decentralization will remain highly limited, some significant reworking of decision-making may occur inside the administrative machine, leading to administrative deconcentration in the regions. Already the *Conférences Administratives Régionales* (CAR) are being delegated broader powers, and local elites are increasingly criticizing their lack of access to it. To the extent that spillover has real force, one can imagine administrative deconcentration provoking demands for allowing regional councils to supervise the CAR and the regional executive.

Alternatively, the differences in formal structures and the difference in national politics between Italy and France may maintain or even widen the difference in the role of regional structures. Direct election may provide Italian regions with greater strength in conflicts against the central government. Already they appear in some cases (particularly those run by the PCI) to play an important role in local decision-making, and may supplant the province as the main intermediary body between center and periphery.

Nonetheless, the fate of regional mechanisms—whether they receive more power and money, whether we see another attempt to change the balance between the capital and various levels of local government—will remain dependent on politics, narrowly understood. Moderate shifts in the political balance among parties and a decrease in interparty tensions are likely in both countries to produce more space for the regions. Drastic political shifts, in any direction, are likely to work against the regions. In a tense political situation, rulers are likely to discover the decision rule that most governments follow: decentralization cedes advantage to your enemies.

CHAPTER 10

DECENTRALIZATION, REGIONALISM AND THE REVIVAL OF PERIPHERAL NATIONALISMS
Some Comparative Speculations

All the present nation-states of Europe were constructed by sub-merging one or more potential "nations." These acts of nation-building appeared until recently to be by-and-large successful. The persistence of local languages, dress, customs, and the like were written off as so much archaic particularism, soon to go the way of the spinning wheel. The recent resurgence of such nationalisms has surprised most of us. The Scots, Basques, Catalans, Croates, Flemish, and Quebecois have all mounted politically powerful challenges to the distribution of power within the existing states of Europe and North America.

In those countries where such challenges are strong, the nationalist controversy has powerfully affected the politics of decentralization. Politicians able to mobilize ethnic identity can exert far greater pressure on behalf of decentralization than those who cannot. Sometimes, unfortunately for the effort to generalize, intensity often produces a counterreaction of repression, leading to an even greater central control than in less

NOTE: For their comments on earlier drafts of this chapter, I wish to thank Suzanne Berger, David Bloom, Milton Esman, Michael Hechter, Patrice Higonnet, Albert Hirschman, Lisa Hirschman, James Kurth, Juan Linz, Charles Lipson, Charles Maier, Tom Naylor, Victor Perez-Diaz, Harvey Rishikof, Judith Shklar, Martin Shefter, Theda Skocpol, Sidney Tarrow, John Zysman, and the participants of seminars at Airlie House, the Center for European Studies, and the Center for International Affairs at Harvard University, Cornell University, and York University.

ethnically diverse countries. Nonetheless, it seems safe to say that, in the twentieth century, the existence of powerful ethnic nationalisms concentrated in certain regions has been a major force, bringing about the revision of the areal distribution of powers. Conversely, where such pressures have been weak, a certain imperative to reform has been lacking. France is one of those countries where peripheral nationalisms, while by no means nonexistent, have been relatively weak. If we can explain that weakness, we may contribute to an understanding of why areal reform has been so limited in France.[1]

This chapter offers an interpretation of French peripheral nationalism (Breton, Basque, Occitan, and Alsatian) in comparative perspective. While the emergence of ethnic consciousness, or concern with ethnic identity, is universal across Europe and North America (or indeed around the globe), nationalist movements are not equally strong: the nationalism of the Scots, the Spanish Basques, Catalans, Croats, Flemish, and Quebecois is far more powerful than that of the Alsatians, Bretons, French Basques, South Italians, and the Occitans. In the latter regions, nationalism remains confined to the folklore level: songs, litera-

---

1. Juan Linz, "Early State Building and Late Peripheral Nationalisms against the State," in *Building States and Nations*, ed. S.N. Eisenstadt and Stein Rokkan (Beverly Hills: Sage, 1973), pp. 32–112; Michael Hechter, *Internal Colonialism* (Berkeley and Los Angeles: University of California Press, 1975); Stein Rokkan, "Dimensions of State Formation and Nation-Building," in *The Formation of Nation-States in Western Europe*, ed. Charles Tilly (Princeton: Princeton University Press, 1975), pp. 562–600; Suzanne Berger, *Peasants Against Politics* (Cambridge, Mass.: Harvard University Press, 1972); Harry Hanham, *Scottish Nationalism* (Cambridge, Mass.: Harvard University Press, 1969); Immanuel Wallerstein, *The Modern World System* (New York: Academic Press, 1974); Perry Anderson, *Lineages of the Absolutist State* (London: New Left Books, 1974); Eugen Weber, *Peasants into Frenchmen* (Stanford: Stanford University Press, 1976). The European Consortium for European Research *Newsletter* of December 1976 (*European Political Data*, 21) announces the publication of two potentially informative books: Meic Stephens, *Linguistic Minorities in Western Europe* (Landysul, Dyfed, Wales: Gomer Press, 1976); Riccardo Petrella, *Les "Régions" de l'Europe: Etude exploratoire sur les cultures régionales dans la Communauté Européenne* (Commission of the European Communities, provisional text X/4671/76F).

ture, language, dress, traditions.[2] It has not broken through existing forms of political action to become an important issue or an organizing force of politics. In the former group of regions, peripheral nationalist demands are significant components of regional and national life, as shown by electoral successes, demonstrations, acts of violence, involvement of militants, and so on, although, of course, not all of these occur in each region. Thus while we may speak of universal trends that are undermining attachment to the traditional nation-state, these trends obviously cannot account for differences in strength among peripheral nationalisms.[3]

NATIONALIST MOVEMENTS COMPARED

Among those regions of Europe and North America which have retained an ethnic distinctiveness into the present, how can we account for the much greater strength of nationalist movements in some of these regions than in others? Regions are not actors; their inhabitants are. If a particular territory becomes nationalistic, we must explain why some of its residents find nationalism attractive, and if the nationalism is new or suddenly much stronger politically, why they have abandoned old appeals for new ones. Regions in complex society have a diverse population, including entrepreneurs, workers, shopkeepers, farmers, bankers, civil servants, students, retired and unemployed persons, employees of foreign corporations, the religious and the anticlerical, and so on. Frequently these differences become the basis of political action. Nationalist movements stress what

2. While this essay was being revised for publication during July 1977, a group of Bretons demanding autonomy for their people set off a bomb at the palace of Versailles. There have also been a number of incidents recently in Corsica, somewhat more than in Brittany. Nonetheless, in comparative terms, Breton and Corsican nationalism remain relatively weak when contrasted with the ability of the Catalan, Quebecois, Spanish Basque, or Scots movements to attract votes or sustain long-term violence.

3. Dov Ronen, "From Class Conflict to Ethnic Separatism" and "Toward a Theory of Self-Rule," mimeographed (Center for International Affairs, The Hebrew University and Harvard University, 1977).

these people have in common: their cultural identity. Under what conditions are such movements likely to be effective?

The argument given here temporarily anthropomorphizes regions; that is, it abstracts from their internal diversity and imputes characteristics to the units as a whole. The argument focuses on the relationship between ethnicity and the geographical congruence, or its absence, between two functions of the modern state: political leadership and economic development. Political leadership, ethnic distinctiveness, and economic development are usually associated with some specific region within each country. Politics in countries where these functions and ethnic differences overlap differ from politics in countries where they do not. The three terms may be defined as follows:

Political leadership. Constructs and maintains strong central institutions common to the whole country (law, police, taxation, army, bureaucracy) and formulates common policies in key areas (trade, defense, foreign policy, and so on). The historical dimension of this activity may be called state-building.

Economic growth and development. Constructs and maintains an industrial economy (involving the building of factories, towns, and transportation systems, investment facilities, technological research and its applications, rationalization and modernization of industry, and so on). The historical dimension of this activity may be called industrialization.

Ethnic potential. The existence of some distinctive characteristic(s) among the people living in a region, such as language, institutions, and/or historical traditions, in that order of importance. The aim here is to differentiate ethnically distinct regions that remain politically dormant from those which become politically active. Since regions without ethnic distinctiveness may also remain dormant, we must have some way of separating in advance nonethnic from ethnic regions, in order to be sure that the dormant condition derives from the relationships considered here rather than from "nonethnicity." Though operationalization is difficult, circularity can be avoided by specifying (however arbitrary it may appear) which regions have ethnic potential and which do not.

Regions that have ethnic potential include: Wales and Scotland; Brittany, Alsace, Occitania (particularly the area near the Pyrenees where some Catalan is still spoken), the Basque departments, and Corsica; the Basque provinces of Spain, Catalonia, and to a lesser degree Andalusia and Galicia; Flanders; Bavaria, Baden-Wurtemberg, and other parts of southern Germany; Sicily, southern Italy, the regions of the former Papal states, Sardinia, perhaps the Venetia; all the regions of Yugoslavia; Quebec.[4] In the United States the independence movement in the South showed that separatism can be based on forces other than ethnic consciousness.

Regions that do *not* have ethnic potential include: the English North; the French Nord, Pas de Calais, Dauphiné, Champagne; Westphalia; Lombardy; Saskatchewan, Alberta, British Columbia; the American South and West.

This chapter is concerned with the regions of the first group, those *with* ethnic potential. Some of them have developed politically significant nationalisms in recent years; others have not. The following propositions seek to account for these differences: (1) Where both political leadership and economic dynamism take place in the same region (that is, where the two types of "core" coincide), peripheral nationalism is weak. Ethnically distinct regions that occupy peripheral positions politically and economically in relation to the center acquiesce in the national union and take their place in it. (2) Where the above activities take place in different regions, one of which has ethnic potential, the latter region is likely to develop strong, politically relevant nationalism. This may occur if the original economic or

4. Specification of core and periphery for Germany is immensely complicated by changing boundaries and borders. Down to 1945 the role of Prussia is clear enough; it was the Catholic South, the free cities, and old kingdoms such as Hanover which resisted the Bismarckian version of unity, but acquiesced. Today, the rump of Prussia in the West still dominates. Bavaria is the most independently-minded but accepts the situation. Southern Italy and other regions had considerable distinctiveness of institutions and traditions until 1870, and considerable variance of language. The discussion does not include areas where the claims are irredentist, seeking to join up with ethnic neighbors in another country, such as Alto Adige and Friuli-Veneza.

political core falters; that is, if it stops promoting economic growth or providing political leadership for the whole country. Or the noncongruence may occur if the peripheral region improves its economic position relative to the original center through the development or the plausible prospect of the development of some resource or newly acquired geographical advantage. (3) If there is no "ethnic potential" in the region, even noncongruence of this type will not produce ethnically based politics, though it may produce regional politics. Tables 5 to 8 present the foregoing information in diagrammatic form.

TABLE 5

Strength of Peripheral Nationalisms and the Congruence of Political and Economic Leadership Functions: For regions having some "Ethnic Potential"

| Periphery Nationalism | Degree of Congruence *Intensity of* | |
	Congruence	*Noncongruence*
Strong		Britain-Scotland
		Spain-Catalonia, Basque Provinces
		Canada-Quebec Belgium-Flanders Yugoslavia-Croatia
Weak	France Italy Britain pre-WWII Belgium pre-WWI	

TABLE 6
Congruence of Functions

COUNTRIES WITH CONGRUENCE	COUNTRIES WITHOUT CONGRUENCE
France	Britain, post-1945
Italy	Belgium, post-1914
Britain, pre-1945	Canada, post-1920
Belgium, pre-1914	Spain
Canada, pre-1914	Yugoslavia

TABLE 7
Regions with "Ethnic Potential"

HAVING STRONG NATIONALISM	HAVING WEAK NATIONALISM
Catalonia	Brittany
Spanish Basque Provinces	French Basque Provinces
Scotland	French "Occitania" or Langedoc
Quebec	region
Croatia	Alsace
Flanders	South Germany
	Southern Italy
	Galicia, Andalusia
	Montenegro, Macedonia

TABLE 8

Regional Location of Economic and Political Leadership Functions

	UNITED KINGDOM	SPAIN	FRANCE	ITALY	GERMANY	BELGIUM	CANADA	YUGOSLAVIA
Function:								
Political leadership								
State-building (pre-1945)	England	Castille	Ile de France	Piedmont	Prussia	Wallonia	Quebec, Ontario	Serbia
Present	England	Castille	Ile de France	Piedmont, Lombardy	Rhine Westphalia W. Prussia	Wallonia	Ontario	Serbia
Economic leadership								
Original industrialization	England	Catalonia, Basque Provinces	Ile de France, North, Lyonnais	Piedmont, Lombardy	Prussia, Western	Wallonia	Quebec, Ontario	Croatia
Present	England, Scotland	Catalonia, Basque Provinces	Ile de France, North, Lyonnais	Piedmont, Lombardy	Rhine-Westphalia	Flanders	Quebec, Ontario, Alberta	Croatia

The remainder of this chapter deals with the experiences of several countries in light of these propositions. The argument is not perfectly worked out nor is it exhaustive; its value lies in systematizing a set of questions about certain relationships. Without such an effort, errors cannot be detected.

The United Kingdom

England constructed the British state and led its industrialization. Wales, Scotland and Ireland were linked first politically, then economically to the English core. For two centuries England was the most dynamic and wealthy region in the Western world. Though Wales and Scotland, as Michael Hechter shows, never equaled the core region in wealth, they did develop industrially by means of their association with that core, and they did share in some of the wealth.[5] Until recently, both regions acquiesced in English dominance. Politically they responded to the same principles of cleavage that prevailed in the English core: religion and class. To some degree, both the Liberal nonconformist nexus and the Labour working class nexus expressed a Celtic alienation from England. Primarily, however, they both constituted links that permitted the Welsh and the Scots to join with their religious and social counterparts in England in the same political formations. Thus the Liberals drew nonconformists from all over Britain against the Tory Anglicans. The shift to Labour, starting in 1890, marked the displacement of religion by class.[6] Wales and Scotland have voted the Labour ticket disproportionately because a disproportionate number of their inhabitants belong to the working class.[7]

5. Unlike Ireland, which remained largely agricultural. Michael Hechter makes a very good case for treating this as the principal reason Ireland was the one which broke away. The absence of industrial development maintained the homogeneity of the economic function of most of the Irish, around which a mass movement could be mobilized. See Hechter, *Internal Colonialism*.

6. P.F. Clarke, *Lancashire and the New Liberalism* (Cambridge: Cambridge University Press, 1971).

7. Some of the deviance from a class model of voting does derive from the hold of Anglican and English identities on the English working class. See Robert Alford, "Class and Party," in S.M. Lipset and Stein Rokkan, *Party*

The period from 1920 to 1945 saw the highest integration politically of the three areas—it was also the period when the seeds of discord were germinating. In the 1870s England lost her commanding position in the world economy to Germany and the United States.[8] She began increasingly to live off the return from overseas investments and other invisibles, and these rewards trickled down to the periphery only very slowly. After World War I, the coal and shipbuilding industries of special importance to Wales and Scotland declined, and unemployment shot up, going far higher than in England. Thus the rot at the core was not perceived. The initial consequence of structural difficulty at the periphery was to strengthen the hold of integrating cleavages, or cleavages common to the whole nation; unemployment strengthened class consciousness, not ethnic consciousness.

After World War II, it became politically clear that the British crisis extended to England as well. Indeed, gradually people came to see it as the root of the problem, just as once it had been the root of the bloom. England proved increasingly unable to compete with other countries in the world economy. Her standard of living fell slowly. Bankers and government remained attached to sterling. The stop-go policies pursued to prevent payments drains inhibited modernization of industrial activity and growth. This hit England hard, but Wales and Scotland worse.

Prior to 1964, it was possible for Labour voters in Wales and Scotland to blame the Conservatives for their plight, and to

---

Systems and Voter Alignments, ed. S. M. Lipset and Stein Rokkan (New York: Free Press, 1967), pp. 67–94; Richard Butler and Donald Stokes, *Political Change in Britain* (New York: St. Martin's Press, 1969; 2d ed., 1976).

8. On the origins of the present British predicament, see David Landes, *The Unbound Prometheus* (Cambridge: Cambridge University Press, 1969); E.J. Hobsbawm, *From Industry to Empire* (New York: Pantheon, 1968); Robert Gilpin, *U.S. Power and the Multinational Corporation* (New York: Basic Books, 1975); for an exploration of the British, German, French, and American responses to stiff international competition see Peter Gourevitch, "International Trade, Domestic Coalitions, and Liberty: Comparative Responses to the Crisis of 1873–1896," *Journal of Interdisciplinary History* 8 (Autumn 1977): 281–313.

await the return of Labour to power. They were disappointed. Wilson, seeking to establish the credibility of Labour management of a capitalist economy, defended the pound.[9] The economy continued to deteriorate. As Hechter shows, the rise of the nationalist vote in Wales and Scotland increased markedly after the election of 1964. Objectively, the situation had been bad for some time. Subjectively, the voters now understood that the English core was itself weak and that leaders appealing to them on the basis of nationwide interpretations were either unwilling or unable to help them. Why stick to the union if it was no longer a good bargain, when the metropole no longer had much to offer? North Sea oil, of course, makes this argument especially pungent in Scotland.[10]

Britain, then, fits the scheme nicely. At first, the combination of state-building and industrializing functions in one region overrode ethnic differences. Then, the economic weakness of the core region undermined the bargain. The core has not been able to solve the problems of the peripheries, which increasingly blame it for this failure. Scotland is the purest case of the contrast between rising periphery and sinking core, and it is therefore not so surprising that nationalism is strongest there, even though it is Wales which retains a much larger percentage of bilinguals.[11]

9. Stephen Blank, "Britain: The Politics of Foreign Economic Policy, the Domestic Economy, and the Problem of Pluralistic Stagnation," *International Organization* 31 (Autumn 1977); special issue, ed. Peter Katzenstein (Madison: University of Wisconsin Press, 1977).

10. Milton Esman, "Perspectives on Ethnic Conflict in Industrial Societies," in *Ethnic Conflict in Industrial Societies*, ed. Milton Esman, forthcoming; and Milton Esman, "Scottish Nationalism, North Sea Oil, and the British Response," *Waverly Papers on European Political Studies*, ser. 1, no. 6 (Edinburgh University, April 1975).

11. See Hechter, *Internal Colonialism*. Ireland fits less well, since Eire broke away during the apogee of British economy and imperial power. An explanation of that fact consistent with the argument here would require deeper analysis of the *types* of economic dominance–dependence between center and periphery, and of the types of people in the periphery drawn into a relationship with the core. Hechter's interpretation is very plausible: Ireland, alone of the Celtic fringe, broke away because Ireland alone had no industrial development; hence there was no industrial enclave within the country having strong ties to the core. More purely agricultural, Ireland was more

Spain

Spain fits the same pattern, with the difference that the discordance among regions has always been greater: the nation-building region has never been the same as the industrializing one.

The marriage of Ferdinand and Isabella linked a trading, commercial area whose monarchy was hedged all around by medieval representative institutions (Aragon) with an agricultural region, not especially prosperous, dominated by the crown (Castille). Castille's initial advantage, like Prussia two centuries later, was organizational; it developed a centralized bureaucracy able to mobilize men and money. Other forces helped it dominate the diverse elements of the Iberian peninsula; the decline of Mediterranean trade routes weakened Aragon; the fortune found in gold from the Americas went to Castille alone, not Spain as a whole; and the rise of the French monarchy divided the Basques and the Catalans along the Pyrenees. Only Portugal escaped, largely because of help from the outside.[12] This dominance nonetheless fell far short of uniformity and integration. Each former kingdom and province retained many of the institutions and practices it possessed at the moment of its link to the Crown of Castille.

Juan Linz suggests that it was the failure to eradicate these differences in the seventeenth century which provided the basis for ethnic nationalism in the nineteenth and twentieth centuries.[13] Certainly a centralization may preempt some kinds of later conflict by stamping out the bases for later divergence. (Compare the linguistic unifomity wrought by the French school system in the nineteenth century.) Nonetheless, the success or failure of national homogenization in this early period

---

homogeneous, hence more easily mobilizable against the metropole. Hechter does examine the other interpretations of Ireland's difference, especially religion. See pp. 266–292.

12. R.B. Merriman, *Six Contemporaneous Revolutions* (Oxford: Oxford University Press, 1935).

13. Juan Linz, "Politics in a Multilingual Society with a Dominant World Language," in *Les Etats multilingues*, ed. Jean-Guy Savard and Richard Vigneault (Quebec: Presses Universitaires de Laval, 1975), pp. 367–444.

does not alone explain the emergence of nationalisms later on. Other countries which were no more centralized or uniform than mid-seventeenth century Spain, or even less so, have formed nation-states which have not faced separatist challenges. Was the France of Louis XIV really more uniform than the Spain of the Count-Duke of Olivares? Italy and Germany did not exist. Prussia was nothing.

Castille's problem is not that it failed to do enough at an early stage, but that coal, iron ore, water power, and transportation links to the outside do not lie within her borders. In the nineteenth and twentieth centuries, mining, smelting, textiles, and other basic industries developed around Bilboa and Barcelona, while Madrid remained the politico-administrative capital of an agrarian plateau. This provided a basis for tension between the two types of region. Basques and Catalans resented Castille for a variety of reasons, one of which was economic. Carlism and the nationalism of the Basque provinces and Catalonia are remarkably complex movements, which I do not mean to disfigure through reductionism.[14] What I wish to suggest is that Castille offered little in the way of economic advantages, while it took a lot, or could be made to appear to do so. Taxes siphoned money into the center, and prevented these two peripheries from having the kind of commercial policies which suited their nascent industrialization. To various elements of the peripheral populations (only close study can tell us who—aristocrat, industrialist, merchant, artisan, laborer, peasant, intellectual) the advantages of membership in the whole appeared dubious and the arguments of separatism quite plausible.

Twentieth-century peripheral nationalism in Spain continues this pattern. Castille has developed industrially. Like other administrative capitals, Madrid has attracted some investments,[15]

14. James Kurth, "Patrimonial Authority, Delayed Development, and Mediterranean Politics," Paper delivered at American Political Science Association, September 1973; idem, "The Political Consequences of the Product Cycle," *International Organization* 33 (Winter 1979): 1–34.

15. Most bureaucratic-military capitals, even those with no special advantages in location or resources eventually attract industrial development. Berlin

but it is Catalonia and the Basque region which still lead Spanish economic development. Thus the political center and the economic center remain different, and the unity of Spain remains contested.

France

The pattern in France, as in Italy and Germany, is initially the English one, but the last phase differs. State-builder and industrializer coincide—the Ile de France, broadly understood, was the royal domain around Paris which provided the base for the formation of the French state, virtually complete by the end of Louis XIV's reign.[16] Industrialization was somewhat more dispersed. Textiles in Lyon, the Nord and Alsace; coal and iron in Lorraine and the Nord—these joined Paris to be the motor of French industrial growth. As peripheries, the North and East benefited from both natural resources and location (transportation, proximity to large markets). The West and South, whose ports had led the economy during the commercial period of the eighteenth century, declined in the nineteenth century.[17] These areas developed the standard relationship of periphery to core: supplier of food, manpower, and politicians; consumer of manufactured products. The highly centralized school system imposed the French of the center upon the whole country. Peripheral nationalism was not a politically salient problem.

In the present period, the same areas continue their economic leadership. The Common Market accentuated the locational advantages of the Paris basin, the North, the East, and the Lyonnais by eliminating the tariff barriers which dampened the pull of the German, Benelux, and Italian markets. The regions lying along the communications link of Marseilles-Lyon-Strasbourg-Nancy-Lille have challenged the Parisian-centered conception of national interests by demanding investments that would improve the infrastructural links between them and the neighboring countries rather than with other parts of France. This is a

---

is the best example, along with Madrid today and perhaps Moscow?

16. Alsace, Franche-Comté, Picardy, and the lands up to the Pyrenees were brought under the crown during the reign of Louis XIV. Lorraine was added in the mid-eighteenth century, Savoy in 1860.

17. Robert Lafont, *La révolution régionaliste* (Paris: Gallimard, 1967); idem, *Décoloniser la France* (Paris: Gallimard, 1971).

challenge to centralization, but it is not peripheral nationalism. Lorraine and the Nord are suffering from changes in their key industries (coal, steel, and textiles) but have not supported "ethnic" or "regional" interpretations of their plight.[18]

Some industrial development has taken place in the peripheries: natural gas near Toulouse, steel mills near Marseilles. These regions remain inferior in income and growth to the dynamic ones. They continue to depend massively on the center for various forms of assistance. These are the regions where some peripheral nationalism has emerged: Brittany, Occitania, and Corsica. Nonetheless, in contrast with Scotland and Wales, the movements in these French areas are extremely weak. Discontent has helped nationalize peripheral politics and reduce the salience of older issues, rather than the reverse. In Catholic areas like Brittany, the left has made gains; in the traditionally anticlerical left areas (such as the Southwest), the right has scored. The polarization of politics in France between left and right helps prevent the translation of peripheral discontent into nationalism. It offers the hope of a massive change in the identity of the rulers of the center as a way of improving the region. Should the left fail to help such regions, we could see the repetition of the English pattern: the perceived failure of the "socialist" or "class" option opens the way to other analysis of the regional situation, including nationalist ones. Even so, for one of the regions to become like Scotland, two more conditions would have to be fulfilled: deterioration of the economic health of the core region, and development of some economic trump in the peripheral region.

Italy

Italy and Germany both follow the French pattern: state-building and industrialization are led by a particular region; that region remains dynamic; midcentury peripheral nationalism has

18. The creation of regional government in France has had little to do with peripheral nationalism, and much more to do with party politics, bureaucratic rivalries, and economic imbalances. See Peter Gourevitch, "Reforming the Napoleonic State: The Creation of Regional Government in France and Italy," in *Territorial Politics in Industrial Nations*, ed. Luigi Graziano, Peter Katzenstein, and Sidney Tarrow (New York: Praeger, 1978). See also Sidney

been relatively weak compared to Spain and Britain. This is interesting in that both Italy and Germany are frequently treated as the main examples of a special category: late-unifying, late-industrializing states.[19]

Italian unification was led by Piedmont, whose institutions were extended to the rest of the peninsula.[20] Other northern regions supported the Piedmontese initiatives, especially Lombardy. Industrialization occurred in these two regions. Rome became the capital because of its symbolic importance, not because it played a conspicuous role either in unification or industrialization. Indeed, as part of the Papal domain, the Lazio was rather a retardant to both processes. The South was integrated into the kingdom as a very inferior member, and probably to the detriment of its economy. Despite the greater severity of the internal colonialism problem there, the Italian South has been far quieter than Scotland or Catalonia or the Basque country.

Since 1945, the original industrializing regions have performed the leadership function with great vigor. Rapid growth has sucked up vast numbers of people from the South. Politics in both North and South have been increasingly nationalized—the same cleavages exist everywhere. As in France, a sharp left-right conflict helps inhibit regionalist interpretations. The principal ethnic problems have been in areas over which there exist border disputes. The Tyrolese and the Slavs of Friuli wish not independence but fusion with a different *patrie*—not at all like the Basques, Catalans, or Scots.

Germany

Prussia is, of course, the quintessential example of unification of the whole through conquest by a part. A completely peripheral region in the seventeenth century, Prussia gained through

Tarrow, *Between Center and Periphery: Grassroots Politicians in Italy and France* (New Haven: Yale University Press, 1977).

19. Alexander Gershenkron, *Economic Backwardness in Historical Perspective*, (Cambridge, Mass.: Harvard University Press, 1962).

20. D. Mack Smith, *Modern Italy* (Ann Arbor: University of Michigan Press, 1960).

politico-military organization (plus French foreign policy) much greater leverage in German and European politics than could have been predicted from her resource base. Even that would not have sufficed had the Congress of Vienna not given her great chunks of the Rhineland, whose industrial potential was not appreciated at the time. This allowed Prussia to become the economic leader as well. The two functions thus were undertaken by the same polity, whose job it was to iron out a variety of disputes. Resentment toward the Prussians never disappeared. Bismarck worried constantly about a revisionist coalition in which particularists wanting to challenge Prussian dominance would join up with socialists, liberals, and other forces. Some historians attribute the strident nationalism and imperialism of the Kaiserreich to this internal insecurity.[21] Mostly, though, people celebrated Bismarck. Once Poland was removed in 1919, the German problem was not that regions wished to leave the nation-state, but that German speakers allegedly wished to get in.

World War II so altered the map and the composition of the population that it is difficult to speak of any region within the Federal Republic as corresponding to the Prussia of old. Rhine-Westphalia comes the closest to being the original industrializing region. It remains today the leader of the German economic revival. Bavaria retains the strongest identity culturally and politically, and has the strongest local nationalism. No region can be called separatist. Politics is dominated by issues which cut across all regions: socialism, property rights, religion, foreign policy.

Germany and Italy together confirm the importance of the location of industrial energy, both in the original push and in susbsequent leadership. If longevity of political unity were enough to prevent late peripheral nationalism, Spain would today be well integrated. If early industrialization were enough, Britain would also have no problems. Germany and Italy are

21. Hans-Ulrich Wehler, "Bismarck's Imperialism, 1862-1890," *Past and Present* 48 (1970): 119-155; Helmut Böhme, "Big Business Pressure Groups and Bismarck's Turn to Protectionism, 1873-1879," *The Historical Journal* 10 (1967): 218-236.

both recently industrialized. The original industrial region remains economically dominant. The peripheries have not abandoned dependence on the superior wealth and energy of the
center; nor do they have resources of their own to tempt them
toward an independent course.

Belgium

Belgium constitutes a blend of the British and Canadian
models. At its formation (in 1830) the country was dominated
both economically and politically by the same region—French-
speaking Wallonia—which led the break from the Netherlands
and led one of the earliest industrializations in Europe. Flanders
played the role of Wales and Scotland, acquiescing, more or less
pacifically, in the dominance of the richer region. In the twentieth century, Wallonia, like England, has faltered economically. Her coal and textiles no longer sustain energetic economic
leadership. As in Canada, economic leadership has shifted to
another region altogether, to Flanders. Where class once organized the electorate in both regions, Flemish nationalism now
cuts across that cleavage.[22]

Yugoslavia

Yugoslavia resembles the Spanish case—nation-builder and
economic leader differ. Loosely speaking, the drive to link up
the diverse peoples of Yugoslavia came from Serbia, which thus
played the role of Castille. Croatia, however, has been more
economically energetic. Industrialization and tourism together
give her more income than any other region in the country, and
have fueled Croatian suspicion that the Serbian-influenced
policy set in Belgrade is biased against them.

Canada

Canada is perhaps the most difficult case to subsume under the
models proposed here because the core and periphery occupied
the same territory, lower Canada or Quebec. What has changed
in recent years is both the relationship of Quebec as a whole to

22. Aristide R. Zolberg, "Splitting the Difference: Federalization without
Federalism in Belgium," in *Ethnic Conflict in the Western World*, ed. Milton
Esman (Ithaca: Cornell University Press, 1977), pp. 103–142.

the political economy of Canada, and the relationship of the Anglophone and Francophone populations within Quebec to each other. These shifts are connected, and help account for the increased political strength of Quebecois nationalism.[23]

Historically, Canadian confederation was based on an alliance between Ontario and Quebec. Together the two provinces were able to impose on the country a set of economic policies favorable to them: high tariffs, railroad building, controlled freight rates, centrally directed banking, and so on. As long as the two provinces worked together, their demographic weight was great enough to overcome the opposition of farmers, fishermen, and entrepreneurs in the Maritimes, the prairie provinces and the Rockies.[24]

In Quebec, the economy was controlled by Anglophones, but Francophones were more numerous and not without political influence. Quebec support of the National Policy at the federal level required mass encapsulation and elite accommodation.

The great majority of Francophone Quebecois lived in the countryside only marginally connected to industrial Montreal. Relations between them and the Anglophone core were mediated by a traditional preindustrial elite composed of the clergy, large landowners, and members of the liberal professions. Quebec politics reflected an asymmetrical compromise between Anglophone control of the economy and Francophone autonomy in culture and religion.

23. For more detailed development of my remarks on Canada, see Peter Gourevitch, "Quebec Separatism in Comparative Perspective," in *The Future of North America: Canada, the United States, and Quebec Nationalism*, ed. Elliot Feldman and Neil Nevitt (Cambridge: Center for International Affairs, Harvard University, 1979), pp. 237–252; Tom Naylor, "The Third Commercial Empire of the St. Lawrence," in *Economics and the National Question*, ed. Gary Teeple (Toronto: University of Toronto Press, 1972); Tom Naylor, *The History of Canadian Business 1867–1914* (Toronto: Lorimer, 1976); Milton Esman, "The Escalation of Communal Conflict in Canada," mimeographed (Center for International Studies, Cornell University, Ithaca, 1977).

24. These tensions among different sectors of the economy during periods of severe international competition were not unique to Canada. Similar things happened in the United States, Britain, France, Germany, and other countries. See Gourevitch, "International Trade, Domestic Coalitions, and Liberty."

Since 1945, these relationships have altered dramatically. With the massive demographic shift into cities and industry, the encapsulation of Francophones is over. The influence of traditional elites has waned. Education gives Francophones training and aspirations. They refuse to accept the subservient positions traditionally offered them. Demands of various kinds increase.

At the same time, the ability of the Anglophone interests of Montreal to satisfy those demands has decreased; Montreal has gradually been losing its strategic place in Canadian life as banking, manufacturing, resource extraction, and agrobusiness have migrated to Ontario and beyond to Alberta, British Columbia, and Saskatchewan, following the supply of resources, American growth to the South and West, and improvements in transportation which bypass Montreal.[25]

Quebecois nationalism is frequently cited as a *cause* of this movement, particularly the flight of head offices from Montreal. Such nationalism can be seen instead as a *consequence* of the westward shift. Had the massive investment gone to Quebec instead of to the western provinces, Quebec would be booming. There would be plenty of opportunity for all kinds of labor skills in the private sector. Business would have been in a stronger position to forge links with some segment of the Francophone community interested in preserving a federally oriented society and economy. French culture and language would be defended without a full break, as the governments of the sixties and early seventies tried to do.

Certainly, many Francophones do support this orientation. Other Quebecois, the nationalists, do not. They explain Quebec's economic problems as the consequence of cultural divisions: Anglophone capital has not been interested, they charge, in developing the province into a modern industrial region, but in extracting resources and profits according to a division of labor favoring Ontario and foreign capital. They propose

25. Garth Stevenson, "Federalism and the Political Economy of the Canadian State," in *The Canadian State: Political Economy and Political Power*, ed. Leo Panitch (Toronto: University of Toronto Press, 1977), and other essays in that volume.

a different strategy, one which would be run by the public centered in the provinces, led by Francophones. Only in a state controlled by Francophones, the nationalists argue, can the economy be developed in a way which will insure the survival of French culture.

This *indépendiste* vision is sustained by the existence of resource wealth: hydroelectric power, asbestos, wood, pulp and paper, aluminium processing facilities, iron ore, uranium, good harbors. These resources play a role equivalent to that of North Sea oil in Scotland. They give at least some plausibility to the separatist case. Were Quebec much poorer or much less developed, the "go-it-alone" strategy might appear much less credible.

Changes in the distribution of economy activity not only augment nationalism in Quebec; they also increase economic tensions throughout the country, diminishing the ability of the federal government to deal with pressures from Quebec. Economic conflicts of interest are visible in quarrels over tariffs, monetary and fiscal policy, taxation, foreign investments, transfer payments, profit flows, and so on. Alberta clashes with the eastern provinces over the distribution of oil revenues. Restrictions on foreign capital are supported by industrially developed Ontario and disliked by the western provinces and the Maritimes. Prairie farmers continue to oppose discriminatory foreign structures. The West and the Maritimes criticize industrial tariffs. Government equalization payments siphon money from Alberta and Ontario to the other provinces. Economic stimulation from Ottawa goes to Ontario, leaving the Maritimes and Quebec underemployed. The flow of profits probably favors Quebec, Ontario, and Alberta.[26]

26. Richard Simeon, "The Regional Distribution of the Benefits of Confederation: A Preliminary Analysis," mimeographed draft (Institute for International Affairs, Queen's University, December 1976); Rodrigue Tremblay, "Présentation des Comptes économiques du Québec, 1961–1975," (Québec: Gouvernement du Québec, 1977); Donald Macdonald, "Provincial Economic Accounts," Dept. of Finance, Press Release 77-63 (Ottawa, 6 June 1977); Gérard Bélanger, "Why do the Balances Differ on Federal Receipts and Expenditures in Québec?" (Montreal: C. D. Howe Research Institute, October 1977); Richard Caves, "Economic models of

So far, the unifying force containing these antagonisms has been the partial convergence of interests in the policy goals of Quebec and Ontario. Despite the clash between them which dominates the news, both provinces continue to derive important benefits from the National Policy begun one hundred years ago. Most Canadian manufacturing still takes place in Quebec and Ontario, shielded behind tariff walls and other federal policies. Much of Quebec manufacturing is especially dependent on protection; it is labor-intensive and uncompetitive in world markets. Quebec understands this. It blames that condition on Anglophone capital and Ottawa's policies. It speaks not of outright independence but of sovereignty-association, by which it hopes to preserve some of the advantages of continued access to Canadian markets. Its arguments can be seen as a way of redressing the balance between Quebec and Ontario concerning the benefits to be derived from their mutual dominance of the Confederation.

Ontario has more capital-intensive industries, but they too are vulnerable and derive important benefits from having a protected Canadian market. Indeed, among the Anglophone provinces, Ontario would be the most shaken by Quebec's departure. Ontario's domination of Ottawa's policy-making has always required the help of Quebec. With no Quebecois deputies in Ottawa, Ontario alone lacks the weight to impose those policies on the other provinces. The other provinces, indeed, are at times sorely tempted to use Quebec as a ruse to break up the whole Confederation, or at least to join Quebec in forcing a drastic reorganization, which would weaken Ottawa and Ontario. The Maritimes would then have the freedom to be a depressed area, open to foreign capital; Alberta and British Columbia could sell their diverse wares on world markets. The prairies could buy cheap manufactured goods. Canadian nationalism may restrain these temptations, and diminish the

---

Political Choice: Canadian Tariff Structure," *Canadian Journal of Economics* (May 1976): 278–300.

propensity to take economic risks. Conversely, in Quebec, nationalism may increase the risk-taking. Just how elites and
masses evaluate the trade-offs remains to be seen.

CONCLUSION

The location of critical political and economic activities within
each country clearly has something to do with the emergence of,
peripheral nationalism. This rapid *tour d'horizon* certainly con-
fers plausibility on the propositions advanced at the beginning
of the discussion. The sharpest cases are Britain and Spain on
one side; France, Italy, and Germany on the other. By the end
of the eighteenth century, Bourbon Spain seemed well on the
way to constructing a nation-state; those efforts foundered
when the Basque provinces and Catalonia took the lead in
industrial development. Similarly, Britain during the period of
English ascendancy looked secure. English weakness plus Scots
oil have very rapidly transformed that condition. In France,
which on the eve of the Revolution was institutionally and
linguistically as diverse as Spain, a much higher level of integration has been attained, against which challenges remain
weak. Germany and Italy, despite the absence of any state at all
before 1870, remain more integrated in these respects than Britain or Spain. Belgium, Yugoslavia, and Canada, in their
various ways, bear out the British and Spanish models.
    From this evidence, we may note several conditions which
serve to increase or decrease the effects of congruence/non-
congruence:
    1. The more severe the core's weakness, the stronger the pe-
ripheral nationalism. Scot's nationalism waxed as the English
economy waned, but not before.
    2. The greater the economic "trumps" available to the
peripheral region, the stronger the nationalism there. Contrast
Scotland, which has oil, to Wales, where there are more
speakers of Gaelic but the nationalism is weaker. Quebec is
buoyed by the promise of natural resources (hydroelectric

power, asbestos, iron ore, pulp and paper). Whether these out-weigh the loss of markets and subsidies is much disputed; con-fusion sustains the plausibility of rival interpretations and political stances toward separation.

3. The stronger the "ethnic potential" or the sense of "eth-nic grievance," the less economic tension between core and pe-riphery is required to produce nationalism. The Scots were more easily integrated into British life than were the Quebecois into the Anglophone Canadian one. The sense of threatened iden-tity is correspondingly much stronger in Quebec than in Scotland, and the Quebecois are much more willing to run eco-nomic risks than are the Scots. Conversely, where there is no sense of ethnic distinctiveness, purely economic grievances are unlikely to give rise to separatist movements; note the contrast between Scotland and the English North (though the precision of the comparison is blurred by the absence of an equivalent in the North to the Scot's oil trump). Nor, in our own country, is New England threatening to break away now that much of that region is in an economic slump.[27]

4. An open international economy, one with low tariff bar-riers and free movement of capital and labor, reduces the economic functions played by the existing state, thereby en-couraging peripheral nationalisms. A closed international sys-tem, conversely, discourages such movements by increasing the advantages of inclusion in a larger economic system.

5. Similarly, the present bipolar configuration of military power encourages peripheral nationalisms by decreasing the salience of the defense function of the traditional national state. Small states in Western Europe and North America are certain of the NATO shield, both certain that it will protect them and certain that they have little choice but to accept that protection. In the more fluid multipolar world before 1914, the defense re-sources offered by the core appeared more attractive. Where Empire once conferred an economic, military, and cultural halo

---

27. Carl Ogelsby, *The Yankee and Cowboy War* (Kansas City: Sheed, An-drews and McMeel, 1976); Kirkpatrick Sale, *Power Shift* (New York: Random House, 1975).

on the core, NATO and American hegemony generate peripheral contempt for it.

What explanation makes the most sense out of these relationships? Spatial differentiation, both political and economic, is both very old and very ubiquitous; China, Russia, Ancient Rome, and the United States all had it and still do, along with the countries examined here. Wherever ethnic differences exist, they become part of the internal division of labor; barriers are created segregating the populations into different types of jobs on the basis of various cultural distinctions (speech patterns, language, skin color). Capitalism, like most other economic systems, makes use of this division of labor, along with other familiar divisions, such as those within a factory or a metropolitan area.

Though the geographic division of labor is universal, the likelihood that it will lead to ethnically based politics varies. Economic distress alone will not produce it, not will ethnic subordination acting alone. So long as the core appears viable, the peripheries appear to accept their situation, even if they are poor and dominated. Ambitious elites in the peripheral regions are drained off to the center or absorbed into its system. They take up intermediary positions at the local level (such as the Italian landowners of the Mezzogiorno), or literally move to the center to take positions there (the stereotypical civil servant in France and Italy is from a well-born family in the south of each country).

Conversely, when the core falters, its attractiveness to the peripheral elites diminishes. Local interpretations of their destiny become more convincing. Some elites continue the national option, but others become tempted by the local one. Ethnicity provides a plausible argument around which elites can organize an appeal to which masses of people are apparently capable of responding. Regional appeals without the ethnic dimension are correspondingly always weaker. The ethnic appeal typically cuts across class lines; it allows elites to mobilize the population around a program from which the local upper and middle as well as lower classes are likely to benefit: higher or lower tariffs, more government spending, more upper-level jobs for ethnic nationalism, and so on. The classic left complaint about such movements—that they ignore the conflict of interests among the different groups within them, that the working class members risk being dominated by the middle class ones—emphasizes what is precisely these movements' greatest strength (the appeal to unity based on blood), which was also the great strength of the older nationalisms presently under attack.[28]

The political coloration of autonomist movements differs widely (left in Catalonia, right in the Basque provinces, at least until recently), but in most cases such movements recruit especially well from the peripheral middle classes, which feel excluded from opportunities in the center, or see greater ones in the periphery. Where class-based conflicts and the parties which organize them are strong (as in Italy and France), peripheral nationalisms are weak. This is not an explanation, however, but a description. The ability of class issues to damp down ethnic ones itself reflects the preponderance of the industrial center over the less industrial periphery. Noncongruence (weakly industrial center, surging core) undermines the grip of both bourgeois and working class organizations over the periphery. Elements of both classes then turn to nationalism. Indeed, the argument in this chapter may be read as a statement of the conditions under which a particular cleavage structure successfully penetrates a whole country: when the core is economically strong, its cleavages dominate; when the core falters, rival definitions of the stakes emerge.

Note that, to tease out of these observations an explanation, it has been necessary to end the anthropomorphizing of the regions; the political behaviors explored here are not those

28. Aristide Zolberg, "Culture, Territory, Class: Ethnicity Demystified" (Paper delivered at the International Political Science Association, Edinburgh, 16–21 August 1976); Karl Deutsch, *Nationalism and Social Communication* (Cambridge, Mass.: MIT Press, 1953); Kenneth McRae, ed., *Consociational Democracy: Political Accommodation in Segmented Societies* (Toronto: McClelland and Stewart, 1974) contains a very excellent summary of the literature on nation-building in countries of this type, including excerpts of the important work by such people as Val Lorwin, Arend Lijphart, Hans Daalder, Jürgen Steiner, along with very useful analytic essays by the editor.

regions, but of people in them. The effects of geographical dis-
tributions of political and economic activity work through individuals and groups.

Cross-class appeals on the basis of ethnic group identity have
in the twentieth century repeatedly clashed with appeals to class
solidarity, and the former have usually won. In the cases examined here, different types of ethnic appeal are in conflict
with each other (existing nation versus new nation). The outcomes of these conflicts will depend partly on the connection
between economics and politics, which has been stressed in this
paper, and partly on the connection between politics and
cultural grievances of a noneconomic kind, which have been
neglected here. Another comparative inquiry might seek out
regularities in the content of these cultural grievances and in the
content of ethnic "self-understandings." But that is another
book altogether.

CHAPTER 11

CONCLUSIONS

The areal distribution of powers has been on the political agenda of France throughout the postwar period. Numerous proposals for reform have been put forward leading to political conflict over what policy to adopt. On several occasions, these conflicts have had a major impact on French political life, most notably with the Referendum of April 1969, whose defeat prompted the resignation of President Charles de Gaulle.

Some of the suggestions for altering center-periphery relations were adopted. The most visible example is the creation of a new political form, the regions. Under the terms of the *loi Frey* of 1972, regions levy taxes, spend money, select executives, meet in deliberative assemblies, and engage in other activities typical of public institutions. Other new units of government include *communautés urbaines, syndicats à vocation multiple*, and a host of special instruments for specific projects such as Fos sur Mer. In March 1977, for the first time in over one hundred years, Paris elected its own mayor. Over the past three decades, a vast array of decrees have provided for numerous reforms: the harmonization of administrative districts, the formulation of regional plans, the strengthening of departmental prefects in relation to agents of other Parisian ministries, the classification of expenditures according to their geographic scope (leading to the deconcentration of decisions concerning smaller jurisdictions), the creation of regional prefectures and other regional structures, and the relaxation of prefectoral *tutelle* over communes.

Together these measures have to some degree altered the ways in which the state conducts its business. New representative bodies give some voice to new geographic entities. Inside the administration, the substantive, geographic, and political criteria on which decisions are based have shifted toward the economic, toward larger units, and toward more "modern" forces (high technology industry, export businesses, and so on). Careers are not made in quite the same way, and there are new routes; the department remains an important framework for shaping promotion, but some talented persons have been attracted by jobs (in the ministries or special delegations) which cut across traditional geographic lines.

Nonetheless, although the areal distribution of power in France has changed since 1945 in real ways, these changes do not add up to a new model of the politico-administrative system in France. Power remains concentrated in the hands of the central government and its agents. The new units have little leverage over decisions while old units remain in place. Social forces and interest groups still aim their efforts at influencing decisions made in Paris. What we have been witnessing is another modernization of the modalities of centralized rule in France, analogous to previous modernizations from the seventeenth through the twentieth centuries.

Indeed, under the Fifth Republic, the influence of the periphery, or local forces, on the center has become, if anything, weaker. New institutions shift power to indirectly elected representatives and to nonresponsible executives and administrative organisms. In the presidential system, the National Assembly (hence the locally elected deputy) has considerably less influence over the national executive. More disciplined parties, or parties heavily dependent on a few leaders (such as the UDR), reduce the leverage of the individual deputy even further. The spread of government, the complexity of contemporary problems, and economic concentration all contribute to the narrowing of the channels of pressure brought to bear on decisions of ever increasing importance. Pierre Grémion has aptly labeled the emerging pattern *l'état rationalisateur corporatiste.*[1]

Moreover, over the past thirty years, all the more far-reaching schemes for reform of the geographical division of powers in France have failed: reduction of the number of departments, suppression of the prefect, creation of departmental or regional executives responsible directly to the electorate or to its elected representatives, the direct election of regional councilors, the elimination of departments, the redrawing of regional boundaries, the creation of *grandes régions* on a European scale, the fusion of the thirty-eight thousand miniscule communes, the equalization of representation at both national and subnational levels, and abolition of the Senate. Despite the clamor for change, despite the endless complaints about centralization, despite the popularity of such general schemes as regionalization, the pressures for reform have been contained or channeled into safe waters.

Why? Throughout this book, I have stressed the power of political constraints in shaping the character of reform of the areal distribution of power in France. Over the past four decades, criticism of the traditional Jacobin model linking Paris to the countryside has increased significantly. Old arguments have been revived, and new arguments invented. It used to be taken as axiomatic that the Jacobin model was the best arrangement for the realization of freedom, control, and rationality. This is now contested. Liberty requires diversity, it is argued, and the opportunity to participate in decision-making in ways other than simply voting or being a party militant. For the purposes of ruling, centralization has for many politicians become counterproductive; it blocks involvement of new social forces, inhibits experimentation, and exposes the government to taking the blame for anything and everything. Finally, it is increasingly argued that traditional Jacobin structures prevent rationality by imposing inappropriate jurisdictions upon the

1. Pierre Grémion, *Le Pouvoir périphérique: Bureaucrats et notables dans le système politique français* (Paris: Le Seuil, 1976).

political process, and by clogging the machinery of government at the center with a mass of details best left to the periphery.

Certainly, the Jacobin tradition is not dead. It remains very much alive and makes its own contribution to the lack of change. Even among the reformers, it is possible to see modes of reasoning which deter reform. Decentralization means fragmentation, and in a fragmented system, policy is the result of some kind of group process. It is still hard to find anywhere in French thinking about the organization of public authority any appreciation of the value of a group process per se. Citizen involvement in decision-making is valued, but not the pushing and shoving of group politics. The collective good continues to be seen as a unitary whole, not the outcome of a process. The Americans have no trouble legitimating this aspect of decentralized government because the tradition of *The Federalist Papers* derives it precisely from the virtues of group conflict. In France, the legitimation of the operational consequences of decentralization (fragmented policy-making) remains more difficult.

Still, other countries without something like the Federalist tradition have managed nevertheless to carry out quite extensive reforms of their systems of local government. It is possible that a careful comparative study of the political culture of the various European countries could demonstrate a particular resistance to decentralization on the part of the French, greater than that found elsewhere. But it is far from obvious that this is so, indeed unlikely. In France, moreover, arguments in favor of extensive reform do exist, and in quantity. While the particular versions of such arguments vary from party to party, even from person to person, there can be identified in each major political formation a strong current of thought capable of legitimating significant change in the territorial distribution of powers in France. Politicians, interest group leaders, civil servants, and the public have no difficulty finding inadequacies with the traditional model, nor in suggesting proposals for change, nor in articulating sophisticated rationales on its behalf.

The problem rather is that these rationales have conflicted repeatedly with political calculations. There are tradeoffs among the values of liberty, control, and rationality, and in France the concern of control understood as requiring centralization has won out over the other two. It may be that, in the long run, the hegemony of the bourgeoisie in France would best be assured by extensive decentralization. Involvement in local government would moderate the left by giving it responsibilities and a stake in the system, and by forcing it to confront pragmatic issues. The best conservative strategy might therefore be extensive reform. Nonetheless, no center or center-right government in France has behaved this way since the war. The Gaullist reforms sought to supplant the center-right, not moderate the party system as a whole. The person who might have been expected to take a reformist conservative line seriously—Giscard—has not done so, certainly not in this domain. Chaban-Delmas might have behaved differently, but the electorate rejected just the kind of moderate strategy he represented.

The center and right have dominated French politics over the past twenty years. Responsibility for the limited extent of areal reform lies therefore with them. The majority's caution arises from two political facts, one having to do with the balance of forces internal to the center-right, the other with the balance between the majority and the left. As the comparison with Italy brings out, the decomposition of a Christian Democratic party has in France weakened the cause of regionalism and decentralization. The Gaullist schemes of the mid-sixties aimed less at decentralization than at undermining the partisan position of its political neighbors. The interest in change was always drastically limited by the presence within the party of strong currents of Jacobin thinking. Thus, during the period when Gaullism stood at the "center," interested in reform, it was antagonistic to those political groups in the center interested in decentralization; as its relations with those formations have improved, the Gaullists have ceased being in the center and have lost interest in certain kinds of change.

Chirac has led the party toward some of its older roots: nationalism and statism. He differs from de Gaulle however in the character of his appeal. While certainly fiercely anti-Communist, the founder of Gaullism also cultivated Communist support. De Gaulle always understood that both his foreign policy of independence and the domestic one of reconstruction required the acquiescence of Moscow and the PCF. Indeed, the foreign policy was double-edged: it was both the cause and the consequence of Communist party support. Chirac, however, has upset this delicate balance. Anti-Communism has been so prominent in his political appeals of recent years, it will be very difficult for Chirac to capture a portion of the left the way de Gaulle managed to do. Increasingly, his principal theme has been nationalism in foreign policy: antisupranationality in Europe, criticism of the United States, and so on. Similar themes are voiced on the left, especially in the PCF, but also among Socialists. Yet cooperation among the left and the *Rassemblement du Peuple Républicain* has been rendered difficult if not impossible by the stridency of Chirac's antileftism. Chirac's policy line is thus in conflict with its political requirements. Under present conditions he cannot come to power by mobilizing the right on the basis of an appeal which makes it impossible to win support in the center and the left. With respect to decentralization, the Chiracian line leads to no change; decentralization could only benefit the left.

Giscard's political situation is somewhat different, but his policy inference in this domain is the same. Giscard has a popular image as moderate and reforming, a man of the center. At the same time, he has very conservative elements among his supporters, and as a liberal committed to accepting the fate dictated by market forces, he is not well placed to do something for those suffering from present economic dislocations (note his willingness to force transformations in the steel industry at the cost of very high unemployment). While Giscard would like an opening to the left, which would detach the Socialists from the PCF and free him from the veto exerted by Chirac, he remains at the same time intensely opposed to the politics of the left alliance. The result has been considerable caution with respect to anything which affects the state's ability to maintain order, in particular, dècentralization. Giscard supports minor changes which presumably improve efficiency, but nothing which would allow the left to capture a significant chunk of power.

Thus the struggle between factions of the majority spills over to the relations between it and the left. Both Chirac and Giscard have chosen to impute a particular meaning to the importance of the left. Since some local governments will always be controlled by the left, including the Communists, giving more power to all local governments means giving some power to the left. Since most local governments are not in the hands of the left, most decentralized power would go to the center and the right. Nonetheless, Chirac and Giscard would rather no one have more power at the local level than allow the left, especially the Communists, to have some of it. At certain key moments, fear of the right has made its own contribution to the status quo, such as in the early days of the Fourth Republic and during the Algerian crisis. But the persistent and recurrent systemic cause of blockage has been fear of the left.

The evolution of the majority's position on decentralization will not, of course, take place in isolation. Left, center, and right are part of a system; the behavior of each depends in part on that of the other and vice versa. Several scenarios are possible on the left. First it is at least conceptually possible, if apparently empirically improbable, that the PCF could become more moderate in ways which diminish the "fear" reflex. It could modify its doctrines, soften its remote and mistrustful stance in relation to other parties, and loosen its internal organization to the point where other parties become willing to accept it as a partner in a parliamentary game. Were the PCF to change in this way, partisan political rivalries would continue, but the interactions would take on a different character. Centralized control would no longer seem indispensable to maintaing the integrity of the regime. The major obstacle to change under such conditions would be the partisan calculations of the majority of the moment—whether a given reform proposal would strengthen or weaken its organizational interests. The experience of other European countries suggests that, where a system threat such as a Communist party is absent or weak, the majority or coalition feels able to manage the reform of local government in such a way as to neutralize any threats to it, or even to profit from the changeover. It is thus not just any partisan political strife which appears to deter decentralization, but a particular kind, one in which the polarization goes beyond a certain point. Were internal change within the PCF to bring it within those limits, the prospects for decentralization would improve, barring the emergence of some other internal threat to the system as a whole.

A second route to further reform could come from a change in the PCF's influence on policy via a shift in relations among the present party formations leading to the French equivalent of the *apertura à sinistra*. A shift to the left, caused by a change in voting behavior, or a major crisis requiring a unity government, or some breakdown in relations between the Giscardians and the Gaullists, would give the left and the PCF more leverage over policy. Since both major formations call for revision of the *loi Frey*, the government could be forced to accept some reform as the price for the coalition. As in Italy, such a government might be willing to make concessions in this domain, rather than in other more costly ones, such as autogestion or major nationalizations.

To some extent the second type of development requires some of the first—in order for something like an opening to the left to come about, some moderation of the PCF is probably necessary. Should such moderation not occur, a crisis or a voting shift could be resolved without the Communists or against them. In that case, the chances for more decentralization would probably drop. Support for decentralization tends to be strongest in the center, that is among the Socialists and the moderate, Catholic, and Radical elements of Giscard's UDF.

One might expect therefore that a center-left coalition would produce more decentralization. If such a coalition came to power only in the framework of an emergency of some kind requiring exclusion of the Communists, the "fear" reflex would allow the Jacobins within the UDF and the PSF to prevail over the reformers.

The prediction generated by the argumnet here is that, in power, the left would in this respect behave much as the right. It would be so insecure about its own hold on office as to be unwilling in practice to give up instruments of rule provided by a centralized system. For a time it appeared this prediction would actually be tested before the publication of this book. Instead, the close call of the elections of March 1978 appears to have only strengthened the reluctance of Giscard to make any concessions.[2]

In one respect the situation of the left is not symmetrical with that of the center-right. The left has always criticized second-degree election of local officials while the right has always found ways of justifying it. As argued above, the left can change the mode of designating regional councilors without, at least initially, touching the balance of powers among different levels of local government. Were the left to come to power, either alone or in coalition, it would probably implement this aspect of its program. It is not likely, however, to do much more; there would be no authoritative consolidation or abolition of existing institutions nor any massive reshuffling of the distribution of power among them.

Putting speculation about the left, center, and right together produces the prediction that over the next ten years, we can expect little dramatic change in the territorial distribution of powers in France, with the one important exception concerning the election of regional councilors. French policy is likely to follow the Italian pattern. Nothing will be done unless there occurs some functional equivalent to the opening to the left. Then existing structures may be democratized, but political

2. *Le Monde*, December 1978.

tensions will continue to block any significant decentralization of powers.

It is at this point that, in the language of Chapter 2, the different modes of interpreting policy toward the areal distribution of power intersect. The left is a source of fear because it proposes sweeping social and economic changes, not revolutionary ones perhaps, more than it would actually do perhaps, but certainly important enough to worry many. The stock market rise the day after the first round of 1978 was certainly instructive in this regard. The government in turn pursues policies which antagonize various social categories, some already on the left, some not. The closing of many steel mills is the best example, and this too increases social tension. Thus, if decentralization is ruled out because of political conflict, such conflicts are themselves connected to economic and social processes and policies. What I have argued here is not that the economic dimension is irrelevant but that there is an intervening type of analysis required as well: the concerns of politicians and parties who have their own outlook and interests. And in their evaluation of risks and rewards, these politicians, as well as administrations, interest group leaders, and the public, are affected by ideological traditions concerning the distribution of authority.

Suppose that somehow the political situation were more favorable to decentralization and some wide-ranging scheme were actually put through? What impact would such changes have upon the French political system? The advocates of reform expect a great deal from it, perhaps too much. If changing the content of policy is the major goal, it is not at all clear what reorganization of local government and administration would do. The social problems of France are not unique to it. Countries with very different center-periphery relations also have considerable income inequalities, urban blight, crowded schools, inadequate housing, regional unemployment, pollution, and the like. In some of these respects, France stands up rather well in comparison, and it is at least plausible that its success derives from the centralized nature of administration. The country whose system is probably the farthest from the

French—the United States—does very badly in some of these areas, and again it is plausible that the fragmentation of American politics is a contributing cause of poor performance; extensive decentralization provides multiple veto points, which make it easier to block the attainment of collective good. Conversely, where France does badly, as it does with income distribution, it is hard to see centralization as the primary cause, or decentralization as the principal force behind more egalitarian patterns elsewhere.

Policy derives from power of which institutional structure is a component. To expect decentralization by itself to provide liberty, rationality, and control is to burden center-periphery relations with an unreasonable load. A parallel may be drawn between decentralization in this respect and education. Christopher Jencks and others have shown that the school system does not by itself reduce inequalities.[3] Inequality is the product of a variety of powerful social forces which education alone does not appear strong enough to overcome. Rather than blame education for its failures in this respect, the appropriate response would appear rather to focus attention on the forces which operate to reproduce great inequality despite the efforts of the school system. It may well be that while education cannot alone do the job, greater equality of opportunity cannot be realized without the help of schooling. In a general program to fight inequality, comprising efforts in the realms of employment, housing, transport, and income distribution, education might then play an important role.

In the realm of the areal distribution of powers, the same relationships may obtain. Decentralization is no panacea. Changing the structures which link the capital to the countryside cannot by itself transform society. If, however, such changes were related to efforts to reform other aspects of society, then decentralization could have a considerable impact upon the pattern of policy and policy-making. Indeed, efforts at social reform which leave out the areal distribution of power

3. Christopher Jencks et al., Inequalities (New York: Basic Books, 1972).

may well abort or mutate unpleasantly. Certainly France has witnessed in recent years a striking growth in awareness of these connections, especially those linking economic democracy with citizen involvement at *la base*.

The consequence of any particular change depends on what else goes along with it. Each piece is part of a system. A particular structure of center-local linkages secretes the interests, ideas, and psychological proclivities that in turn sustain it and resist change. The Tocquevillians focus on the psychological-cultural dimensions of this circle. The socio-economic theorists (of whatever coloration) focus on economic interests. I have focused on the partisan political stakes. Each of these interacts with the other, but has some autonomy. Each is a constraint on the others. Compared with the Tocquevillians and the socio-economic-centered theorists, I have been impressed by the latitude allowed by psychology, culture, and economic interests, and by the limits imposed by partisan rivalries. I take no particular pleasure from this. My programmatic visions do not require a Jacobin straitjacket; my sympathies lie with those who would prefer a decentralized model. To the extent that attainment of such ends depends on party relationships, we are in for a very long wait.

BIBLIOGRAPHY

This bibliography presents those materials on which I have particularly relied or which may be of special interest to the reader. It is impossible to list all the publications which have appeared in recent years.

Allen, Kevin, and Maclennan, M. C. *Regional Problems and Policies in Italy and France.* London: George Allen and Unwin, 1970.

Andrews, William G. "The Politics of Regionalization in France." In *Politics in Europe*, edited by Martin O. Heisler, pp. 293–322. New York: McKay, 1974.

Ashford, Douglas. *National Resources and Urban Policy.* Chicago: Maroufka Press, 1979.

Bancal, Jean. *Les Circonscriptions administratives de la France.* Paris: Receuil Sirey, 1945.

Beer, Samuel. "Federalism, Nationalism, and Democracy in America." *American Political Science Review* 72 (March 1978): 9–21.

Berger, Suzanne; Gourevitch, Peter; Higonnet, Patrice; and Kaiser, Karl. "The Problem of Reform in France: The Political Ideas of Local Elites." *Political Science Quarterly* 84 (September 1969): 436–460.

Berger, Suzanne. "Politics and Antipolitics in Western Europe in the Seventies." *Daedalus* 108 (Winter 1979):27–50.

Blackmer, Donald, and Tarrow, Sidney, eds. *Communism in Italy and France.* Princeton: Princeton University Press, 1975.

Bodiguel, J.-L.; Camous, P.; Dubedout, H.; Jourdan, A.; Lecomte, P.; Leleu, C.; Martin, J.F.; Pouyet, B.; Quermonne, J.-L.; Schneider, J.-P.; and Souchon, M.-F. *La Réforme régionale et le Référendum du 27 avril 1969.* Paris: Editions Cujas, 1970.

Bourjol, Maurice. *Les Institutions régionales de 1789 à nos jours.* Paris: Berger-Levrault, 1969.

Castells, Manuel, and Godard, Francis. *Monopoville: l'entreprise, l'état, l'urbainism.* Paris: Mouton, 1974.

Cohen, Stephen. *Modern Capitalist Planning.* Cambridge: Harvard University Press, 1970.

Commission de Développement des Résponsabilités Locales (La Commission Guichard). *Vivre ensemble.* Paris: La Documentation Française, 1976.

Crozier, Michel. *The Stalled Society.* Translation of *La Societé bloquée.* New York: Viking Press, 1973.

Crozier, Michel. *The Bureaucratic Phenomenon.* Chicago: University of Chicago Press, 1964.

Crozier, Michel; Friedberg, Erhard; Grémion, Catherine; Grémion, Pierre; Thoenig, Jean-Claude; and Worms, Jean-Pierre. *Où va l'administration française?* Paris: Les Editions d'Organisation, 1974.

Dayries, Jean-Jacques, and Dayries, Michèle. *La Régionalisation.* Series *Que sais-je,* no. 1719. Paris: Presses Universitaires de France, 1978.

de Savigny, Jean. *L'Etat contre les communes.* Paris: Le Seuil, 1971.

Esman, Milton, ed. *Ethnic Conflict in the Western World.* Ithaca: Cornell University Press, 1977.

Fried, Robert. *The Italian Prefects.* New Haven: Yale University Press, 1963.

Gourevitch, Peter Alexis. "The Reemergence of 'Peripheral Nationalisms': Some Comparative Speculations on the Spatial Distribution of Political Leadership and Economic Growth." *Comparative Studies in Society and History* 21 (July 1979): 303–322.

Gourevitch, Peter Alexis. "The Reform of Local Government in France: A Political Analysis," *Comparative Politics* 11 (October 1977): 69–88.

Gourevitch, Peter Alexis. "Reforming the Napoleonic State: The Creation of Regional Governments in France and Italy." In *Territorial Politics in Industrial Nations,* edited by Sidney Tarrow, Peter Katzenstein, and Luigi Graziano. New York: Praeger, 1968: 28–63.

Gras, Christian, and Livet, Georges. *Régions et régionalism en France du XVIII'e siècle à nos jours.* Paris: Presses Universitaires de France, 1976.

Gravier, Jean-François. *Paris et le désert française*, 2d ed. Paris: Flammarion, 1972.

Grémion, Catherine. *Profession: décideurs—Pouvoir des hauts fonctionnaires et réforme de l'Etat.* Paris: Gauthier-Villars, 1979.

Grémion, Pierre. *Le Pouvoir périphérique: Bureaucrats et notables dans le système politique français.* Paris: Le Seuil, 1976.

Grémion, Pierre. *La Structuration du pouvoir départemental.* Paris: Copédith, 1969.

Grémion, Pierre, and Worms, Jean-Pierre. *Les Institutions régionales et la société locale.* Paris: Copédith, 1968.

Hansen, Nills M. *French Regional Planning.* Bloomington: Indiana University Press, 1968.

Hansen, Nills M., ed. *Public Policy and Regional Economic Development.* Cambridge, Mass.: Ballinger, 1974.

Hayward, J.E.S. "Presidential Suicide by Referendum." *Parliamentary Affairs* 22 (Autumn 1969): 289–319.

Hechter, Michael. *Internal Colonialism.* Berkeley and Los Angeles: University of California Press, 1975.

Kesselman, Mark. *The Ambiguous Consensus.* New York: Knopf, 1967.

Kesselman, Mark. "Political Parties and Local Government in France," and "Research Perspectives in Comparative Local Politics: Pitfalls, Prospects, and Notes on the French Case." In *Comparative Community Politics*, edited by Terry Clark. New York: Halstead, 1974.

Lafont, Robert. *Décoloniser la France.* Paris: Gallimard, 1971.

Lafont, Robert. *La Révolution régionaliste.* Paris: Gallimard, 1967.

Lajugie, Joseph. "Aménagement du térritoire et développement économique en France (1945–1964)." *Revue d'Economie Politique* 74 (January–February 1964): 278–336.

Levesque, Morvan. *Comment peut-on être breton?* Paris: Le Seuil, 1970.

Linz, Juan. "Early State Building and Late Peripheral Nationalisms Against the State." In *Building States and Nations,* edited by S.N. Eisenstadt and Stein Rokkan. Beverly Hills: Sage, 1974.

Maass, Arthur, ed. *Area and Power.* Glencoe: Free Press, 1959.

MacArthur, John, and Scott, Bruce. *Industrial Planning in France.* Cambridge, Mass. Harvard University Press, 1969.

Machin, Howard. *The Prefect in French Public Administration.* London: Croom Helm, 1977.

Mény, Yves. *Centralisation et décentralisation dans le débat politique française 1945-1969*. Paris: Librairie Générale de Droit et de Jurisprudence, 1974.

Monod, Jerome, and Castelbajac, Philippe. *L'Aménagement du térritoire*. Paris: Presses Universitaires de France, 1972.

Peyrefitte, Alain. *Le Mal français*. Paris: Plon, 1976.

Peyrefitte, Alain; Crozier, Michel; Thoenig, Jean-Claude; Geliner, Octave; and Sultan, Elie. *Décentraliser les résponsabilites*. Paris: La Documentation Française, 1976.

Rokkan, Stein. "Dimensions of State Formation and Nation-Building." In *The Formation of Nation-States in Western Europe*, edited by Charles Tilly. Princeton: Princeton University Press, 1975..

Servan-Schreiber, Jean-Jacques. *Le Pouvoir régional*. Paris: Editions Bernard Grasset, 1971.

Tarrow, Sidney. *Between Center and Periphery: Grassroots Politicians in Italy and France*. New Haven: Yale University Press, 1977.

Tarrow, Sidney; Katzenstein, Peter; and Graziano, Luigi, eds. *Territorial Politics in Industrial Nations*. New York: Praeger, 1978.

Thoenig, Jean-Claude. *L'Ère des technocrates: le cas des Ponts et Chaussées*. Paris: Editions d'Organisation, 1973.

Wahl, Nicholas, and Hoffmann, Stanley. "The French Constitution of 1958." *American Political Science Review* 53 (June 1959): 332–382.

Weber, Eugen. *Peasants into Frenchmen*. Stanford: Stanford University Press, 1976.

Worms, Jean-Pierre. "Le Préfet et ses notables." *Sociologie du Travail* 3 (July–September 1966): 249–275.

Wright, Vincent, and Machin, Howard. "The French Regional Reform of July 1972: A Case of Disguised Centralization." *Policy and Politics* 3 (March 1975): 3–28.

INDEX

Italy and Italians, 4, 5, 50, 53, 136, 138, 211–212, 221, 234; Communist Party of (PCI), 138, 175, 180–198; Christian Democrats of (DC), 175, 181–193, 230; Socialist Party (PSI), 175, 180; and contrast with France concerning regions, 179–181, 193–198; creation of regional government in, 179–198, Fascism and Fascists in, 180–181, 188; and Constitution of 1947, 181; and foreign policy and implications for regional reform, 181; and Hot Autumn, 181, 189; and ideology concerning center-local relations, 181–184; and Marxism, 183; *legge Scelba* of, 186; and role of bureaucracy compared to France, 186; and electoral law of 1967 for regions, 187–189; monarchists in, 188; and regional elections of 1970, 189; and regional elections of 1975, 190–193; Red Belt in, 192, 195; and riots in Reggio Calabria, 197; South Italians, 200; and peripheral nationalism, 213–214

Jacobin and Jacobinism, 9–11, 15, 16, 17, 19, 23, 24, 27–28, 33, 38, 39, 41, 43, 48, 61, 103–104, 119, 122, 141, 153, 154–159, 161, 168, 183, 194, 228–229, 234; hardline Jacobinism, 61; modernized Jacobinism, 62
Japan, 26
Jeanneney, Jean-Marcel, 116, 120, 123, 137, 143
Jeanson, André, 164
Jencks, Christopher, 236

Krivine, Alain, 171

Lafont, Robert, 161, 168
Languedoc-Roussillon, 137, 196
Lecanuet, Jean, 143, 146
Left: and ideas about local govern-

ment reform, 19–22, 154–163; and party politics, 163–176; and comparison to Italy, 179–198
Legge Scelba. See Italy
Legislative elections: of 1967, 121, 170; of 1968, 114; of 1978, 146–147, 151, 235
L'Huillier, Waldeck, 12, 13, 14
Liberal critique, 24, 33
Liberation, 10, 64–65, 68, 72
Liberty and local government reform, 15–26
Liguria, 192, 195
Limousin, 137, 140, 196
Linz, Juan, 210
Local government reform: explanations of, 37–56; social-psychological explanations of, 37–41, 237; political culture interpretation of, 39–41, 237; socio-economic explanation of, 41–46, 237; and regional imbalances, 44–46; and strength of local implantations, 50–51; and party alliance strategies, 51–53; and common program, 52; and distribution of voting strength, 53; partisan political interpretation of, 55–56; and executive, 62; options, 60–64; and economic democracy, 173–174
Loi d'orientation. See Education Law of 1968
Loi Frey, xi, 42, 44, 64, 96, 140, 143, 147, 149–150, 226, 233
Loi Marcellin, 96, 134
Lombardy, 203
Lorraine, 132, 212–213
Louis-Napoleon, 21, 128
Lyon, 76, 109

Madison, James, 2
Marcellin, Raymond, 122, 134
Marches of Italy, 192, 195
Maritime Provinces of Canada, 219–220
Marseilles, 140
Marx and Marxists, 9, 10, 16, 19,

Designer:	Wendy Calmenson
Compositor:	Freedmen's Organization
Printer:	McNaughton & Gunn, Inc.
Binder:	McNaughton & Gunn, Inc.
Text:	EditWriter Garamond
Display:	EditWriter Garamond
Cloth:	Joanna Arrestox B 34000
Paper:	50 lb P&S offset vellum, B-32

FH

NIIIHFP

GOUREVITCH